The Fatal Gift of Beauty

BOOKS BY A. B. C. WHIPPLE

The Fatal Gift of Beauty: The Final Years of
Byron and Shelley
Tall Ships and Great Captains
Pirate: Rascals of the Spanish Main
Yankee Whalers in the South Seas

FOR YOUNGER READERS

Hero of Trafalgar
Famous Pirates of the New World

The
Fatal Gift
of
Beauty

THE FINAL YEARS OF BYRON AND SHELLEY

A. B. C. Whipple

Harper & Row, Publishers

NEW YORK, EVANSTON, AND LONDON

This one is for
JANE

Illustrations

(following page 144)

1. BYRON'S MOTHER, painted by Thomas Stewardson, courtesy of Sir John Murray
2. AUGUSTA LEIGH, courtesy of the British Museum Print Room
3. NEWSTEAD ABBEY, courtesy of the Public Libraries, Nottingham, England
4. THOMAS MOORE, painted by Sir Thomas Lawrence, courtesy of Sir John Murray
5. JOHN CAM HOBHOUSE, engraved by James Hopwood, courtesy of the National Portrait Gallery, London
6. LADY CAROLINE LAMB, Devonshire Collection, Chatsworth, courtesy of the Trustees of the Chatsworth Settlement
7. ANNABELLA MILBANKE, from a miniature by Charles Hayter
8. BYRON IN ALBANIAN DRESS, painted by Thomas Phillips, courtesy of the National Portrait Gallery, London
9. CLAIRE CLAIRMONT, painted by Amelia Curran, courtesy of the Public Libraries, Nottingham, England
10. PERCY SHELLEY, from an engraving by Amelia Curran, courtesy of the National Portrait Gallery, London
11. MARY SHELLEY, by R. Rothwell, courtesy of the National Portrait Gallery, London
12. VILLA DIODATI, engraved by Edward Finden from a drawing by W. Purser
13. LORD BYRON AT THE VILLA DIODATI, courtesy of the New York Public Library, Prints Division
14. MARGARITA COGNI, engraved by Henry Thomas Ryall from a drawing by George Henry Harlow, courtesy of the National Portrait Gallery, London

Italia! oh, Italia! thou who hast
The fatal gift of Beauty, which became
A funeral dower of present woes and past—
On thy sweet brow is sorrow ploughed by shame,
And annals graved in characters of flame.

BYRON: Childe Harold, IV

Foreword

One day more than a century ago, Percy Bysshe Shelley sat at his desk overlooking the Arno in Pisa, Italy, and wrote:

Man is an instrument over which a series of external and internal impressions are driven, like the alternations of an ever-changing wind over an Aeolian lyre, which move it by their motion to ever-changing melody. But there is a principle within the human being, and perhaps within all sentient beings, which acts otherwise than in the lyre, and produces not melody alone, but harmony, by an internal adjustment of the sounds or motions thus excited to the impressions which excite them.

Harsh were the winds over the lyre of Percy Bysshe Shelley. In the three years before he wrote these lines, in his essay *A Defence of Poetry*, both his daughter and his son died. In the year after writing these lines, Shelley would die himself.

This book is about the external and internal impressions on the lives—and the poetry—of Percy Shelley and of George Gordon, Sixth Lord Byron, who lived in Italy during the same short period of four years. The beauty of Italy, like wind over a lyre, inspired Shelley and Byron to the most melodious harmonies of their poetic careers. It also produced one of the most dramatic tragedies in literary history.

I have tried, through the story of the interrelationship of the two poets and through the narrative of these Italian years, in combination with the poetry written during these years, to show how Italy inspired and doomed both poets, and why Byron referred to Italy's "fatal gift of beauty." In more than a century since Shelley's drowning and Byron's death of fever, many brilliant studies have been made of the two men. None, to my knowledge, has concentrated on this short Italian climax, on the interrelationship of the two poets during this time, and on the influence of Italy's beauty upon their poetry.

That is what my book attempts to do. The attempt could never have been made without the definitive groundwork of the great Byron and Shelley scholars. The most important of their works are described in a separate chapter at the end of this book. But it would be an injustice for me not to mention at the outset those scholars who have, through their books or in person, helped me in the process of writing my own narrative of Byron and Shelley in Italy.

Leslie A. Marchand, author of the classic biography of Byron, has been most generous and helpful. So has Peter Quennell, author of the justly popular *Byron in Italy*. I doubt if anyone could write a book about Shelley in Italy, or Byron for that matter, without the assistance of Dottoressa Vera Cacciatore, curator of the famous Keats-Shelley Memorial in Rome. Nor could the full story of Byron's consuming love affair with Teresa Guiccioli be told without the brilliant pioneering done by Marchese Iris Origo. And my gratitude must also be happily expressed to the following: Sergio Rossi, Professor of English Literature, Catholic University, Milan; Giovanna Foà, Professor of English Language and Literature, Bocconi University, Milan, and author of *Lord Byron, Poeta e Carbonaro*; Anna Maria Crinò, Professor of English Language and Literature, Poetical and Economic Faculty, Florence University; Sergio Baldi, Professor of English Literature and Language, Teaching Faculty, Florence University; Carlo

Izzo, Professor of English Language, Bologna University; Alieto Benini, author of *Byron a Ravenna*; Riccardo Marchi, authority on Byron's and Shelley's activities in Leghorn. Not to mention Peter Dragadze, genial guide, interpreter and student of poetry himself; Count Ottavio Zasio, walking (and I mean *walking*) authority on Byron in Venice; and David Lees, photographer *extraordinaire*.

But most of all I must thank my wife, Jane, who shared both the pleasant field trips in Italy and the much longer months of research in countless libraries—and who also shared, in growing measure year by year, the inspiring realization of Percy Shelley's phrase, "A poem is the very image of life expressed in its eternal truth."

The Fatal Gift of Beauty

[I]

Venice in 1818 was a great city-state gone into decline. The Venetian Republic, heir of Rome and once the most formidable power in the western world, had subsided into impotence and dalliance. Two decades earlier, the 120th doge had been deposed and Napoleon had swept over Venice. The great bronze horses, symbol of the Republic's days of power, were shipped to Paris; so was the winged lion; and the jewels from St. Mark's treasury went to adorn a crown for Josephine. Napoleon moved on to Waterloo, and Venice was handed over to other rulers, the Austrians. But the Venetians seemed not to care. When Napoleon erected a Tree of Liberty in St. Mark's Square, Venetians pranced around it as if they had been liberated instead of conquered. When the Austrians returned the bronze horses to St. Mark's, the Venetians pretended to ignore them. And now, as Venice's authority waned, Venetians played on, heedless of their city's political disintegration and moral rot.

As the rest of Europe recovered from the aftereffects of Napoleon, British travelers began to rediscover the Continent. And Venice, in her dance of death, attracted one Englishman in particular. George Gordon, Sixth Lord Byron, had shocked all England and had sailed from home in a cloud of scandal. Now he appeared to be attempting to accomplish the much more difficult task of achieving the same notoriety in Venice. At the same time he tried rendering the plight of Venice into poetry.

> In Venice Tasso's echoes are no more,
>   And silent rows the songless Gondolier;
>   Her palaces are crumbling to the shore,
>   And Music meets not always now the ear:
>   Those days are gone—but Beauty still is here.
>   States fall—Arts fade—But Nature doth not die,
>   Nor yet forget how Venice once was dear,
>   The pleasant place of all festivity,
> The Revel of the earth—the Masque of Italy![1]*

On an August afternoon in 1818, another Englishman came to Venice to call on Lord Byron in his palazzo on the Grand Canal. The visitor reclined in his gondola as it swung down the mainstream of the city's central waterway and eased up to the steps of the Palazzo Mocenigo, which Byron had rented from a member of Venice's fading aristocracy. Holding a handrail to avoid slipping on the slime-covered steps, the visitor leaped ashore. Inside the entranceway, in the damp and cavernous ground floor, he could make out the shapes of a carriage and rows of cages and could hear the squawks, mutterings, squeals and whimpers of countless unidentifiable animals. The visitor walked toward the back of the dark room, to the wide staircase. Climbing the steps—and ducking around a snarling

---

* Superior numbers refer to a section of notes beginning on page 284.

monkey chained on the landing—he reached the large entrance hall. And there he was greeted by a cry of surprise from a servant. It was William Fletcher, Byron's manservant, who called out to the next room: "Your Lordship! Mr. Shelley is here!"

Percy Bysshe Shelley was led into a big, bright room whose high ceiling danced with the lights reflected from the canal. And then Lord Byron came hobbling across the room to take his hand.

Shelley could see that his friend's sturdy figure had taken on a little fat, indicating some truth behind the rumors Shelley had heard of Byron's profligate living in Venice. But the Byronic profile was as handsome as ever, and Shelley was again impressed with the proud, even haughty carriage, somehow enhanced by the limping gait of Byron's clubfoot. For his part, Byron could see that his young friend had altered little in two years. Slight, frail, diffident, Shelley seemed the same gentle aesthete Byron remembered from their summer together in Geneva.

Now Byron, at thirty, had become even more the literary lion of London, but he showed no inclination to return to the country where he still was both famous and infamous. Shelley too had left England in self-exile, and though he had become a figure of scandal, his literary fame was far less than that of Byron. And instead of plunging into a bachelor's life of debauchery like Byron, twenty-six-year-old Shelley had come to Italy with his twenty-one-year-old wife and two children.

And one other. She was a one-and-a-half-year-old girl, the illegitimate daughter of Byron and Mrs. Shelley's half-sister. The little girl's name was Allegra, and she was to become the central link between the two poets in a four-year Italian adventure they were about to share.

It was Allegra, and the question of her immediate future,

3

which brought Shelley to the Palazzo Mocenigo on this August afternoon. But at the outset Byron was more interested in talking to his old friend about Italy and Venice and poetry, and in taking Shelley in his gondola for a ride to the Lido. As they rode across the lagoon, Byron carried on a spirited monologue, recounting ribald tales of his various mistresses and reciting the verses of *Childe Harold* that he had written the night before. On the Lido horses were waiting, and they pounded along the barren beach, inhaling the sea air and watching the sinking sun tinge the Adriatic. Then they rode home across the lagoon again, and Shelley was overwhelmed with the spectacle of Venice at sunset. Looking across the rippling water that reflected the lighted fairyland of the city, he was oblivious to the chatter of his host, and lost in a world of beauty all his own.

> I rode one evening with Count Maddalo
> Upon the bank of land which breaks the flow
> Of Adria towards Venice: a bare strand
> Of hillocks, heaped from ever-shifting sand,
> Matted with thistles and amphibious weeds,
> Such as from earth's embrace the salt ooze breeds,
> Is this . . .
> How beautiful is sunset, when the glow
> Of Heaven descends upon a land like thee,
> Thou Paradise of exiles, Italy! . . .
> Though bent on pleasant pilgrimage, we stood
> Looking upon the evening, and the flood
> Which lay between the city and the shore,
> Paved with the image of the sky. . . .
> Said my companion, "I will show you soon
> A better station"—so, o'er the lagune
> We glided; and from that funereal bark
> I leaned, and saw the city, and could mark

4

How from their many isles, in evening's gleam,
Its temples and its palaces did seem
Like fabrics of enchantment piled to Heaven. . . .[2]

This was how, on the afternoon of August 23, 1818, the Italian adventure began. It would end in personal tragedy, but it would leave a lasting poetic heritage to the world. For both Byron and Shelley the adventure had started many years earlier, and many miles away.

[II]

It could be said that Byron's troubles started even before he was born; his ancestry is colored with the escapades of eccentrics. In the eighteenth century tales were told all over London and Newstead, the family seat, of the wild doings of the "Wicked Lord," Byron's great-uncle. His grandfather, "Foul Weather Jack" Byron, circumnavigated the world, managing to miss most of the islands in the Pacific, then returned home to scandalize his wife with his amorous escapades, including an open liaison with a servant girl whom he established in a London flat after she had been discovered in the Admiral's bed. By the time "Foul Weather Jack" Byron died, the mantle of disrespectability had fallen onto the shoulders of "Mad Jack" Byron, the Admiral's eldest son and the father of the poet.

"Mad Jack" had a Continental education in a French military academy, and he returned to England, where the old Admiral had bought him a commission in the Guards. He served for a period in America during the Revolution, but was soon back, living the life of a Guardsman dandy in the drawing rooms and bedrooms of London. At twenty-two, his path crossed that of the handsome, wealthy and headstrong Lady Carmathen. Mother of three and wife of a marquis, she nevertheless followed the example of many another London lady and ran off with romantic young Mad Jack Byron. The marquis responded with a divorce, through an Act of Parliament, and she and Jack were married and escaped Jack's creditors to the Continent. They lived together for five years, during which time the marchioness bore Mad Jack three children. The only one who survived was a daughter, Augusta. Her mother died the following year. But Mad Jack recovered quickly and brought the infant Augusta with him when he returned to England to look for another heiress.

This was in the spring of 1785. At that time George Gordon Byron's mother-to-be was a twenty-year-old girl down from Scotland to spend the season at Bath. She was irrepressible, adventurous, dangerously naïve and one of the wealthiest young ladies in Bath that season. She was also quite plain, so that it was no difficult matter for young Captain Jack Byron of the Guards to sweep her off the dance floor into church. On May 13, 1785, Catherine Gordon became Mrs. Jack Byron. And within little more than a year, her spendthrift husband, no doubt helped by earlier creditors, had squandered her fortune. Fleeing creditors again, he escaped to France. Catherine followed him, but now she was pregnant, and the harassing, debt-ridden, free-spending life her husband continued to lead, in a foreign land where she was baffled by the language, was too much for her. She returned to England. With her came four-year-old Augusta,

7

Captain Jack's daughter by his first wife; the life he was living was too profligate for a young daughter, and Augusta's maternal grandmother agreed to take her in for the time being. Catherine Gordon Byron found inexpensive quarters in London and waited for her child to arrive. Captain Jack sneaked back, hiding out in the country and coming to London only on Sundays, when debtors were free from arrest. In such circumstances, on January 22, 1788, in a furnished back drawing room on the first floor at 16 Holles Street, George Gordon Byron was born. The first thing the doctor noted was that the baby had a deformed right foot.

George Gordon Byron's mother and father lived a tempestuous few years, quarreling and separating, then coming back together again. Catherine Byron could not make the complete break from her handsome, feckless husband, but she could not live with him long without upbraiding him for his spendthrift ways. Finally her family managed to pay him off and send him away. He went back to France in 1790 and moved in with his sister, whereupon he continued to sink lower into degradation and debt. Within a year he was dead, and his widow was frantic with grief. His son was three and a half years old—"not so young," he said later, "but that I perfectly remember him; and had very early a horror of matrimony, from the sight of domestic broils."

Young Byron's early years were a blurring combination of genteel poverty, of alternate outbursts of adoration and abuse from his mother, of schoolboys' taunts at his lameness and of the painful but futile efforts to correct it. Braces, exercises and corrective boots helped little if at all, and already the crippled foot was beginning to cripple his personality. Then one day the master of his grammar school in Aberdeen called him in to tell him that his great-uncle had died and that he was now the Sixth Baron Byron of Rochdale. He was ten years old.

His great-uncle, the colorful old "Wicked Lord," had died childless. Because the old lord had been preceded in death by his brother, Admiral Byron, and the Admiral's eldest son, Captain Jack, the title descended directly to Captain Jack's son. And now Catherine Gordon Byron's income was increased from about £100 per year to nearly £2,000. From their cramped quarters in Aberdeen, Scotland, the young Lord Byron and his mother set out south for England and Newstead Abbey, the Byron family seat, leaving Scotland and the early, impoverished formative years behind.

The once-proud oaks of Newstead Abbey were rotting stumps. The farms surrounding the estate were in near ruin. Part of the manor house was roofless, and some rooms were stuffed with hay for animals, which were quartered in other rooms because the outbuildings had fallen into decay. Most of the furniture had been taken away by creditors, and Mrs. Byron discovered that nearly all of her son's inherited income would be taken up, at least for a year or two, in discharging debts incurred by the old "Wicked Lord" in his last years. But as August turned into early autumn, the decrepit manor house still retained some of its charm. There were 3,200 acres of parks, lakes and rolling English countryside. The estate included sixteen tenant farms, which showed some promise of providing a comfortable income if given better management. And for ten-year-old Lord Byron the Gothic ruins were full of romance and wonder.

By the time Byron was thirteen, his income, largely through the careful management of John Hanson, who had been appointed by the Court of Chancery to manage the estate, was sufficient for the boy to be sent to Harrow School, though during that time Byron's mother was often destitute. And now the son began to show habits reminiscent of his father, quickly adopting and often outdoing the profligate habits of his fellow lords and future dukes at Harrow. His Harrow years were also years of boredom with Greek translations, prowess at swimming, further torturing attempts to straighten his clubfoot, and early evidences of a talent for versifying. It was also a time for an early romantic infatuation with one Mary Chaworth, an infatuation which came to a cruel end when he heard that Mary had said: "Do you think I could care anything for that lame boy?" And during the Harrow years, when he was sixteen, he started a correspondence with his half-sister Augusta: ". . . you are *the nearest relation* I have in *the world both by the ties of Blood* and *affection.*"

He was at odds with his mother, more and more as his increasingly spendthrift ways antagonized her. Here in his sister he found a close relative who did not nag him about his failings, to whom he could confide his feelings and with whom he could feel relaxed. The letters continued, through the last year at Harrow and into the Cambridge period. Through these years it was not Byron's mother but his half-sister Augusta who was his confidante.

It was to Augusta that he wrote of his impressions of Cambridge: "I am now most pleasantly situated in *Super*excellent Rooms . . . I am allowed 500 a year, a Servant and Horse, so Feel as independent as a German Prince who coins his own Cash, or a Cherokee Chief who coins no Cash at all, but enjoys what is more precious, Liberty." And it was to Augusta that he wrote explaining that what he had called the "best allowance in College" was not sufficient for his chosen way of life, and asking if she would "be joint Security with me for a few Hundreds a person (one of the money lending tribe) has offered to advance. . . ." He was still a minor, and she was twenty-three. Despite an increased income, after years of work to improve the yield of Newstead Abbey's farms, Byron had begun to turn, like his father, to the moneylenders.

And like his father Byron soon found how easy it was to borrow money, so long as he signed a note at heavy interest. One debt led to another, and the loans mounted until word reached his mother, who wrote Hanson, the estate's business manager, in agony: "God knows what is to be done with him— I much fear he is already ruined. . . ." Her son meanwhile skipped most of Cambridge's lectures, took part in amateur dramatics, ran down to London for balls and banquets, displayed his expertise at swimming and diving, and practiced at target shooting. He acquired a ferocious-looking bulldog which he named Smut, and was distressed when it was pointed out to him that college rules forbade keeping dogs in students' rooms. He responded by substituting a bear; there were no written rules about keeping bears in the rooms. It was a placid bear, and it went along quietly when he took it for walks on its chain, despite the curious undergraduates who usually followed. When one of the authorities asked Byron what he meant by bringing a bear to the university, he replied that the bear intended to sit for a fellowship. "The answer," he reported to a friend, "delighted them not." At Cambridge the versifier of Harrow turned to half-serious, half-mocking love lyrics.

> Away with your fictions of flimsy romance,
>   Those tissues of falsehood which Folly has wove;
> Give me the mild beam of the soul-breathing glance,
>   Or the rapture which dwells on the first kiss of love.
>
> Ye rhymers, whose bosoms with phantasy glow,
>   Whose pastoral passions are made for the grove;
> From what blest inspiration your sonnets would flow,
>   Could you ever have tasted the first kiss of love. . . .
>
> Oh! cease to affirm that man, since his birth,
>   From Adam, till now, has with wretchedness strove;

Some portion of Paradise still is on earth,
And Eden revives, in the first kiss of love.

When age chills the blood, when our pleasures are past—
For years fleet away with the wings of the dove—
The dearest remembrance will still be the last,
Our sweetest memorial, the first kiss of love.[3]

But perhaps the most significant event of Byron's stay at Cambridge was his meeting with an undergraduate who was to become his closest friend and confidant. John Cam Hobhouse was one of those campus leaders whom all undergraduates wanted to emulate. He was the son of a Member of Parliament who was on his way to becoming a baronet. As in all schools and colleges, Hobhouse was a leader of a clique which attracted and at the same time scorned most of the fellow students. Byron had been with them but not of them at first. Finally, as Byron explained it in a letter, Hobhouse "took me into his good graces because I had written some poetry. I had always lived a great deal, and got drunk occasionally, in their company—but now we became really friends in a morning." It was the beginning of a friendship that would last through Byron's lifetime, and have a deep effect on both men.

For Byron, however, Cambridge palled. After the Christmas holidays in 1807, he did not return, but instead found rooms in Dorant's Hotel in London. To Hobhouse, who had returned to the university, Byron bragged: "I am buried in an abyss of Sensuality." Byron's drinking companions in London were highly amused when the "young man" Byron had passed off as his cousin unexpectedly had a miscarriage, "to the inexpressible horror of the chambermaids, and the consternation of all the house." And as Byron indulged in more elaborate and ludicrous escapades, he sank deeper into debt.

To escape the stews of London for a while, Byron "retired" to the family seat at Newstead, and gradually Newstead Abbey took on the same atmosphere of debauchery as his London quarters had. When a gardener brought in a skull he had unearthed in the garden, Byron had it made into a drinking cup, from which he and his fellow carousers would drink wine through an evening that also included such games as chasing servant girls about the Gothic galleries. Hobhouse sometimes came down to join the fun, and to compose poetry of his own while Byron tried to concentrate on some verses in between parties.[4] But Newstead, like London and Cambridge, was boring Byron, and he proposed to Hobhouse a grand tour of the Continent and the Middle East.

This seemed to Hobhouse an excellent suggestion. He had just had a bitter disagreement with his father and did not want to return home. Because of the disagreement, Hobhouse had no money. Byron, who was already some £13,000 in debt, managed to arrange another loan, at an outrageous rate of interest, and the two friends prepared to set out on their great adventure.

Their departure was delayed by these financial negotiations. But in June of 1809, the last trunk was packed and the two friends rode down to the coast. Byron's exuberantly expectant mood when at last they set sail came through in the lilting lines he wrote as they bucked and plunged across the Channel.

> . . . From aloft the signal's streaming,
>   Hark! the farewell gun is fired;
> Women screeching, tars blaspheming,
>   Tell us that our time's expired.
>   Here's a rascal
>   Come to task all,

Prying from the Custom-house,
Trunks unpacking,
Cases cracking,
Not a corner for a mouse
'Scapes unsearched amid the racket,
Ere we sail on board the Packet.

Now our boatmen quit their mooring,
And all hands must ply the oar;
Baggage from the quay is lowering,
We're impatient, push from shore.
"Have a care! that case holds liquor—
Stop the boat—I'm sick—oh Lord!"
"Sick, Ma'am, damme, you'll be sicker
Ere you've been an hour on board." . . .

"Hey day! call you that a cabin?
Why 'tis hardly three feet square:
Not enough to stow Queen Mab in—
Who the deuce can harbour there?"
"Who, sir? plenty—
Nobles twenty
Did at once my vessel fill."—
"Did they? Jesus,
How you squeeze us!
Would to God they did so still:
Then I'd 'scape the heat and racket
Of the good ship Lisbon Packet." . . .[5]

It was an adventure which Byron would never forget and
which would color the rest of his life. Only a little more
than a week after sailing from Falmouth, he was writing home
from Lisbon that already he had eaten oranges, talked "bad
Latin to the monks," ridden a mule, learned to swear in Portu-

guese and experienced both mosquito bites and diarrhea. He had also engaged in his first impressive swimming feat, crossing Lisbon's Tagus River against tide and wind in two hours.

At Puerta Santa Maria, near Cádiz, Byron found his first bullfight a repulsive spectacle, and he was mesmerized with horror to the extent that he remembered it with gory clarity much later while writing the first canto of *Childe Harold*.

Foiled, bleeding, breathless, furious to the last,
    Full in the centre stands the Bull at bay,
    'Mid wounds, and clinging darts, and lances brast,
    And foes disabled in the brutal fray:
    And now the Matadores around him play,
    Shake the red cloak, and poise the ready brand:
    Once more through all he bursts his thundering way—
    Vain rage! the mantle quits the conynge hand,
Wraps his fierce eye—'tis past—he sinks upon the sand!

Where his vast neck just mingles with the spine,
    Sheathed in his form the deadly weapon lies.
    He stops—he starts—disdaining to decline:
    Slowly he falls, amidst triumphant cries,
    Without a groan, without a struggle dies.
    The decorated car appears—on high
    The corse is piled—sweet sight for vulgar eyes—
    Four steeds that spurn the rein, as swift as shy,
Hurl the dark bulk along, scarce seen in dashing by.

Such the ungentle sport that oft invites
    The Spanish maid, and cheers the Spanish swain.
    Nurtured in blood betimes, his heart delights
    In vengeance, gloating on another's pain. . . .[6]

The travelers found Gibraltar "the dirtiest most detestable spot," but Malta was better, partly because Byron fell into an agreeable love affair with a visiting Englishwoman, Constance Spencer Smith. He also enjoyed the bravado of challenging a British army captain to a duel, over what he could scarcely remember later. The duel was canceled by mutual agreement, and the love affair ended when Constance Spencer Smith sailed for home to return to Mr. Smith.

The adventurers sailed on to Greece. Byron was enchanted with the wild country inland and northward along the Albanian border. Hobhouse complained of the washed-out trails, the rocky roads, the rain-soaked bedding, the fleas. But Byron was enthralled by a visit to Tepelenë and the Ali Pasha, absolute ruler of all the countryside from Albania to the Gulf of Corinth. "The Albanians in their dresses," Byron wrote his mother, "the Tartars with their high caps, the Turks in their vast pelisses and turbans, the soldiers and black slaves with the horses . . . couriers entering or passing out with dispatches, the kettle drums beating, boys calling the hour from the minaret of the mosque, altogether, with the singular appearance of the building itself, formed a new and delightful spectacle to a stranger." The Albanian spectacle would affect Byron's poetry for many years thereafter.

Trekking back toward Athens, Byron went bird hunting, and was surprised at his reaction when he hit one. It was "an *eaglet*, on the shore of the Gulf of Lepanto, near Vostitza. It was only wounded, and I tried to save it, the eye was so bright; but it pined, and died in a few days; and I never did since, and never will, attempt the death of another bird."

In and around Athens, Byron and Hobhouse toured the historic sites and marveled at the plains of Marathon. They visited Piraeus, where they saw chests containing soon-to-be-famous marble sculptures from the Acropolis, about to be shipped to England by the British archaeologist Lord Elgin.[7]

They managed to get lost in the caves near Cape Colonna. And they admired the view from the cape, where from the southeast promontory of Attica the green islands spring up in the blue Aegean as far away as the eye can see.

Sailing on to Smyrna and Constantinople, they were detained by bad weather—and while waiting near the Dardanelles Byron was seized with the urge to emulate Leander by swimming the Hellespont. On April 15, 1810, with a lieutenant of marines, Byron waded into the water on the European side and set out for the Asiatic shore, a mile away. After an hour, fighting tide and frigid water, they gave up. But on May 3 they tried again; and this time, after an hour and ten minutes, they made it. Byron never ceased bragging about this undeniably formidable feat of swimming.

> If, in the month of dark December,
>   Leander, who was nightly wont
> (What maid will not the tale remember?)
>   To cross thy stream, broad Hellespont!
>
> If, when the wintry tempest roared,
>   He sped to Hero, nothing loth,
> And thus of old thy current poured,
>   Fair Venus! how I pity both!
>
> For *me*, degenerate modern wretch,
>   Though in the genial month of May,
> My dripping limbs I faintly stretch,
>   And think I've done a feat to-day.
>
> But since he crossed the rapid tide,
>   According to the doubtful story,
> To woo, and—Lord knows what beside,
>   And swam for Love, as I for Glory;

17

'Twere hard to say who fared the best:
Sad mortals! thus the Gods still plague you!
He lost his labour, I my jest:
For he was drowned, and I've the ague.[8]

One of the first sights to greet Byron and Hobhouse in Constantinople was that of two dogs worrying a human body. But they found the city's social life attractive, once they became accustomed to it, though Byron was already forming an intense hatred of the Turks. In Constantinople Byron and Hobhouse climbed towers, inspected mosques, wineshops and seraglios. Then, after a year's traveling together, the two companions decided to part at last. In July Hobhouse set out for England and home. And Byron headed for Greece, where he planned to stay an entire year before going home himself.

So for a year Athens became the hub of his life, a life of traveling to Morea, to Tripolis, to Piraeus again. Always he returned to Athens, for there he became engaged in what became one of the most famous of his young love affairs—with Theresa Macri.

She was twelve years old, in a part of the world where twelve amounted to near maturity; she was one of three daughters of a widow, Mrs. Tarsia Macri, in whose home Byron and Hobhouse had taken lodgings when they first reached Athens. Theresa was dark-haired, with sparkling black eyes set in a pale face. She and Byron had parted emotionally when he had sailed for Constantinople; and now on his return they took up again. Theresa's wily mother tried to lure Byron into marriage with her daughter. Failing that, she calmly rented Theresa out to him. The affair went on through much of his time in Athens, and is preserved forever in one of his best-known early poems.

> Maid of Athens, ere we part,
> Give, oh give me back my heart!
> Or, since that has left my breast,
> Keep it now, and take the rest!
> Hear my vow before I go,
> Ζωή μου, σᾶς ἀγαπῶ. . . .⁹

The poem's sentiment indicates absence and reflection a bit more than does Byron's comment at the time: "I was near bringing away Theresa," he wrote on leaving Greece, "but the mother asked 30,000 piastres!"

Byron arrived home on July 14, 1811, two years after he and Hobhouse had set forth from Falmouth. He brought with him impressions that would always affect his poetry, and four thousand lines he had already written. These he gave to a friend, Robert Dulles, to pass along to a publisher, saying: "They are not worth troubling you with, but you shall have them all if you wish." The lines included a long work which he titled *Childe Harold's Pilgrimage*. The publisher, John Murray, took one look and accepted the work with alacrity.

Byron's pleasure at this reception was shortly clouded by sadness and perhaps remorse. On his return to England he had not taken the time to visit his mother at Newstead, and two weeks after his return he received word that she was ill. He was trying to borrow against his literary prospects when, one day after the first message, another arrived reporting that she had died.

No doubt shocked at the sudden realization of his thoughtlessness and irresponsibility, Byron plunged into a new arena, the House of Lords.

He chose a dramatic time. In late 1811, Nottingham, England, was convulsed by one of history's earliest reactions against automation. Bands of weavers, incensed by the introduction of textile frames that were putting them out of jobs, were rioting and smashing the frames. So destructive had the rioting been that troops were called into the area, without quelling the uprisings entirely. The Tories, in full charge of Parliament, were in no mood to temporize with rioters, and a bill proposing the death penalty for frame breakers went through the House of Commons and on to the House of Lords.

Lord Byron had read about, and indeed had seen, the poverty-stricken conditions of the weavers put out of work by the introduction of stocking frames. On February 27, 1812, the twenty-four-year-old lord rose to make his maiden speech, in defense of the frame breakers and advocating a bill to alleviate their poverty rather than to punish them. "I have been in some of the most oppressed provinces of Turkey," he said, "but never under the most despotic of infidel governments did I behold such squalid wretchedness as I have seen since my return in the very heart of a Christian country. . . . How can you carry the Bill into effect? Can you commit a whole country to their own prisons? Will you erect a gibbet in every field, and hang up men like scarecrows?" The bill was modified in the House of Lords, by a committee on which Byron was asked to sit. But the modification was then wiped out by the House of Commons.

At that point, however, Byron was forced to forget politics. His poem *Childe Harold* was published, and his life was changed overnight.

Neither Byron nor his publisher, John Murray, had dreamed of the sensation that *Childe Harold* would produce. The first edition was confined to five hundred copies, which were gone in three days. Further editions kept selling at the same rate, the fifth going in one day. Everyone talked about the romantic new epic hero, and the romantic new poet. The Duchess of Devonshire wrote that *Childe Harold* "is on every table, and himself courted, visited, flattered, and praised whenever he appears . . . in short, he is really the only topic almost of conversation—the men jealous of him, the women of each other."

Especially the women. On some days there were traffic jams in St. James's Street, as the carriages stopped to deliver invitations to the new literary lion of London. The curly-haired young man with the Greek profile, the mocking smile, the arrogant carriage and the limping gait was a refreshing sight to the bored ladies of London society, and they swept him into their circle of salons, balls and banquets. Byron enjoyed acting his part, and he was soon engulfed in the social round and in a seemingly endless series of attachments as the ladies competed for his favors. The society that swarmed around him was ultra sophisticated and ultra immoral. The first salon Byron found himself frequenting, for example, was that of Lady Holland, whose previous husband had divorced her, naming Lord Holland as corespondent. And one of the first women to catch his eye at the salon was the former mistress of Lady Holland's first husband.

She was Lady Caroline Lamb, the spoiled, impetuous twenty-seven-year-old wife of William Lamb, a spineless husband who either did not care about or could do nothing to prevent his wife's reckless behavior. When she first heard of Byron's reputation, Lady Caroline described him in her journal as "mad—bad—and dangerous to know"; after meeting him she added: "That beautiful pale face is my fate." Her wildly passionate affair with Byron supplanted the talk of Byron alone as the main subject of London gossip, so completely did Caroline Lamb give up all pretense and discretion. Through the spring months of 1812 they made love, battled, made up and scandalized everyone with their public display of affection. One unwritten law of London society was that such affairs were conducted surreptitiously. Caroline Lamb paid no attention to the warnings of her friends or even of her worldly wise mother-in-law, Lady Melbourne, who had had a number of affairs of her own, but who had never flaunted her misbehavior. Nearly the only person involved who did not warn Lady Caroline was her husband. "He was privy to my affair with Lord Byron," she confessed, "and laughed at it. His indulgence rendered him insensible to everything."

But then Lady Caroline began to realize that Byron had an indolence of his own, which let him drift into attachments like this and also made it difficult for him to break off when he wanted to. After a few months of their stormy relationship, he did want to break off from Caroline, but he could not bring himself to it. On her side, as she sensed his growing disaffection, Caroline became frantic. When Byron made excuses to avoid her, she besieged him. It reached the point where she disguised herself as a page to sneak into his rooms. At length her strong-willed mother-in-law, Lady Melbourne, talked her son, William Lamb, into taking his wife away to Ireland. And Byron, and many others who had been involved, breathed a sigh of relief. There was a final scene some ten months later, when Lady Caroline evidently became so hysterical that she tried to stab herself. But the notorious affair was ended, amid recriminations, protestations and tears.

Others had already taken Caroline's place, the most striking of them being Jane Elizabeth Scott, Countess of Oxford. Eighteen years earlier she had married the Fifth Earl of Oxford, a mild-mannered man who, when she told him of her indiscretions, replied that "her candour and frank confession were so amiable that he entirely forgave her." So many liaisons had she previously acquired that her children were cattily called the "Harleian Miscellany," after a series of manuscripts published by Lord Oxford's library.

Lady Oxford was sixteen years older than Byron when they met, but he found her maturity relaxing after the frenetic youth of Caroline Lamb. Lord Oxford continued to be permissive, and Byron spent weeks at a time at the Oxford country home while the lord of the manor obligingly pursued his own amusements in London. Byron unabashedly recounted his amorous exploits to Caroline's mother-in-law, Lady Melbourne, who had become his confidante. Lady Melbourne, in the wisdom of her experience and her sixty-two years, calmly listened to Byron's accounts and as calmly advised him on how to avoid Caroline. Byron found the welcome at Melbourne House as warm after his break with Caroline as before, and in fact his intimate correspondence with Lady Melbourne continued until her death in 1818. And it was at Melbourne House that he met the woman who was to become his wife.

Few ladies of the London society of the time could have provided a more striking contrast to the women with whom Byron had been consorting than Annabella Milbanke. Annabella was Lady Melbourne's niece, the only daughter of Lady Melbourne's brother, Sir Ralph Milbanke. Like many of the other ladies of fashion in the social whirl inhabited by Byron, Annabella was spoiled and self-centered. But where the others were superficially bright and wittily sophisticated, Annabella Milbanke was a country girl, introspective and thoughtful and nearly devoid of any sense of humor or self-deprecation. While Caroline Lamb, for example, had learned to read in her teens (and had then taken to simple versifying), Annabella at twenty was a scholar in mathematics, the classics and philosophy. She was intelligent, learned, moralistic, priggish and nearly everything else that contrasted with all the other women Byron had encountered in the salons and ballrooms of London's social whirl. Byron was impressed by her after all the giddy glamour girls, but his main interest at first, he confessed to Lady Melbourne, was in Annabella's fortune. Partly attracted by her accomplishments but perhaps mostly interested in her money, he made an offhand proposal of marriage. She turned him down.

Shrugging the incident off, he turned to other amours. He put Annabella out of his mind and they did not cross paths again for six months. By this time Byron had become involved in the most scandalous affair of his scandalous London life.

Augusta Byron Leigh was five years older than her half-brother. She was the daughter born to "Mad Jack" Byron and his first wife, before her death and Jack Byron's marriage to Catherine Gordon, by whom he became the poet's father. Despite their correspondence, brother and sister had seen little of each other, and Augusta had, at the age of twenty-four, married her cousin, Colonel George Leigh. By 1812 she was the mother of three daughters, the lady of the manor at Six Mile Bottom, near Newmarket, and deeply in debt because of her husband's infatuation with betting on horse races. Colonel Leigh was rarely home, preferring to follow the horses all over England, and Augusta was properly bored. Her memories of Byron were a sentimental mixture of recollections of him as a baby and half-envious admiration of the gay life he was leading up in London. Now their paths crossed again.

Byron found that the gangling girl he remembered had grown into attractive maturity, with a handsome profile, a sensuous curl of the lip and an offhand sense of humor often lacking in the precious parlor ladies of his London acquaintance.

His most recent inamorata, Lady Oxford, had been spirited away to the Continent by her husband, and Byron found the easy, pleasant companionship of Augusta a great comfort. Shortly it became more than that.

Colonel Leigh was off at some racetrack or other, and Augusta's children had been having all of the usual childhood diseases. So she was delighted to come up to London and plunge into the round of balls and parties to which her brother was constantly being invited. And Byron, in the same heedless manner that had led him into so many entanglements, became infatuated with Augusta. Added to his natural disinclination to care about the proprieties was, in this case, the added allure of knowing how wrong it was. In his young years of libertinism he had tried everything else; but he had never committed incest.

As for Augusta, for all her attractions she was an empty-headed girl, easily tempted and unable to withstand anyone so persuasive as Byron. Then, too, she may have rationalized that he was only her half-brother, a fact that might have swayed Byron as well. Actual proof of incest has never been established conclusively. But of evidence there was plenty, particularly in the words of Byron, who could no more resist bragging about or hinting at his sins than he could resist sinning. To Lady Melbourne he wrote about Augusta: "Forgive my follies, and like me as much as you can." To his old friend the poet Tom Moore he wrote: "I am at this moment in a far more serious, and entirely new, scrape than any of the last twelve months,—and that is saying a good deal. It is unlucky we can neither live with nor without these women." In his daily journal he wrote: "It is quite enough to set down my thoughts, —my actions will rarely bear introspection." And when Moore asked him to write the words for a song, Byron replied with:

I speak not, I trace not, I breathe not thy name,
There is grief in the sound, there is guilt in the fame:
But the tear which now burns on my cheek may impart
The deep thoughts that dwell in that silence of heart.

Too brief for our passion, too long for our peace,
Were those hours—can their joy or their bitterness cease?
We repent, we abjure, we will break from our chain—
We will part, we will fly to—unite it again!

Oh! thine be the gladness, and mine be the guilt!
Forgive me, adored one! forsake, if thou wilt;
But the heart which is thine shall expire undebased,
And *man* shall not break it—whatever *thou* mayst.

And stern to the haughty, but humble to thee,
This soul, in its bitterest blackness, shall be:
And our days seem as swift, and our moments more sweet,
With thee by my side, than with worlds at our feet.

One sigh of thy sorrow, one look of thy love,
Shall turn me or fix, shall reward or reprove;
And the heartless may wonder at all I resign—
Thy lip shall reply, not to them, but to *mine*.[10]

Rumors of the affair permeated the London social circle
immediately. And for once Byron worried. He wrote fewer
letters to Lady Melbourne, perhaps unable to come out with
the truth and afraid that he would. He even gave up writing his daily journal for a while, evidently unwilling to confess in writing. Once he apparently did set down a statement
on the subject, but then tore out the pages and destroyed them.
He sank into a bad temper, and found that "sleep is no friend
of mine." At last Byron the libertine seemed to have shocked
even himself. And at that point he received a letter from
Annabella Milbanke:

"It is my nature to feel long, deeply and secretly. . . . Early in our acquaintance, when I was far from supposing myself preferred by you, I studied your character. . . . How often have I wished that the state of Society would have allowed me to offer you my sentiments without restraint!"

So began a renewal of the courtship, first carried out by an exchange of archly worded letters—an odd form of courtship for Byron, as nearly every other aspect of his relationship with this strange girl was out of the ordinary. Reacting to the gossip about his relationship with Augusta, tormented by the affair himself, he seized on this opportune avenue of escape. The letters at length led to one in which, in much the same reckless way he had before, he made an overture toward another proposal. "When I believed you attached, I had nothing to urge—indeed I have little now, except that having heard from yourself that your affections are not engaged, my importunities may appear not quite so selfish, however unsuccessful. It is not without a struggle that I address you once more on this subject. . . ."

What he intended Annabella to read between these lines is a mystery. He might only have been inquiring if her first refusal had been because of someone else. In any case, Annabella chose to read the letter as a second, more serious proposal. She quickly replied: "I am almost too agitated to write—but you will understand. It would be absurd to suppress anything —I am and have long been pledged to myself to make your happiness my first object in life. . . . I will *trust* to you for all I should look up to—all I can love. . . . This is a moment of joy which I have too much despaired of ever experiencing." She added that she was also sending a "few lines" from her father.

Byron was at dinner with Augusta when Annabella's acceptance arrived. He read it, handed it across to Augusta and said: "It never rains but it pours."

Annabella Milbanke became Lady Byron on January 2, 1814. Hobhouse was present to watch his friend go through the simple ceremony at the Milbanke country home. He helped hand Lady Byron into the carriage and wished her happiness. She replied, "If I am not happy, it will be my own fault." The carriage drove off. Hobhouse wrote in his diary: "I felt as if I had buried a friend."

It was a hopeless marriage from the start. The last thing Byron could sustain was domesticity; though he had fooled himself into thinking it would be good for him, he knew as soon as the marriage vows had been taken that he had walked into a trap. On the morning after the wedding he greeted his bride with: "It is too late now. It is done, and cannot be undone." And when Annabella replied that she had no regrets, he was furious. As the days went on he tried every way he knew to taunt her, to arouse her anger, to inject some spice into the placidity that he saw enveloping him. The more he goaded her, the more Annabella tried to calm him by a soft answer, a noncommittal response, a turning away of wrath. It had the opposite effect. Byron insulted her, bragged of his previous love affairs and talked of infidelities he planned in the future. No doubt he found the prim Annabella sexually unresponsive, particularly in contrast to the passionate Caroline Lamb and the experienced ladies with whom he had been consorting. And as he continued his campaign of taunt and insult, Annabella began to respond more in pity than forbearance. This was too much. Byron realized that he had maneuvered himself into what for him was untenable—marriage. There were rare times when Annabella relaxed and laughed with him, or talked intelligently about something that interested him, and when he could say that he enjoyed her company; but what he could not stand, he now knew for a certainty, was any woman's constant company. Once he said to Annabella: "If any woman could have rendered marriage endurable to me, you would." Her answer to such remarks was a calm and confident claim that he would learn to love her yet; his answer was: "It is too late . . . it is my destiny to ruin all I come near." As if he excused himself by blaming destiny, he set out to ruin the marriage. And Annabella, try as she would, was unable to prevent it. As Byron's manservant Fletcher said: "It is very odd, but I never yet knew a lady that could not manage my Lord, *except* my lady."

More and more Byron retreated to his study. Annabella was unable to tell when he was composing poetry or simply hiding out, and so she often interrupted him when he was at work, a transgression he never forgot. His rudeness in driving her from the room was something she could not forget either. Meanwhile Byron's debts mounted and he borrowed and tried to put off the collectors. At one point a bailiff forced his way into the house and refused to leave until part of one creditor's loan was paid—by borrowing from yet another. And so it went, with the marriage running swiftly downhill. Plagued by his debts, by boredom and by his wife, Byron turned back to the solace he knew best—his sister Augusta.

At first he planned to visit her alone at the Leighs' country house at Six Mile Bottom. Colonel Leigh might or might not be in residence; more often he was off following the horses. It didn't matter. Byron and Augusta could enjoy each other's company undisturbed whether her husband was there or not; he seemed not to care. But Annabella cared, and she insisted on coming along. With a shrug, Byron agreed, and the young couple arrived at Six Mile Bottom on March 12, 1815. Ever afterward Annabella wished she had not gone along.

It was obvious from the moment of their arrival that Byron and his sister were happiest in each other's company, alone. Evening after evening they chattered to each other, through dinner and on afterward for hours until Annabella finally tired of listening and went to bed alone. On an occasion when she decided to stick it out, Byron finally turned to her and said with a sneer: "We don't want you, my charmer." In tears Annabella went to their room. And when, many hours later, Byron came to bed, she was awakened by hearing him curse Fletcher and fall into bed. If, as she did once, she moved toward him, he cried out: "Don't touch me!" Annabella may or may not have realized that her husband had been drinking too much. Whatever the reason, the two-week visit was the first excruciating trial of the many she would experience before their marriage reached its inevitable end. During the visit Augusta tried to be hospitable to Annabella, but Byron was determined to humiliate his wife, and his sister could do nothing to ameliorate the situation he insisted on creating over and over again. The only pleasant periods Annabella could later remember from this visit were when occasionally Byron would lose himself in playing with Augusta's children. In fact, said Annabella: "I should like to have him painted when he is looking at Medora."

When they moved up to London, things only got worse. Byron took up with other women, including an actress named Susan Boyce, whom he described years later as "a transient piece of mine." He spent more and more time out of the house, and when he was home seemed to devote most of his time, when he was not writing, to drinking. The fact that Annabella was pregnant and about to deliver their child seemed only to annoy him more, with the obvious threat of entangling him deeper in the coils of domesticity. The night of the baby's birth was a nightmare for Annabella, with Byron in the study below her bedroom roaring around, drinking and knocking the heads off the bottles with the fire poker. The baby was a girl, and Byron paid scarcely any attention to the creature, beyond proposing that she be named Augusta Ada.

As she recovered from childbirth and watched her husband's eccentricities and humiliating behavior increase all the more, Annabella at last began seriously to believe that he was losing his mind.

In desperation Annabella turned to Augusta for help, inviting her to visit them. But finally she decided that, for her safety and that of her baby, she must leave. Augusta was with them at the time, and Byron and his sister were sitting together when Annabella came into the room.

"Byron, I come to say good-bye." She held out her hand.

He rose and walked to the mantel, where he stood for a moment saying nothing. Then he smiled and asked: "When shall we three meet again?"

"In heaven, I trust."

She turned and went to her room. By her account she slept soundly—"as I believe is often surprisingly the case in such cases of deep sorrow." Next morning early, as the carriage waited, she paused at Byron's bedroom door, standing beside the large mat where his Newfoundland dog often lay. But she did not go in; she went down the hall and out to the carriage. The horses lurched ahead and the wheels rattled away from Piccadilly Terrace. Byron never saw her or his daughter again.

For a time Annabella worried about her husband's insanity, as she chose to see it, and humored him by writing affectionate letters. But little by little absence dimmed Byron's effect upon her, and her innate coolness reasserted itself. Finally the marriage was completely dead.

And now Byron, who had not wanted her when he had her, felt that he wanted her more than ever. He complained to anyone who would listen that he was lost without his wife and daughter. He wrote her fervent love letters. "Bell, dearest Bell . . . I can only say . . . that I love you, bad or good, mad or rational, miserable or content, I love you, and shall do, to the dregs of my memory and existence. . . ." But Annabella kept to her resolve, and turned to a lawyer to file the necessary papers for a separation; divorce was more of a scandal than she could face. And she hoped that the separation procedure could be kept as quiet as possible; for she was by now convinced of what she had tried not to believe for months—that her husband was involved in an incestuous relationship with his half-sister.

Byron did little to object to the separation, and on March 17 the agreement was reached. Augusta Ada, whom Annabella hereafter referred to as Ada, was to remain with her mother. And Byron, in his half-self-conscious remorse, turned to poetry.

> Fare thee well! and if for ever,
>   Still for ever, fare *thee well*:
> Even though unforgiving, never
>   'Gainst thee shall my heart rebel.
> Would that breast were bared before thee
>   Where thy head so oft hath lain,
> While that placid sleep came o'er thee
>   Which thou ne'er canst know again:
> Would that breast, by thee glanced over,
>   Every inmost thought could show!
> Then thou wouldst at last discover
>   'Twas not well to spurn it so. . . .

Though my many faults defaced me,
  Could no other arm be found,
Than the one which once embraced me,
  To inflict a cureless wound? . . .
And when thou wouldst solace gather—
  When our child's first accents flow—
Wilt thou teach her to say "Father!"
  Though his care she must forego? . . .
But 'tis done—all words are idle—
  Words from me are vainer still;
But the thoughts we cannot bridle
  Force their way without the will.
Fare thee well! thus disunited—
  Torn from every nearer tie—
Seared in heart—and lone—and blighted—
  More than this I scarce can die.[11]

He also turned to more drink. And, not surprisingly, he
turned to other women. Among them there was one who
seemed only a passing interest at the moment. But she was to
affect Byron's life far more than any of the others in all those
years in London.

An utter stranger takes the liberty of addressing you. It is
earnestly requested that for one moment you pardon the intrusion,
and laying aside every circumstance of who or what you are, listen
with a friendly ear. A moment of passion or an impulse of pride
often destroys our own happiness and that of others. If in this
case your refusal shall not affect yourself yet you are not aware
how much it may injure another. It is not charity I demand, for
of that I stand in no need. . . .
I tremble with fear at the fate of this letter. . . . Mine is a
delicate case; my feet are on the edge of a precipice; Hope flying
on forward wings beckons me to follow her, and rather than resign
this cherished creature I jump, though at the peril of my life. . . .

If a woman whose reputation has yet remained unstained, if without guardian or either husband to control, she should throw herself upon your mercy, if with a beating heart she should confess the love she has borne you many years, if she should secure to you secresy and safety, if she should return your kindness with fond affection and unbounded devotion, could you betray her, or would you be silent as the grave?

I am not given to many words. Either you will or you will not. Do not decide hastily, and yet I must entreat your answer without delay, not only because I hate to be tortured by suspense, but because my departure a short way out of town is unavoidable, and I would know your reply ere I go. Address me as

E. Trefusis
21 Noley Place, Mary le Bonne

The notorious Lord Byron received letters like this one regularly during his years of glory in London. He ignored it. But Miss E. Trefusis was not so easily put off. At length she wrote that she needed to see him on a matter of "peculiar importance." Byron replied: "Ld. B. is not aware of any 'importance' which can be attached by any person to an interview with him, and more particularly by one with whom it does not appear that he had the honour of being acquainted." But evidently the persistence of the young lady had begun to intrigue him. He added: "He will however be at home at the hour mentioned."

Her name was Mary Jane Clairmont. During the next few years she would change her name with her changing whim, from Clara to Clare and finally to Claire (which we might as well call her from the outset). Miss Clairmont's family was an odd one, to put it mildly. Her widowed mother was now the second wife of William Godwin, the nonconformist philosopher whose writings advocated political radicalism, atheism and free love. Despite his principles, Godwin had married his first wife, Mary Wollstonecraft, and on her death had married Mrs. Clairmont, whose children, including Claire, now lived in a mixed and chaotic household with Godwin's children by his first wife and one child by the present Mrs. Godwin.

Claire was now eighteen, a brunette who would have been handsome except for a prominent nose. She was multilingual, a student of German literature, loquacious, intense, single-minded and pertinacious. At the moment she fancied an acting career, and her overt reason for approaching Byron was that he was on the committee of the Drury Lane Theater. Byron was at first put off by so mundane a request and referred her to a friend on the committee. But something kept him from turning away from her completely, and when she suggested that she was interested in writing too, he realized that this curious, intense young girl was indeed interested mostly in him. Her single-mindedness should have warned him of trouble. But in his usual heedless manner, never pausing to consider the consequences, he encouraged her visits and letters. Then came one that brought matters to a head.

. . . I do not expect you to love me: I am not worthy of your love. I feel you are superior, yet much to my surprize, more to my happiness, you betrayed passions I had believed no longer alive in your bosom. . . . I may appear to you imprudent, vicious, my opinions detestable, my theory depraved, but one thing at least time will show you, that I love gently and with affection. . . .

Have you then any objection to the following plan? On Thursday Evening we may go out of town together by some stage or mail about the distance of ten or twelve miles. Then we shall be free and unknown; we can return early the following morning. . . .

So the affair started.

But it was to be short-lived, in London at least. The reason was that Byron had made the dramatic decision that he must exile himself from England. The conviction had been growing on him, as he read the accusations against him in the gossip columns and listened to his former acquaintances cluck disapprovingly at his behavior. But the situation came to a spectacular climax on the evening of April 8, 1816, at a ball given by his friend Lady Jersey.

Byron attended with Hobhouse—and with Augusta. She made her entrance into the crowded ballroom on the arm of her brother, as she had on so many occasions in the past few months. But this time a flutter and then a wave of shock went through the room. Augusta was pregnant.

One, then another, then others and finally every lady present turned and swept grandly out of the ballroom. Byron masked his astonishment and outrage with one of his studied sardonic smiles. As he and Augusta stood watching the humiliating procession, one young lady, a Miss Mercer Elphinstone, tiptoed over to him, gave him a coquettish nod and said: "You should have married *me*, and then this would not have happened to you." At the moment Byron was neither amused nor intrigued by the obvious invitation. In fact, so outraged was he by this cruel insult to Augusta that he made the decision he had been approaching all along. He would leave this callous and sanctimonious society for good. He would exile himself from England.

When he set about in earnest making his plans to go to the Continent, Claire Clairmont was overjoyed. She too was planning to visit the Continent, and she asked Byron to agree to a meeting in Switzerland, where both would be that summer. Byron consented, not so much because he looked forward to seeing Claire again as because of her announcement that her companions in Geneva would be her stepsister Mary Godwin and Mary's lover, the young poet Percy Bysshe Shelley. Byron was among the small minority of Englishmen who had read the poetry of Shelley, and he looked forward to the prospect of meeting this intense, rebellious, obviously talented young man.[12]

[III]

[III]

Percy Shelley was four years younger than Byron. Like Byron he could look back on an assortment of eccentric ancestors. The Shelley family line could be traced to James I, even to William the Conqueror with a little imagination. But the family's wealth had not been well preserved, and Percy Shelley's great-grandfather had even endured the humiliation, for an old aristocratic English family, of emigration to America. It had been Percy's grandfather Bysshe, born in Newark, New Jersey, who had restored the Shelley fortunes—by marrying well not once but twice, both by elopement. Not only had he married two heiresses, but he had also won himself a baronetage, and by the time his grandson Percy was born, Sir Bysshe Shelley had become a conservative, comfortable country squire. How many sons Sir Bysshe had fathered, including bastards, was not known for certain, perhaps even by him.

But his oldest legal son, Timothy, named *his* first son Percy Bysshe, and old Sir Bysshe fondly watched his grandson and namesake grow into an intelligent and attractive young boy. Hopefully looking forward to a proper scion who would maintain the family honor, marry well and perhaps enter Parliament, Sir Bysshe arranged his will to make sure that his estate would be passed on through Timothy to young Percy Bysshe.

At first his grandson showed heartening promise. His teachers were impressed by Percy's Latin and English versifying, but his real forte was science. Young Percy was fascinated by his discoveries through the telescope, and he was seized by the concept that many of the planets were inhabited, perhaps by a higher order of life. He was forever conducting experiments, and when at twelve he left for Eton, his room at home still smelled oddly from his many scientific experiments. At Eton he electrocuted a cat. He delivered a numbing shock to a tutor who had the misfortune to touch one of Shelley's galvanic batteries. And one of his chemical formulas almost blew him up.

But meanwhile Eton was becoming the turning point in Shelley's life, the formative period when the normal country boy developed into the rebellious nonconformist, when Sir Bysshe's young scion became the atheistical "Mad Shelley." All unprepared by his sheltered life at home in Field Place, Sussex, the favorite grandson was thrown into the jungle of a boys' school. Eton in 1804 was at once the fostering and testing ground of the boys who would grow to be England's leaders. But that fostering and testing, as Wellington innocently described it a few years later, took place more on the playing fields than in the classrooms of Eton. The school provided every sort of game from cricket to hoops and from football to kites. A spirit of zealous, even brutal, competition was encouraged, and there was no sympathy, in fact there was downright scorn, for any boy who did not engage heartily in these character-building activities. Proficiency in the classroom was secondary to performance on the famous playing fields.

Shelley despised this preoccupation with athletics. But to his fellow students such an attitude could have only one cause: Shelley was effeminate and inferior to his burly classmates, however poorly their intelligence compared with his. And so Shelley became the butt of the Etonians' ridicule, especially when they found how easily he could be taunted into a maddened reaction.

A schoolmate would yank at Shelley's arm, spilling his books. Someone would flick at his posterior as he bent to pick them up. He would come up swinging on his tormentor, who would duck away to be replaced by another, who would dump Shelley's books again or rip off his jacket. Another would peg a muddy ball at him; another would trip him or jostle him off the walk or into a door. Meanwhile the others would dance around him, pointing at him, hooting and calling him names. After the first few encounters of this type, Shelley realized that reacting would only encourage his attackers, so he tried to control his temper. But he rarely could take such harassment for long without striking back in a blind, frenzied—and futile—counterattack. His eyes, one of his colleagues later remembered, would "flash like a tiger's, his cheeks grow pale as death, his limbs quiver." His hysterical flailings were nearly always in vain, though once he did have the satisfaction of sticking a fork through the hand of a tormentor. Usually these scenes were harmless, diverting sport for the young Etonians, and "Shelley baits" became a favorite Etonian amusement.

Little by little Shelley withdrew into himself and cultivated the manner and behavior of an outcast. He affected sloppy dress—no shoelaces or hat, with little attention to how, or how often, he wore the rest of his clothes. He cultivated a reputation as the school rebel, and his antagonism toward his schoolmates extended to insurrection against school authority and all the accepted custom for which the school stood. "Mad Shelley" he was called, and "Shelley the atheist," though he was not an avowed disbeliever in the Almighty yet; that would come later. He even, perhaps as a last gesture of defiance of his rough-and-ready colleagues of the football field and cricket pitch, adopted the effete pose of a writer of verse.

Oxford in 1810 seemed to Shelley as intellectually barren as Eton. The arrogant lassitude of those around him only increased his spirit of separateness and rebellion. But in one fellow Oxfordian he did find a friend and soul mate, one who would be a sympathetic, if sometimes errant, companion through the trying years ahead. Thomas Jefferson Hogg was the spoiled son of a successful attorney in New York. Intelligent, cynical, interested in the law but also willing to entertain some of the more radical ideas, Hogg found the vague-mannered but stimulating young man from Eton worth a few idle hours of conversation. Casual friendship grew into companionship, and Shelley and Hogg found themselves sharing most of their free time, of which there was a great deal at Oxford in those days.

Through the long afternoons and evenings, the talk of science and its promising future turned to the social sciences and their unpromising present. The discussion naturally came around to a social scientist whom they both had read and who would have a far greater effect on their lives than they could have guessed.

Their intellectual hero was the same William Godwin whose

stepdaughter Claire Clairmont was to pursue Lord Byron. Godwin's most famous book bore the long-winded title *An Enquiry Concerning Political Justice, and Its Influence on General Virtue and Happiness*. Better known as *Political Justice*, the treatise virtually advocated anarchy. In his theoretical philosophy Godwin was against all government, all laws, all property, all religion. And Shelley was soon referring to the book as "the regulator and former of my mind."

Timothy Shelley, Percy's father, was not the brightest member of the family. He was generally content with the placid, ordered—and dull—life of a country gentleman. But he had the perception to spot the waywardness of his son at an early stage. Like most fathers, he was prepared for youthful rebellion; the attitudes being struck by his son, however, seemed extreme. He wrote the young man, admonishing him to give up such evil influences as the books of Godwin and the companionship of Hogg. Percy's reaction was expressed in a note to Hogg which had overtones of those earlier days at Eton: "I am reckoned an outcast; yet I defy them and laugh at their ineffectual efforts." And then came the explosive event which Timothy Shelley feared and which Percy welcomed.

In the show window of a bookstore in Oxford appeared a few copies of a little volume entitled *The Necessity of Atheism* (sixpence, author anonymous). Shortly there occurred a dramatic encounter in the common room of University College, Oxford. Shelley was summoned to appear before the Master, who produced a copy of the book and asked Shelley if he was the author. Shelley refused to answer yes or no, asking instead what evidence the Master had. The Master put the question to him again. And again Shelley refused to answer. The Master said: "I desire that you quit the College early tomorrow morning at the latest."

Shelley marched out of the common room and back to his

quarters, where his friend Hogg waited for him. Still in a state of shock, Shelley could say nothing but, "Expelled! Expelled!" Hogg reacted by sending a note to the Master, protesting and asking him to give his friend Shelley another chance. The Master responded by summoning Hogg and asking him what part he had played in this business. Hogg refused to answer, except to say that if his friend Shelley was guilty he, Hogg, was equally guilty. That was sufficient for the Master. Hogg too was expelled. Early in the morning of March 26, 1811, Shelley and Hogg climbed aboard the stage and set out for London and a new life.

Shelley's father was appalled and made one last effort to save his son. Obviously the real trouble lay in the influence of young Hogg on his son's fertile mind. So Timothy Shelley hurried up to London to make a final offer: if his son would make a complete break with this diabolical companion, his father would pay for a tutor.

When Timothy Shelley confronted the two young men, they mocked his arguments, laughed at his country pronunciation and sauntered away from him as if he were beneath their contempt. In the blind rage of humiliation brought on by his own son, Timothy Shelley went home. He would never forgive Percy Shelley as long as he lived.

Whether young Shelley ever had cause to reflect on and regret this juvenile act of cruelty is not known. At the moment, however, he was engrossed in the free life of London, in the plays and parties, in the literary life (particularly a new book, *English Bards and Scotch Reviewers*, by Lord Byron), and in a love affair. Her name was Harriet Westbrook. She was a friend and classmate of Shelley's sister in her boarding school and reputed to be the prettiest girl in the school. Harriet's father, John Westbrook, was a retired tavernkeeper.

Harriet was pleasant, rather ingenuous and, despite her

prettiness, flattered by Shelley's attentions. She was attracted by his intelligence and earnestness and intrigued by his rebellious spirit. His expulsion from Oxford only made him more interesting. And, no doubt influenced by Shelley's gay London life in contrast to her own in boarding school, Harriet wrote him to confess that her schoolmates were discriminating against her because she had admitted a connection with such a renegade. There were more letters and more visits. And on August 25, 1811, Shelley, who was nineteen, and Harriet, who was sixteen, eloped to Scotland.

It was a torturous, anguished union. Shelley let himself be induced into formal marriage, and then fretted over this betrayal of his principles of free love. His father cut off all funds, as did Mr. Westbrook, in an attempt to starve them out. Shelley borrowed whenever he could, at ruinous rates of interest, meanwhile writing his father demanding money and taunting him with hypocrisy: "How then can your boasted professions of Christianity appear to the world, since if you forgive not you can be no Christian—do not rather these hypocritical assumptions of the Christian character lower you in real virtue below the *libertine* atheist?" Fleeing his creditors, Shelley brought his bride back to England, and his friend Hogg moved in with them to help save on living expenses. When Timothy Shelley appeared momentarily to relent, his son went to confront him and to demand what he regarded as his rightful share of the family fortune. And while he was away, Hogg tried to seduce Harriet.

When Shelley returned, empty-handed, and Harriet told him of his friend's treachery, Shelley forgave Hogg, explaining that he refused to be bound by conventional traditions of monogamy. "I told him that I pardoned him freely, fully," Shelley wrote. "His vices and not himself were the objects of my horror and my hatred. I told him I yet ardently panted for his *real* welfare."

Timothy Shelley and Harriet's father finally relented enough to provide the young couple with a small income, since they were obviously starving. But Shelley kept moving about restlessly, to Ireland, to Wales and to London again. Hogg continued to move in and out of the rootless, disordered household. And Harriet's sister Eliza came to live with them, precipitating an animosity between Harriet's husband and her sister which would increase as time went by.

The income parceled out by his father and father-in-law was not enough for Shelley's expenses, more because of his careless generosity than his style of living. So Shelley frequently borrowed more, at even higher rates of interest than before. Knowing that his grandfather's estate would sooner or later come to him, he was able to find moneylenders who would buy "post-obits," i.e., pay him a small amount now in return for the promise of rich repayment when Shelley came into his inheritance. One of the post-obits at this time, promising £8,000, brought Shelley only £2,593 and 10s. Meanwhile he continued to badger his father for a larger share of the family income. His father refused, even when Shelley employed lawyers to press his case.

During this time Shelley was writing seriously—political and philosophical pamphlets and poetry, including his first major work, *Queen Mab*, published when he was almost twenty-one years old. This argument against the "tyranny" of Christianity only saddened—and hardened—his father's heart more than ever.

In June, 1813, eighteen-year-old Harriet gave birth to a daughter; and Shelley's pleasure turned to disappointment when Harriet wanted to name the baby Eliza after the sister he detested. They settled for Eliza Ianthe, the middle name taken from the heroine of *Queen Mab*. Immediately Harriet's sister, who had been attending her, took over the care of Eliza Ianthe, to Shelley's acute anger. At one point he wrote: "I sometimes feel faint with the fatigue of checking the overflowings of my unbounded abhorrence of this miserable wretch." This was not long before Shelley found himself involved with another woman.

Mary Godwin was the daughter of philosopher William Godwin and his first wife, Mary Wollstonecraft. Shelley's fascination with Godwin and his theories had led him to write the philosopher and then to call on him in his home in London. At first the young disciple had been so engrossed in his talks with Godwin that he had paid little attention to the oddly assorted children of the Godwin household: the two children of Godwin's second wife (one of them Claire Clairmont); the illegitimate daughter of Mary Wollstonecraft and the artist Gilbert Imlay before her marriage to Godwin; her son by Godwin; and Mary, her daughter by Godwin. As Mary blossomed into a fair-skinned sixteen-year-old, Shelley began to realize that the girl was interested in him, and characteristically he responded. During long afternoons when Godwin was out, Shelley and Mary Godwin talked together and went on walks together. Mary led him to the quiet graveyard where her mother was buried. And there one afternoon, sitting by Mary Wollstonecraft's grave, Mary Godwin confessed her love for Shelley.

It was in July of 1814, and Harriet Shelley was in Bath with her mother and father. She was taken aback to receive an anguished letter from Shelley, telling her of his love for Mary Godwin and proposing a *ménage à trois*, with Mary as his wife and Harriet as his "sister."

Harriet was in no doubt over how it had happened; "Mary was determined to seduce him," she wrote later. Harriet took the only course that seemed practical—going straight to William Godwin. The idealistic philosopher had been pleased with the adulation with which his young disciple Shelley had absorbed his teachings advocating atheism and free love. But when he heard that Shelley was about to put the teachings into practice with Godwin's own daughter, he was outraged. Immediately, to Harriet's satisfaction, Godwin told Shelley to get out of his home and stay out. He lectured his daughter on her indiscretion and forbade her to have anything more to do with the young renegade. Mary, also a believer in her father's preachings, must have been puzzled; she dutifully broke off from Shelley, or at least made the appearance of trying.

Shelley reacted by trying to poison himself. That was enough for Mary. She decided that Percy Shelley's fate was hers, come what might, and only half suspecting all that would. Early in the morning of July 28, 1814, Shelley and Mary Godwin rode off in a chaise for Dover and the Continent.

But the fleeing lovers were not alone. With them, overtly to act as their interpreter in France, went Mary's stepsister Claire Clairmont. Though brought up in the same household, the two girls were unrelated. Claire's mother, no doubt goaded by Godwin's eccentricities, had become something of a shrew, and Claire had been searching for an excuse to flee the unpleasant atmosphere of the Godwin household. Now she saw her opportunity to escape the tyranny of her nagging mother for a longer period. Mary, for reasons she might have rejected had she been less flustered by the whole affair, welcomed the offer of a French-speaking guide on the Continent. As for Shelley, evidently he was so infatuated with the prospect of running away with his inamorata that he too did not give a second, sober thought to the proposition of taking Claire along. A traveling companion, even on an elopement, was not uncommon in those days. And perhaps the presence of Claire did not seem so unpleasant after the nagging presence of Harriet's sister Eliza. So, in a rented boat whose helmsman barely made it through a Channel storm, the trio fled to France.

It was anything but a holiday. From the first day they were low on funds. On his birthday, August 4, Shelley sold his watch and chain so they could eat. To save money they tried a walking tour. Shelley and then Claire grew lame. Mary, who was already pregnant, became ill. They bought a mule and tried taking turns riding it, found this did not work, and sold it at a loss. They were going through the area between Paris and the Swiss frontier, where in 1814 Napoleon had fought to save Paris. The countryside was devastated from the warfare, and the people were understandably inhospitable. After staying in a succession of cheap, filthy inns and still wondering how they would pay their way, they finally turned back to England.

They returned to face the scorn of everyone, including Godwin, who still could not forgive Shelley for putting Godwin's preachings into practice. Harriet was unrelentingly furious, especially when Shelley blandly turned to her for financial help.

For the next six months Shelley and Mary, sometimes with Claire along and sometimes without her, moved about England, keeping one jump ahead of Shelley's creditors. In February of 1815, Mary gave birth to a girl; she lived only two weeks. Mary became desperately ill. So did Shelley, who consulted a doctor and was told that he was dying of consumption. Meanwhile Godwin, who still would not speak to Shelley,

48

nevertheless kept nagging his daughter to ask Shelley for money.

Shelley's economic picture suddenly showed signs of improvement when his grandfather, Sir Bysshe Shelley, died at the age of eighty-three. Sir Bysshe left an estate of £200,000. His will, as he had promised, settled most of the estate on his grandson, Percy Bysshe Shelley, but with his son, now Sir Timothy Shelley, entitled to the lifetime use of the estate. One portion, worth £800 a year, went direct to Percy. But Percy was too hard-pressed financially to wait out his still-vigorous father's life in order to receive the full estate, and he discovered that some £18,000 left by an uncle was part of the estate but not willed to his father's use. After some negotiating, he signed a contract in which he relinquished his rights to his uncle's money, in return for £7,400 and an annuity of £1,000.

This small relief from indebtedness and poverty was further reduced by his odd generosity, considering the circumstances, in making more loans and gifts to Godwin. But by the end of the year Shelley and Mary were able to make plans to return to the Continent, this time in comfort. And on January 24, 1816, Mary gave birth to a son, who was healthy and normal. They named him William. The outlook was improving for Shelley and Mary, if not for the disconsolate Harriet.

It was at this point that Claire Clairmont, prompted partly by her new interest in the theater but mostly by an unreasoning desire to match Mary's accomplishment by finding a poet of her own, launched her reckless campaign to become the mistress of Lord Byron.

And so it was that, virtually in the same week, at the end of April, 1816, both Lord Byron and Percy Shelley left England for Continental Europe, where their mutual adventure in exile would begin.[18]

[IV]

For all his eloquence on the subject of the sea, Lord Byron
was a poor sailor. On April 25, 1816, his boat fought Channel
head winds for sixteen hours. Byron stood it well until, as he
wrote Hobhouse, "a damned 'Merchant of Bruges' capsized his
breakfast close by me, and made me sick by contagion." As usual,
Byron took with him a huge equipage, along with three servants
and a doctor as a traveling companion and interpreter. The
doctor, a young but already slightly pompous man named John
William Polidori, knew French and Italian and fancied himself
a writer, and he immediately started to keep a diary toward the
time when he would publish his account of Byron's Continental
tour. One of his first entries in the diary noted that, on landing
at Ostend, they had scarcely been shown their rooms at the inn
when Byron assaulted the chambermaid.

The tour started off in an aimless fashion, up through Holland and into Belgium, Byron pausing wherever he was intrigued by a museum, a military installation or any ordinary sightseers' attraction. He found that he "utterly detested, despised and abhorred" the Flemish school of painting, and his opinion of Rubens was even lower—"the most glaring—flaring—staring—harlotry impostor that ever passed a trick upon the senses of mankind. . . . I never saw such an assemblage of florid nightmares as his canvas contains; his portraits seem clothed in pulpit cushions." Byron did not think highly of the Flemish landscape itself, nor was he especially impressed by Belgium—until he reached Waterloo.

Byron had been fascinated by Napoleon from the start. While the more common British attitude toward France's dynamic leader had been one of dread and hatred, Byron had always felt a certain fascination for the charismatic quality of the man. Napoleon personified many of the qualities that Byron praised and admired in much of his poetry. And now that the menace to England had been removed, at Waterloo, Byron could indulge his belief that the British "tyranny" was little better than that of Napoleon which it had defeated. At Antwerp Byron had found himself fascinated by the naval basins Napoleon had had prepared for the great cross-Channel invasion that had never come off. And now at Waterloo Byron walked over the battlefield with a friend as guide, so lost in contemplation that his friend thought he was not paying attention. Not content with this one visit, Byron returned next day with Polidori, on horseback, and the two galloped across the fields in as headlong a cavalry charge as any that had taken place at Waterloo one year earlier. "This place of skulls, the grave of France, the deadly Waterloo," it seemed to Byron. And he returned to his hotel room to write furiously away at what were to become some of the most famous lines of *Childe Harold:*

There was a sound of revelry by night,
And Belgium's Capital had gathered then
Her Beauty and her Chivalry—and bright
The lamps shone o'er fair women and brave men;
A thousand hearts beat happily; and when
Music arose with its voluptuous swell,
Soft eyes looked love to eyes which spake again,
And all went merry as a marriage bell;
But hush! hark! a deeep sound strikes like a rising knell!

Did ye not hear it? No—'twas but the Wind,
Or the car rattling o'er the stony street;
On with the dance! let joy be unconfined;
No sleep till morn, when Youth and Pleasure meet
To chase the glowing Hours with flying feet—
But hark! that heavy sound breaks in once more,
As if the clouds its echo would repeat;
And nearer—clearer—deadlier than before!
Arm! Arm! it is—it is—the cannon's opening roar!

. . . there were sudden partings, such as press
The life from out young hearts, and choking sighs
Which ne'er might be repeated; who could guess
If ever more should meet those mutual eyes,
Since upon night so sweet such awful morn could rise!

. . . Ardennes waves above them her green leaves,
Dewy with Nature's tear-drops, as they pass—
Grieving, if aught inanimate e'er grieves,
Over the unreturning brave—alas!
Ere evening to be trodden like the grass
Which *now* beneath them, but *above* shall grow
In its next verdure, when this fiery mass
Of living Valour, rolling on the foe
And burning with high Hope, shall moulder cold and low.

Last noon beheld them full of lusty life;
Last eve in Beauty's circle proudly gay;
The Midnight brought the signal-sound of strife,
The Morn the marshalling in arms—the Day
Battle's magnificently-stern array!
The thunder-clouds close o'er it, which when rent
The earth is covered thick with other clay
Which her own clay shall cover, heaped and pent,
Rider and horse—friend—foe—in one red burial blent![14]

The tour led on across Belgium and into Germany, to Cologne, where Byron was fascinated by a church exhibit of "11,000 virgins' bones"—and where he found another chambermaid, this time to the embarrassment of his landlord, who mistakenly thought his wife was in Byron's room. As Byron regaled Hobhouse with the account, the landlord "stood swearing at the door . . . till the mystery was developed by his wife walking out of her own room & the girl out of mine."

Traveling along the Rhine and enjoying the spetacular scenery, Byron and his entourage crossed the river at Mannheim and went down through Karlsruhe, pausing for more sightseeing and for Dr. Polidori to recover from a fever. Moving on through the Black Forest, they crossed into Switzerland at Basel and headed for Lake Geneva.

And on the night of May 25, 1816, after a hard, day-long drive from Lausanne, Byron signed the register at the Hotel D'Angleterre in Sécheron, just outside Geneva. Exhausted by the ride and irritated by all the questions asked on European hotel registers, Byron answered the question "Age" with the figure "100." He had just climbed wearily into bed when a boy knocked at the door with a note from Jacques Dejean, the proprietor, who in a proper, humorless Swiss manner requested the correct answer.

Next morning Byron found another note awaiting him: "I am sorry you are grown so old, indeed I suspected you were 200, from the slowness of your journey. I suppose your venerable age could not bear quicker travelling. Well, heaven send you sweet sleep—I am so happy. Clare."

On May 6, while Byron had been crossing Belgium into Germany, the Shelleys had reached Paris, on a more direct route to Geneva. From Paris Claire wrote to Byron to express an unlikely notion: "I have no doubt you think my affection all a pretence. Or that you are handsome and my passions are excited. First, I have no passions; I had ten times rather be your male companion than your mistress." She then got to the point:

In five or six days I shall be at Geneva. I entreat you to write a little note for me. . . . I know not how to address you. . . . I cannot call you friend, for though I love you, yet you do not feel even interest for me. Fate has ordained that the slightest accident that befel you would be agony to me: but were I to float by your window drowned all you would say would be: "Ah, voila." . . . A few days ago I was eighteen; people of eighteen always love truly and tenderly, and I, who was educated by Godwin, however erroneous my creed, have the highest adoration for truth. Farewell, dear Lord Byron. I have been reading all your poems and almost fear to think of your reading this stupid letter, but I love you.

Byron did not answer this letter, if in fact it ever reached him. Meanwhile the Shelleys and Claire went on toward Geneva. And as so often happened with Shelley, in contrast to Byron, the direct route turned out to be more harrowing than Byron's roundabout one.

Shelley, Mary and Claire went southwest to Dijon and Dôle and across the Swiss border at Poligny. The way then led along a narrow road toward Champagnole. At first the path was illuminated by bright moonlight that picked out and accentuated the steep ravine on one side and the echoing precipice on the other. Then heavy clouds swept in across the moon. Rain began to fall. It changed to snow. At Les Rousses the steep roads and the snow forced them to hire more horses and men, in the middle of the night, to help them get through the mountain pass. Finally, with the break of day, they found themselves coming down into the warm sunny area around Geneva. In Sécheron they registered at the Hotel D'Angleterre and started to recover from the ordeal, to enjoy the beauty of the countryside and, in Claire's case, to wait for the arrival of Byron.

While Claire daily searched the registers of the local hotels, Mary walked in the gardens. Shelley set out to find a boat. He was even less an accomplished sailor than Byron; but even more than Byron, he felt drawn to the water. He was soon drifting about on Lake Geneva, oblivious to wind and currents but at once tranquilized and inspired by the sounds of water against the bow, the aimlessness of his course and the isolation from land. So on Monday, May 27, 1816, Shelley was probably on his way down to his boat when the historic meeting took place.

Byron, ignoring the note left at the hotel by Claire, had gone with Polidori into Geneva and from there had ridden out to look at a house. It was the Villa Diodati, owned by a descendant of a friend of John Milton's—which must have intrigued Byron. But the house at first seemed a bit small, and he was not sure he wanted it, despite its location on a hill with a sweeping view of the city on one side, the soaring mountains on the other and a great stretch of lake in the center. When Byron returned to the hotel he found more notes from Claire awaiting him. He ignored them too; but late that night he was awakened by the delivery of another. He realized that he could not long continue to avoid her.

Next morning, Monday, he had himself rowed across the lake for another look at the Villa Diodati. This time he was told he was too late: the villa had been taken by an English family. Riding back across the lake, he stepped out of the boat and was limping along the landing when, finally, Claire found him. With her were Mary and Shelley.

Anyone watching the meeting of the two poets would have been struck by the surface dissimilarity—the arrogant pose of one and the self-effacement of the other; the patronizing manner of the famous writer condescending to comment politely on the work of the struggling unknown; the confrontation of success with aspiration, of master with acolyte, of sybarite with aesthete, of genius with talent. Yet to a large degree the meeting was one more of similarity than of contrast. Both men were rebels against the English establishment of the time. Both were self-proclaimed exiles from the same land. Both were serious poets concerned with the poet's craft and the poet's place in life. And, most important, each sincerely held the other in high regard. Shelley had a great admiration for Byron's *Childe Harold;* and Byron was one of the few Englishmen of the time who appreciated Shelley's poetic powers, especially as demonstrated in *Queen Mab.*

The two men took to each other immediately, and acquaintance rapidly developed into companionship. Byron was delighted and secretly flattered at the way their personalities complemented each other—Shelley praising his friend's work in his selfless manner, meanwhile showing, almost despite himself, a passionate understanding of the meaning of good poetry and articulating his beliefs, in conversation anyway, better than Byron could. The earnest conversations went on through the afternoons and evenings and sometimes until dawn, with neither noticing or caring about the hour. Byron found himself joining his friend for breakfast, for lunch, for tea. When the Shelleys, searching for less expensive lodgings than the hotel, rented a cottage across the lake, Byron tried again to take the Villa Diodati and this time succeeded; the other family had changed its plans. The villa was only a ten-minute walk from the Shelleys' house.

So for weeks the two poets were inseparable. Through rainy afternoons or long evenings they discussed politics, agreed on the mystique of Napoleon and argued over the nature of poetry. Byron broke off these sessions only long enough to continue his *Childe Harold*, of which he was writing the third canto. Even then he no doubt noticed the effect Shelley was having on his writing—particularly those Wordsworthian touches he certainly would have avoided had Shelley not been arguing the merits of the poet Byron had heretofore disliked so much.

Shelley led Byron onto Lake Geneva, where hours were whiled away with Shelley daydreaming at the helm. One evening the whole party was in the boat, "animated by our contest with the elements," as Mary described it, when Byron said: "I will sing you an Albanian song . . . give me all your attention." He broke into "a strange, wild howl," Mary recalled, "as, he declared, was an exact imitation of the savage Albanian mode." From that time on Mary and Claire gave Byron their own nickname: "Albe."

Bad weather only drove them in by the fire, usually in Byron's living room. On the stormy night of July 15, 1816, the little group sat around Byron's fireplace telling ghost stories. With a burst of inspiration Byron made a proposal: why didn't each of them write a ghost story, in an informal contest? All agreed. Shelley started on his next day, but grew bored with it

57

and never finished it. Claire scarcely got started with hers at all. Byron made some progress with a gloomy tale of a secret oath betrayed by a misunderstanding; but he too became disenchanted and dropped the project unfinished. Mary Shelley meanwhile wrote nothing, searching for a plot and worrying over her failure to live up to her promise. Then a few nights later the conversation around the Villa Diodati fireplace turned to the secret of life itself.

"Perhaps a corpse would be re-animated . . ." Mary recalled, "perhaps the component parts of a creature might be manufactured, brought together, and endued with vital warmth. . . ."[15] Mary lay awake most of that night, caught up with the notion of artificial creation of life, and with the natural and supernatural results of such a scientific attempt to endow a human being with the warmth of life but without the saving grace of the human soul. Next day she set down the beginnings of a novel to which she would give the title *Frankenstein*.

And while she worked at her story, Byron and Shelley set off on a cruise of Lake Geneva. For Byron it was an escape from Claire; in his easygoing manner he had let her slip back into his bed, and he was now wishing he had not. For Shelley the cruise was simply a chance to spend more time on the water. The cruise took eight days, during which they circumnavigated the forty-mile-long lake. On sunny days they lolled against the side of the boat as the breeze swept them past the wooded shores. In a storm they nearly capsized; Shelley confessed that he could not swim and Byron prepared to save him; but Shelley insisted that he preferred going down with the boat. The squall suddenly subsided and, bailing furiously, they made it to shore. But Byron was appalled at Shelley's attitude and commented on it often thereafter.

The most impressive event of the cruise, however, was the sighting of the looming battlements of the Castle of Chillon, near the head of the lake. They went ashore and walked through the gloomy caverns below the castle, where a guide cheerfully embroidered on the popular legend of the castle.

In 1532 one Francis Bonivard so enraged Charles III, Duke of Savoy, with his antiroyalist political activities that the Duke had Bonivard committed to the dungeon of Chillon's castle, and it was four years before Chillon's prisoner was set free. The guide invented the simultaneous imprisonment of two of Bonivard's brothers. Not content with this embellishment, he went on to claim that all three brothers were chained to pillars alongside each other, in such darkness that Francis could not see his brothers but could only hear their voices weaken as they slowly died.

Shelley was vastly impressed by this image of a modern Prometheus. As for Byron, when a few days later they were forced to wait out bad weather at Ouchy, he closed himself up in his room and wrote, all in a rush, his solemn, majestic poem *The Prisoner of Chillon*, ending with the poignant lines:

> . . . It was at length the same to me,
> Fettered or fetterless to be,
> I learned to love despair.
> And thus when they appeared at last,
> And all my bonds aside were cast,
> These heavy walls to me had grown
> A hermitage—and all my own!
> And half I felt as they were come
> To tear me from a second home:
> With spiders I had a friendship made,
> And watched them in their sullen trade,
> Had seen the mice by moonlight play,
> And why should I feel less than they?
> We were all inmates of one place,
> And I, the monarch of each race,
> Had power to kill—yet, strange to tell!

In quiet we had learned to dwell;
My very chains and I grew friends,
So much a long communion tends
To make us what we are: even I
Regained my freedom with a sigh.

On his return to the Villa Diodati Byron let Claire make the
fair copy of his poem. And, perhaps lulled by the eight days of
absence and abstinence, he let the affair resume. Again he shortly
grew exasperated by her, resenting his weakness and taking his
resentment out on Claire. For all his bravado he was somewhat
appalled at the strong-willed manner in which she dominated
their relationship—the clinging vine whose gentle twines were
so persistent, parasitical and tough. The more her coils wrapped
around him, the more he sought escape. He even started avoiding the Shelley villa, rowing across the lake to a château where
the famous Mme. de Staël was attracting the intellectuals of
Geneva. Byron found the atmosphere in Mme. de Staël's salon
arid, and retreated, only to be captured by Claire again. His
dilemma was apparent. Much as he liked the company of
Shelley, he could no longer stand the company of Claire. Then
came the final blow: Claire announced that she was pregnant.

It was Shelley who came to the rescue. Perceiving that the
situation was becoming intolerable, and thinking more of Claire's
heartache than of the price Byron was paying for his selfishness,
Shelley decided that it was time to return to England, at least
for a while. He had a valid excuse: his finances were once again
in near-calamitous disorder.

Byron's relief at the news was crushing to Claire, who still
refused to accept the inevitable, though she had been warned
from the start. She made her last visit to the Villa Diodati on
August 25, to insist that they come to an agreement on the
future of their child. Confronted with a reality he had so far

put out of his mind, Byron made the offhand proposal that the child be handed over to his half-sister Augusta for upbringing —and was startled at the outraged reaction of Claire. The anguished argument ended with a grudging promise from Byron, according to Claire's account of it, that the child "should live with him—he promised faithfully never to give it until seven years of age into a stranger's care. I was to be called the child's aunt and in that character I could see it and watch over it without injury to anyone's reputation." No doubt the truth of the matter was that Byron eagerly agreed to whatever Claire proposed, if she would just go away—with no intention of regarding it as an agreement after she had gone.

Whatever the promise, it was forgotten next day with the arrival of his old friend John Cam Hobhouse from England. Shortly they were making plans for a trip through the Alps to the vale of Chamonix, for an excursion through the Bernese Oberland, and for a winter in Venice.

The Shelleys, with Claire, left for England on August 29. Byron entrusted to Shelley his manuscript of the third canto of *Childe Harold* and the manuscript Claire had copied of *The Prisoner of Chillon*. There was no further parting scene between Byron and Claire, whom he was carefully avoiding. She wrote him a farewell letter: "I should have been happier to have seen and kissed you once before I went. . . . Tell me one thing else—shall I never see you again—not once again?" She never would.

Slowly making their way through the Rhone Valley and the Simplon Pass, Byron and Hobhouse crossed into Italy. They journeyed down the shores of Lake Maggiore and across the Lombardy plains until in the distance they could see the spires of the great Cathedral of Milan.

An Italian ambience infected Byron almost immediately. He reserved a box at the Teatro alla Scala. He met and enjoyed the company of the intellectuals of the city. He was pleased to find that his reading knowledge of Italian quickly became a workable conversational Italian. He listened to the Italians' political troubles; Napoleon's departure had meant Austrian dominance over the province, and Byron sympathized with the Italian patriots who resented Austria's authoritarian rule. John Polidori, who had left Byron, at Byron's suggestion, in Switzerland, now rejoined him in Milan—until he blundered into a scrape with an Austrian officer. Byron got Polidori out of jail but could not prevent the doctor's being exiled from Milan,[16] and the high-handed attitude of the Austrian officials made an impression on Byron which he would not forget.

But for the time being he enjoyed Milan's Teatro Re, the popular theater of the masses. He became fascinated with the Ambrosian Library, where he surreptitiously pocketed part of an exhibited lock of hair from the infamous and reputedly incestuous Lucrezia Borgia. And on November 3 Byron and Hobhouse set out, in high spirits and anticipation, for Venice.

They paused to inspect the amphitheater and the reputed tomb of the Capulets in Verona. By the seventh they were in Padua, where Hobhouse wanted to do some more sightseeing. But by now Byron was impatient to reach Venice. At his insistence they drove along the Brenta to Mestre, where they could take a gondola. By the time they reached an inn, a rainstorm had come up. Still Byron would not wait. A covered gondola was ordered and they set out across the lagoon. For more than an hour they rode imprisoned in a black box with nothing but driving rain and roiling water around them. Then, in an instant, lights danced at the windows. Gondola traffic swished past them. Tall buildings seemed to sway to and fro alongside them. Suddenly they heard the echoing splashing that meant they were under a bridge. And as they listened, a boatman called: "The Rialto!" Within minutes they were climbing out of the gondola at the landing stage of the Hotel of Great Britain. And minutes later they were looking out at the lights of Venice dancing across the surging waters of the Grand Canal. Lord Byron, like Childe Harold, had reached his destination, and the stage was set.

After the fogs of London and the primness of Geneva, Byron was overjoyed by the sunny warmth of both Venice and the Venetians. In the first weeks he could only marvel at the golden sunsets across the lagoon, at the soft lapping of the canals against the steps, at the gentle roll of the gondolas, at the hospitable Venetian women speaking their "soft bastard Latin" and doting on the wealthy visitor from abroad.

Such a Venetian woman was Marianna Segati. She was the twenty-two-year-old wife of Byron's landlord, a draper with a shop in the Frezzeria, a tiny street around the corner from St. Mark's. Pietro Segati rented rooms above his shop, and Byron moved in, accepting, as an unspoken part of the bargain, the draper's wife. Byron was soon writing to his friend Tom Moore back in England:

I have fallen in love, which, next to falling into the canal . . . is the best or worst thing I could do. . . . Marianna (that is her name) is in her appearance altogether like an antelope. She has the large, black, oriental eyes, with that peculiar expression in them which is seen rarely among *Europeans*—even Italians—and which many of the Turkish women give themselves by tinging the eyelid, —an art not known out of that country, I believe. This expression she has *naturally*,—and something more than this. In short, I cannot describe the effect of this kind of eye,—at least upon me. . . .

Venice also had her intellectual attractions, of a sort. Shortly after their arrival Byron and Hobhouse had been introduced to the *conversazioni* of Countess Isabella Albrizzi, who regarded herself as the Mme. de Staël of Venice. The countess considered her salon the best in Venice, and she did attract most of the intellectual and artistic leaders then in the city. Hobhouse, however, called Countess Albrizzi "a very poor copy indeed" of Mme. de Staël, "though she seems a very good natured woman." Byron and Hobhouse also enjoyed the opera at the Teatro Fenice, which Byron described as "the finest . . . I have ever seen: it beats our theatres hollow in beauty and scenery." But then Hobhouse decided to take a trip south to Rome, and Byron turned to another source of intellectual inspiration.

Soon after their arrival in Venice the two visitors had gone out to a small, bare island in the lagoon—San Lazzaro, site of an Armenian monastery. The two *inglesi* had been received hospitably by the learned friars. Both Byron and Hobhouse had made a superficial acquaintance with the Armenian language during their trip through the Middle East, and Byron in particular had found it fascinating and challenging. Here in Venice, in contrast to the easy life with Marianna, Byron found the Armenian language "something craggy to break my mind upon," and he plunged into a project of learning the difficult syntax. With Hobhouse gone, Byron concentrated on the project even more wholeheartedly. Part of the lure of San Lazzaro, he admitted, was the peace and quiet of the book-lined library and the tree-shaded terrace looking out across the lagoon, and the example of Father Pasqual, with whom he studied the language. San Lazzaro was a refuge from the fleshpots of Venice, and Byron fled to the refuge every day to relax in the comtemplative atmosphere and to exercise his mind.[17] For physical exercise he rowed himself out to the island, and sometimes he swam most of the way back while his gondolier followed.

To Tom Moore Byron smugly recounted an anecdote told him by the friars, perhaps not without an ulterior motive. "Four years ago the French instituted an Armenian professorship. Twenty pupils presented themselves on Monday morning, full of noble ardour, ingenuous youth and impregnable industry. They persevered, with a courage worthy of the nation and of universal conquest, till Thursday; when *fifteen* of the *twenty* succumbed to the six-and-twentieth letter of the alphabet. It is, to be sure, a Waterloo of an alphabet—that must be said for them. But it is so like these fellows, to do by it as they did by their sovereigns—abandon both."

Byron realized that if he were to repay the Armenian friars with money, the gesture would be resented. Instead he arranged to publish an Armenian dictionary, to be edited jointly by him and Father Pasqual and to be paid for by Byron. It was a project in odd contrast to the life he was leading the rest of each day and night along the Grand Canal. But the good fathers of San Lazzaro and the pious intentions of Byron were forgotten, at least temporarily, when carnival time came to Venice with the first days of 1817.

Everywhere there were riotous balls and masquerades and parties, with night turned into day and no sense of what was the hour or even the day of the week. On and on the festivities whirled, with Byron swept along in their midst, sometimes with Marianna, sometimes with any other attractive Venetian who presented herself. The festivities were not in the least dampened by the news which Byron received in January from Mary Shelley: "Shelley being in London on business I take upon myself the task and pleasure of informing you that Clare was safely delivered of a little girl yesterday morning (Sunday, January 12) at four. She sends her affectionate love to you. . . ."

Byron paused only long enough to comment defensively, in a letter to another friend: "I never loved nor pretended to love her, but a man is a man, and if a girl of eighteen comes prancing to you at all hours, there is but one way. . . ." He continued his night-long revelry until he collapsed with a fever. He was ill, unable to rise from his bed, for two weeks, lovingly nursed by Marianna.

> So we'll go no more a-roving
> So late into the night,
> Though the heart be still as loving,
> And the moon be still as bright.
>
> For the sword outwears its sheath,
> And the soul wears out the breast,
> And the heart must pause to breathe,
> And Love itself have rest.
>
> Though the night was made for loving,
> And the day returns too soon,
> Yet we'll go no more a-roving
> By the light of the moon.[18]

Writing to Hobhouse, who had reached Rome, Byron jocularly described his siege: ". . . after a week of half-delirium, burning skin, thirst, hot headach, horrible pulsation, and no sleep, by the blessing of barley water, and refusing to see any physician, I recovered. It is an epidemic of the place," he added, "which is annual, and visits strangers." This was his first encounter with one of the fevers that plagued so many English visitors to Italy.

The fever and the weather made Venice somewhat less attractive. Chilling fogs, almost as bad as those of London, swept in across the lagoon. Cold rain washed the city and piercing winds smashed the gondolas against the pilings. The Venetians huddled in damp, sheltered corners. The idea of joining Hobhouse in Rome suddenly seemed much more appealing. Rome would be sunny and gay. Byron tried to persuade Marianna to go along with him. She refused—not because of her husband, who no longer counted, but because of her child. So Byron bid her a temporary adieu and set forth.

As it had before, travel inspired him. In the past few weeks in Venice, partly because of his illness, he had begun to think he could not write again. But on the open road he became alive and was inspired to observe and ponder and render into poetry what would later become part of the fourth canto of *Childe Harold*.

Riding southwest by way of Padua, across the sluggish Po and into Ferrara, Byron paused to contemplate the story of Tasso, imprisoned in a tiny, airless and sunless cell. Byron wrote: "As misfortune has a greater interest for posterity . . . the cell where Tasso was confined in the hospital of St. Anna attracts a more fixed attention than the residence or the monument of Ariosto—at least it had this effect on me." Then he went on through Bologna and across the Apennines to Florence, where he paused before starting the last leg south.

> Italia! oh, Italia! thou who hast
> The fatal gift of Beauty, which became
> A funeral dower of present woes and past—
> On thy sweet brow is sorrow ploughed by shame,
> And annals graved in characters of flame.[19]

And then Rome. Hobhouse was waiting for him, to take him touring through the beauties and antiquities of what Byron soon called a "city of the soul." Byron had brought his horses, so he and Hobhouse could ride through the city at will, without being hindered by Byron's lameness. Here, Byron never forgot, once strode the giants of imperial Rome; here were the gaunt and massive mementos of their classic reign: the Forum, where "still the eloquent air breathes—burns with Cicero"; the Colosseum, "this long-explored but still exhaustless mine of contemplation"; Hadrian's Temple, "Imperial mimic of old Egypt's piles, Colossal copyist of deformity"; and all the ancient and honored glories of the place where "a world is at our feet. . . ."

> Where is the rock of Triumph, the high place
> Where Rome embraced her heroes? where the steep
> Tarpeian? fittest goal of Treason's race,
> The Promontory whence the Traitor's Leap
> Cured all ambition. Did the conquerors heap
> Their spoils here? Yes; and in yon field below,
> A thousand years of silenced factions sleep . . .
>
> . . . Here a proud people's passions were exhaled,
> From the first hour of Empire in the bud
> To that when further worlds to conquer failed;
> But long before had Freedom's face been veiled,
> And Anarchy assumed her attributes;
> Till every lawless soldier who assailed
> Trod on the trembling Senate's slavish mutes,
> Or raised the venal voice of baser prostitutes.[20]

Not only Rome's past magnificence struck him, but the vibrant activity of the living city as well. "As a *whole, ancient* and *modern,*" he wrote his London publisher, "it beats Greece, Constantinople, every thing—at least that I have ever seen." He sampled the fine restaurants, visited the gardens, even put aside his hatred of traveling Englishmen to dine with Lord

Lansdowne, who was passing through Rome. But Byron's reputation had followed him all the way from England. At St. Peter's he was seen by another English traveler, Lady Liddell, who was visiting Rome with her daughter. Lady Liddell wrote later of her shock at recognizing who it was. "And what came over me I cannot describe, but I felt ready to sink, and stood as if my feet were rooted to the ground, looking at him, as Mrs. Blakeney told me, as if I were horror-struck." With a maternal impulse, Lady Liddell turned to her daughter, Maria, and told her to keep her eyes down. "Don't look at him, he is dangerous to look at."

Not dangerous, perhaps, but a figure of brooding romance, and a conscious one at that. Hobhouse urged Byron to sit for the Danish sculptor Bertel Thorvaldsen, who had a studio in Rome. Byron finally consented, but with misgivings; there was something posthumous about a bust. And when it was done, though Hobhouse and Byron's other friends admired the likeness, Byron did not; "It is not at all like me; my expression is more unhappy." He had said it in his drama *Manfred*:

> Look on me! there is an order
> Of mortals on the earth, who do become
> Old in their youth, and die ere middle age,
> Without the violence of warlike death;
> Some perishing of pleasure, some of study,
> Some worn with toil, some of mere weariness,
> Some of disease, and some insanity,
> And some of withered or of broken hearts;
> For this last is a malady which slays
> More than are numbered in the lists of Fate,
> Taking all shapes, and bearing many names.
> Look upon me! for even of all these things
> Have I partaken; and of all these things,
> One were enough; then wonder not that I

Am what I am, but that I ever was,
Or having been, that I am still on earth.[21]

Hobhouse was heading on south, to Naples, and urged Byron to come along. But the lure north was greater, back to "Venice and its marine melancholy"—and to Marianna. Byron hurried north, not pausing this time in the towns along the way. And on arrival, on May 28, he found Marianna just recovering from the same fever that had debilitated him before he had left.

She was well enough to give him a warm welcome home, however, and he settled in as if Venice—or Italy, at least—was now really his home.

But as May turned into June and Venice became hot, Byron looked about for escape from the heat, the effluvia of the canals and the fevers which had struck him and Marianna. In 1817 wealthy Venetians escaped not to the Lido, which was still a bare strand along the Adriatic, but to the higher ground on the mainland. Most of them established themselves in Palladian mansions along the river Brenta, a short distance inland from Venice. And here Byron leased a big square palace that had once been a convent and later the villa of the patrician Foscarini family. The Villa Foscarini was not particularly attractive, and there was not enough furniture to make all of its rooms comfortable. It stood on the road to Padua, in an area called La Mira, seven miles from Venice, and the traffic on the road to Padua often filled the air with choking dust. But there was a garden, and the high-ceilinged rooms were cool, and the summer sunsets along the Brenta were among the most beautiful in the world. Byron moved in on June 14.

Two days later his publisher in London brought out Byron's *Manfred*, which he had completed while in Rome. Critics attacked it as scandalous. One of them wrote: "*Manfred* has exiled himself from society, and what is to be the ground of our compassion for the exile? Simply the commission of one of the most revolting of crimes. He has committed incest!" There it was again, the charge that, more than anything else, had turned England against him and him against England.

> . . . Thou lovedst me
> Too much, as I loved thee: we were not made
> To torture thus each other—though it were
> The deadliest sin to love as we have loved.
> Say that thou loath'st me not—that I do bear
> This punishment for both—that thou wilt be
> One of the blessed—and that I shall die . . .[22]

In London, his half-sister Augusta reacted to the literary criticism and the parlor gossip by writing Lady Byron to ask her advice on how to deal with it. Annabella answered primly: "You can only speak of *Manfred* . . . with the most decided expressions of your disapprobation."

If news of the review reached La Mira, Byron was apparently unconcerned. By day he made his visits to Venice, to talk with his cronies, occasionally to go sightseeing with the rare friend from England, more often to enjoy the summer breeze along the Lido and the refreshment of a marathon swim. Then home to La Mira, for supper and for love—before settling down to the serious writing which could go on through most of the early hours. To Tom Moore Byron wrote: "I am just come out from an hour's swim in the Adriatic; and I write to you with a black-eyed Venetian girl before me, reading Boccaccio." Marianna was not only his solace but in some ways his inspiration. She settled him down and relaxed him so that he was in a frame of mind to compose some of his best work. And through the long quiet hours after Marianna and the rest of the world had gone to sleep, Byron sat at his desk in the villa's vaulted room, writing the lyrical fourth canto of *Childe Harold*.

The Moon is up, and yet it is not night;
    Sunset divides the sky with her; a sea
    Of glory streams along the Alpine height
    Of blue Friuli's mountains; Heaven is free
    From clouds, but of all colours seems to be,
    Melted to one vast Iris of the West,
    Where the Day joins the past Eternity;
    While, on the other hand, meek Dian's crest
Floats through the azure air—an island of the blest! . . .

Cypress and ivy, weed and wallflower grown
    Matted and massed together, hillocks heaped
    On what were chambers, arch crushed, column strown
    In fragments, choked up vaults, and frescos steeped
    In subterranean damps, where the owl peeped,
    Deeming it midnight: Temples—Baths—or Halls?
    Pronounce who can; for all that Learning reaped
    From her research hath been, that these are walls—
Behold the Imperial Mount! 'tis thus the Mighty falls.

He dedicated this canto to his old friend John Cam Hobhouse ("to one, whom I have known long and accompanied far, whom I have found wakeful over my sickness and kind in my sorrow, glad in my prosperity and firm in my adversity, true in counsel and trusty in peril,—to a friend often tried and never found wanting"). And then Hobhouse himself arrived at La Mira.

Faithful, loyal, but still the Englishman, Hobhouse was shocked at what he found. He had left his friend in Venice, seven months earlier, at least pretending to board with the draper Segati and his family. Now Marianna lived at La Mira in open sin. And far from disapproving, Marianna's husband visited La Mira on weekends in order to be near a ladylove of his own. Not only that, but the local priest had sent a present to Signora Segati—"This," the scandalized Hobhouse wrote, "to a woman living in open adultery. . . ."

But Hobhouse was able to accustom himself to the situation, and soon he and Byron were everywhere together—in the theaters and salons of Venice, along the Grand Canal and, most pleasant of all, riding horseback along the placid Brenta as the sunset turned the river to gold. And it was here, as Byron rode horseback along the Brenta, that he met his newest and most fascinating love.

The Brenta rolled gently through the countryside down to Venice and the sea. By day it was yellow, turgid and sluggish. But in the cool of the August evening it was a moving mirror for La Mira's brilliant sunsets. Willows, pines and sandy paths wound along the shore. After the heat of the summer afternoon, the cooling ride was a refreshing part of the day, with no sound save the soft creak of saddle leather, the clump of hoofs along the path, the occasional clatter of a passing wagon, and the moan of cattle across the hills. There was usually a light breeze whispering off the Adriatic. Everywhere people bobbed and curtseyed to milord. And the countryside was bathed in that liquid gold so characteristic of Italy in the late afternoon. In *Beppo* Byron described the welcome contrast between Italy and England.

> I like on Autumn evenings to ride out,
> Without being forced to bid my groom be sure
> My cloak is round his middle strapped about,
> Because the skies are not the most secure;
> I know too that, if stopped upon my route,
> Where the green alleys windingly allure,
> Reeling with *grapes* red wagons choke the way—

In England 'twould be dung, dust, or a dray.

I also like to dine on *becaficas*,
  To see the Sun set, sure he'll rise to-morrow,
Not through a misty morning twinkling weak as
  A drunken man's dead eye in maudlin sorrow,
But with all Heaven t'himself; the day will break as
  Beauteous as cloudless, nor be forced to borrow
That sort of farthing candlelight which glimmers
Where reeking London's smoky cauldron simmers.

I love the language, that soft bastard Latin,
  Which melts like kisses from a female mouth,
And sounds as if it should be writ on satin,
  With syllables that breathe of the sweet South;
And gentle liquids gliding all so pat in,
  That not a single accent seems uncouth,
Like our harsh northern whistling, grunting guttural,
Which we're obliged to hiss, and spit, and sputter all.

It was on such an evening, as the sunset touched the Brenta with its magic, and Byron and Hobhouse rode along the river, that they saw the two girls. They were in a group, but they stood out from the crowd and Byron noticed them immediately. There was no question of their noticing Byron.

As the two *inglesi* rode grandly by, the townspeople nodded their greeting. It had not been a prosperous summer in the area and Byron had, in his generous and lordly way, helped out those who had been worst afflicted. Now, as his horse pranced past, one of the girls called out: "You have helped others; why not us?"

Byron reined in his horse, swung about and studied the girl's strong face, her snapping black eyes, her insolent carriage, her full figure.

"My sweet," he replied, with a studied Byronic smile, "you are far too pretty to need help from me."

She held his eye, tossing her long black hair as she replied: "If you saw my hut and my food, you would not say so."

"All this passed half-jestingly," Byron recounted later. But though he and Hobhouse rode on, he could not forget the flashing eyes, the sauntering stance, the animal magnetism of the girl. Next evening, as he rode out along the Brenta again, he looked for her—and the next evening and the next. And then—there she was again, eyeing him and seemingly taunting him. With her was the same companion of a few evenings earlier, and Hobhouse began to look appraisingly at her. This time their conversation was longer and more to the point. A rendezvous was arranged for next evening.

They arrived with a third girl. She was, Byron wrote, "cursedly in the way." The girl Hobhouse fancied now "took fright" and she and the third girl fled. Here was an example of Venetian morality: Hobhouse's intended was a cousin of this tall, dark girl, but she was unmarried, and only married women engaged in such affairs.

Byron too found himself frustrated, for a brief time. Her husband, the girl explained, was "somewhat ferocious." Byron was unconvinced; surely the man could not be more ferocious than this leonine creature. He persevered. And, "in short, in a few evenings we arranged our affairs. . . ."

Her name was Margarita Cogni; because her husband was a baker, her nickname was La Fornarina. Not only the baker but Marianna reacted angrily. La Fornarina silenced them both. To Marianna she shouted: "*You* are *not* his *wife; I* am *not* his *wife; you* are his *donna,* and *I* am his *donna. Your* husband is a cuckold, and *mine* is another. . . . If he prefers what is mine to what is yours, is it my fault?" And yet, when Byron permitted Marianna to remain at La Mira, La Fornarina showed that she could not care less. She knew, she said, that he would keep coming back to her. And he did. Night after night his horse could be seen waiting outside the hut of La Fornarina, while Marianna waited alone at La Mira and La Fornarina's husband presumably drowned his humiliation in his neighbor's wine and in the solacing thought that in the Venice of those times he was not alone.

As for Byron, his new double life seemed to be stimulating. Just as he spent his afternoons with Marianna and his nights with La Fornarina, he worked on two very different subjects and styles at the same time. In the quiet early mornings in the tall-ceilinged rooms at La Mira, after his return from La Fornarina's hut and before retiring at dawn, he drank his gin and water and wrote the sonorous, prophetic stanzas of *Childe Harold:*

> Roll on, thou deep and dark blue Ocean—roll!
> Ten thousand fleets sweep over thee in vain;
> Man marks the earth with ruin—his control
> Stops with the shore; upon the watery plain
> The wrecks are all thy deed, nor doth remain
> A shadow of man's ravage, save his own,
> When, for a moment, like a drop of rain,
> He sinks into thy depths with bubbling groan—
> Without a grave—unknelled, uncoffined, and unknown.[23]

And at the same time he wrote the sprightly lines of *Beppo,* almost in the manner of a nineteenth-century Ogden Nash:

> Shakespeare described the sex in Desdemona
> As very fair, but yet suspect in fame,
> And to this day from Venice to Verona
> Such matters may be probably the same,
> Except that since those times was never known a
> Husband whom mere suspicion could inflame

76

To suffocate a wife no more than twenty,
Because she had a "Cavalier Servente."

If Byron thought that La Fornarina would be a fleeting summer romance, La Fornarina thought otherwise. When in the fall he moved back to Venice, she forced her husband to buy an oven in the city, and Byron's nocturnal visits continued. Inevitably he moved out of Marianna's house, leasing the magnificent Palazzo Mocenigo on the Grand Canal. La Fornarina moved in and took over.

Byron's household was transformed. La Fornarina cut the food bills in half, screeching and cursing at the servants and tradesmen who had made a good thing out of the extravagant Englishman for so long. Lazy servants were beaten into line. Even Byron was awed by this dominating creature with "a face like Faustina's, and the figure of a Juno—tall and energetic as a Pythoness, with eyes flashing, and her dark hair streaming in the moonlight." She was the only woman to stand up to his towering temper tantrums, giving him every bit as good as she got. She also cajoled him, pampered him and mothered him like a tigress. Byron had stabled his horses on the Lido, the sand spit between Venice's lagoon and the open Adriatic, because he enjoyed riding along the lonely beach. One late afternoon he was returning from his daily canter when a sudden squall swept across the lagoon. The waters were churned to a froth and all was hidden in the rain-lashed darkness. As the skies lightened and Byron's gondola came lunging up to the steps of the palazzo, there stood the drenched Medea-like figure of La Fornarina. Over the rumble of the thunder and the crash of the water she screamed: "Dog of the Virgin, is this the time to go to the Lido!" Byron tried to calm her, in vain. For nearly an hour she ranted and shrieked—at Byron, at his gondolier and at the other gondoliers, who had been afraid to take her out looking for her man in the howling storm.

In the midst of Byron's overwhelming affair with La Fornarina, two seemingly unrelated events occurred. One was the sale, at last, of Newstead Abbey, which allowed Byron to pay off his debts in England and still have a comfortable annuity left over. The second event was the departure for home of his companion and moderating influence, John Cam Hobhouse. On a cold January afternoon they had their last gondola ride across the lagoon to the Lido and their last canter along the Adriatic. That evening Byron gave the final polish to the fourth canto of *Childe Harold*. At midnight the two friends said good-bye. The next day Hobhouse left for England, carrying the manuscript of *Childe Harold* with him.

> Farewell! a word that must be, and hath been—
> A sound which makes us linger; yet—farewell!
> Ye! who have traced the Pilgrim to the scene
> Which is his last—if in your memories dwell
> A thought which once was his—if on ye swell
> A single recollection—not in vain
> He wore his sandal-shoon, and scallop-shell;
> Farewell! with *him* alone may rest the pain,
> If such there were—with *you*, the Moral of his Strain.[24]

Now, with a newly increased income, and with his last anchor to respectability gone, Byron ran wild.

It was carnival time again. And again the city came alive with the spectacle of glowing gondolas gliding through the canals, with the ring of revelry across the open piazzas, with the parade of glittering countesses sweeping grandly across the ballroom floors. Again the balls, the feasts, the floating processions went on through the night. Again convention, caution, morality were forgotten and abandon swept the city. At the nightly theater performances, grand receptions and masked balls, the gowns were the most décolleté and the male plumage the most dandified; even the Papal Nuncio wore a mask. The noble lord from England was a familiar sight at the Teatro Fenice, at the salons and at the balls, in his own quixotic, dramatic way surpassing even the most flamboyant Venetians. His notoriety fed on itself. Women who heard tall tales of his licentiousness were drawn toward him. And in his lordly, selfish way he took whatever was offered. In an endless stream, grandes dames with an appetite for intrigue, ladies of easy virtue, famous courtesans and plain harlots visited the great bedroom looking out on the Grand Canal. And Byron prowled the other palazzi, intriguing with wives, outwitting the defenses of jealous fathers to seduce their young daughters. Once he clung to the window grating near a palazzo balcony for nearly an hour until the coast was clear. Once he hobbled the length of his gondola, stumbled and fell into the canal, but proceeded, "all dripping like a Triton," as he fondly described it, to his lady of the evening. And often Venetians returning late to their homes would see across the canal the flickering light of a lantern, bobbing on a plank pushed ahead to light the way as Byron swam home from his latest tryst.

But always he returned to La Fornarina, as she said he would. Occasionally she would give in to jealousy, as when she snatched the mask from a lady who was too obvious in her approach to Byron during one of the balls. La Fornarina knew, though, that wherever he roamed, she would win him back. After a week or perhaps only a night, he would be off on some new conquest, returning with no apology and no remorse. She expected none. She waited patiently for each liaison to end. It always did.

But more and more the pace began to tell. Byron ate little

or nothing; always he was fighting off the fat which grew too readily and which made it more painful to hobble about the piazzas and over the steep bridges on his lame foot. Still he treated himself as if his strength were boundless. One evening he was introduced to Cavalier Angelo Mengaldo, a veteran of the Napoleonic wars who had escaped the enemy by swimming the Danube. Byron could not, of course, resist matching Mengaldo's boasts with his own account of swimming the Hellespont. The verbal contest ended in a challenge to race each other from the Lido to the Grand Canal, a full three miles. After a few hours of sleep, Byron woke at ten in the forenoon, made love, rose and rode out to the Lido. He and Mengaldo started swimming at four-thirty, and did not reach Venice until eight-fifteen, at which time Mengaldo, miles behind, was calling for a gondola. Byron swam on down the canal, dressed, went about his social rounds and was making love again early that evening, before settling down for another long night of composition at his desk in the palazzo.

Often the palazzo study itself was overwhelmed by the wild parties that ranged through the big rooms; and at such times passersby could see Byron crouched by a lantern in his gondola, rising and falling alongside the blue-and-white posts, writing his poetry while the music and cries of revelry came through the big lighted windows of the palazzo.

Finally it was all too much for him. One night he collapsed at a ball. By mid-February he was down with a fever, exhaustion and venereal disease. His doctors told him he must slow down or he would kill himself. This was the atmosphere in which Byron heard from Shelley. The Shelleys were coming to Italy, bringing with them Claire and Byron's new daughter.

[V]

It had been a year and a half since Byron and the Shelleys had gone their separate ways from Geneva, and the period had been a particularly trying one for Shelley, Mary and Claire. They had scarcely settled in Bath when the first tragedy struck: Fanny Imlay, who evidently had never overcome the stigma of illegitimacy as the daughter of Mary Wollstonecraft before her marriage to Godwin, committed suicide, leaving a note which reflected her years of brooding over her situation: "I have long determined that the best thing I could do was to put an end to the existence of a being whose birth was unfortunate, and whose life has only been a series of pain to those persons who have hurt their health in endeavouring to promote her welfare. . . ." Shelley and Mary were still recovering from the shock when even worse news reached them: the body of Harriet Shelley was found in the Serpentine, and Harriet's sister, the

Eliza so much despised by Shelley, received a suicide note
". . . Do not regret the loss of one who could never be any
thing but a source of vexation and misery to you all. . . . Now
comes the sad task of saying farewell. Oh! I must be quick. God
bless and watch over you all. . . . My children—I dare not
trust myself there, they are too young to regret me and you
will be kind to them for their own sakes more than mine. My
parents—do not regret me, I was unworthy of your love and
care. . . ."

The death of Harriet left Shelley free to marry again. He
and Mary Godwin went through an offhand civil ceremony,
nearly as much disturbed by this retreat from their radical
principles as by the suicide of Harriet. Marriage did not help
their case when a judge refused to give Shelley custody of his
children by Harriet. Mary gave birth to another child, a daughter, whom they named Clara Eveline. But whatever equilib-
rium they had achieved was disturbed again with the birth of
Claire's daughter by Byron. During this time Shelley renewed
his friendship with Leigh Hunt, the poet and critic, who had
been among the few to praise Shelley's work in print. And
through Hunt, Shelley met and became fascinated by another
young poet, John Keats. But Keats shied away from the close
friendship which Shelley offered. At this time Mary Shelley
completed the "ghost story" she had started in Geneva, and
Frankenstein became an immediate success—which only served
to emphasize the popular failure of Shelley's own writings.

The Shelleys, with Claire and her infant daughter, moved to
Marlow, outside London, where Shelley enjoyed sailing on the
Thames and taking long walks through the countryside (even
including the thirty-two-mile hike to London). But Marlow
was cold and wet, and the big house they rented was difficult
to heat. By the time the second winter approached, the Shelleys

were making plans to leave England for a warmer climate, preferably in Italy.

Shelley had come back to England chiefly to see if he could talk his father into a more favorable financial arrangement, but he had had little success. His father had insisted that any further settlements be used to settle Shelley's long-standing debts, and what little was left after that was wheedled out of him by the perennially impoverished Godwin. So Shelley found himself borrowing again, and sinking further into debt than ever.

The situation was made all the more disconcerting by the presence of the unmarried Claire and her daughter, and their pretense that Claire was the baby's aunt was unconvincing. Shelley felt that Byron should assume some responsibility for his child. So the odd little group prepared to go to Italy, and Shelley wrote Byron asking him to meet them in Milan.

But first, again contrary to their principles but because the documents would be useful when they had to cross borders on the Continent, they had all three children christened. This raised the problem of a name for Claire's daughter. She had chosen Alba, a name that meant "dawn" and also carried overtones of their nickname for Byron: Albe. But Shelley now wrote Byron to ask what name he preferred, and Byron replied that he liked Allegra, a euphonious Italian name. The baby was christened Allegra.

And Allegra, with her mother, the Shelleys and two nurses, left England on March 12, 1818, to go to Milan to meet her father.

From Calais the Shelleys pushed on to Lyons in seven days, where they rested for a while and where Shelley wrote Byron, to confirm that they were on the way. They went through the

Mont Cenis Pass into Cisalpine Italy at Susa. Next stop wa
Turin, and then Milan, where they moved into the Hotel Real
on April 4.

Byron was not there. Nor was there any message. The
waited a few days, assuming that he had not expected then
to make such good time. Shelley and Mary went out to Lak
Como to look for a cottage for the summer. They returned t
Milan to find that still there was no word from Byron. Shelle
wrote him again:

"Will you spend a few weeks with us this summer? Ou
mode of life is uniform, and such as you remember it a
Geneva, and the situation which I imagine we have chose
(the Villa Pliniana) is solitary and surrounded by scenery o
astonishing grandeur, with the lake at our feet. If you woul
visit us—and I don't know where you could find a heartie
welcome—little Allegra might return with you."

Finally an answer came. Byron declined the invitation. A
for Allegra, he would indeed like to have her, and he wa
sending a messenger to bring the girl and her nurse to Venice
He assumed that Claire was surrendering the child completely

Claire exploded. "Your messenger will remain here," sh
wrote Byron, "at my request until I hear from you again.
cannot send my child under the impression produced by you
letter of the 17th to Shelley. And the messenger has been tol
that her health, which is not perfectly good, makes it necessar
that we should write and hear again from you before she ca
depart. Pardon me, but I cannot part with my child never t
see her again. Only write me one word of consolation. Tel
me that you will come and see Shelley in the summer, or tha
I may be somewhere near her—say this, and I will send he
instantly. . . . On this point I am firm. If you will not regar
me as her mother, she shall never be divided from me. . . ."

84

Shelley was equally surprised by what seemed to him unnecessary cruelty on Byron's part. He wrote a long letter, the first of many he would be writing in the role of mediator in the months and years to come.

. . . You write as if from the instant of its departure all future intercourse were to cease between Clare and her child. This I cannot think you ought to have expected, or even to have desired. . . . What should we think of a woman who should resign her infant child with no prospect of ever seeing it again, even to a father in whose tenderness she entirely confided? . . . Surely, it is better if we err, to err on the side of kindness, than of rigour. . . . I am a third person in this painful controversy, who, in the invidious office of mediator, can have no interest, but in the interests of those concerned. I am now deprived of the power to act; but I would willingly persuade. . . .

There followed an exchange of letters in which Byron appeared more reasonable, without making any specific promises. And then the Shelleys found that the Villa Pliniana was not available after all. So they made plans to go to Pisa, a city favored by many English visitors to Italy. Claire had to decide: should she take Allegra along or send her to Venice? After an anguished few days she concluded that Allegra's prospects with her father outweighed her mother's pain of separation. So, on April 28, she sent her daughter, with the nurse Elise, to Venice.

And, as if to occupy her mind with the distraction of travel, the Shelleys left immediately for Pisa. Riding through the high roads of the Apennines and down across the valley of the Arno, they reached Pisa in a week. They found some of the city's architecture attractive, including the famous Leaning Tower. They enjoyed the beauty of the sunset on the Arno. But they were depressed by Pisa's poverty and the harsh atmosphere of Austrian rule. They tried going on a few miles to Leghorn. There they discovered congenial fellow expatriates when Mr and Mrs. John Gisborne called on them. Twenty years earlier Mrs. Gisborn had been Mrs. Reveley, a close friend of Godwin and Mary Wollstonecraft. When Mary Wollstonecraft had died, Mrs. Reveley had taken the baby Mary into her own home, and when Mr. Reveley had died two years later, Godwin had proposed to Mrs. Reveley. She had declined politely. Now she was married to John Gisborne, a businessman who had made enough money to retire to Italy. And the baby whom Maria Reveley had taken care of was now Mary Shelley.

Mary was pleased to see her "godmother." Shelley too liked Maria Gisborne, though he found John Gisborne rather a bore. But even Mrs. Gisborne could not make up for the disadvantages of Leghorn. The Shelleys found the city dirty, noisy and largely inhabited by sharp traders, Italian and English—"the Wapping of Italy." Mary called it "a stupid town," and Shelley characterized it as "the most unattractive of cities." As the heat of summer approached, they looked for a cooler climate and pleasanter aspect.

They found it in the little town of Bagni di Lucca, not far north of Pisa. Perched on the side of the Pistoiese mountains, the town seemed to cling to the brink. Roads wound around and around the steep hillsides. Houses rose one above the other like outcroppings. The mountains were heavily forested, and through the town raced the clear, cold waters of the Lima River, plunging from its source high on the mountaintop. It was said that the mothers of Bagni di Lucca tied their babies to the doorknobs to keep them from rolling down the mountainside. Everything about the town and the surrounding forests seemed primitive, wild and beautiful—a far contrast to the gentle meadows of England or the crowded streets of Milan and Leghorn.

On June 11 the Shelleys moved into the Casa Bertini, on one of the more level streets of the town, with a back yard that fell away abruptly to the river rushing below. At last, after the cold winter of Marlow and the seemingly ceaseless wanderings since, they felt that they had found comfort and peace. Mary described it in a letter.

When I came here I felt the silence as a return to something delightful from which I had long been absent. We live here in the midst of a beautiful scene. . . . We are surrounded by mountains covered with thick chestnut woods—they are peaked and picturesque and sometimes you see peeping above them the bare summit of a distant Apennine. Vines are cultivated on the foot of the mountains— The walks in the woods are delightful. . . . We see the fireflies in the evening—somewhat dimmed by the brightness of the moon— So we lead here a very quiet pleasant life— reading our canto of Ariosto—and walking in the evening among these delightful woods—

A path from the villa led into the forest. At the top of a hill Shelley found a spot where the river catapulted over a rock ledge and formed a deep, swirling pool. He described it in a letter which revealed how he too had recovered from the toil and trouble of England.

I bathe in a pool or fountain formed in the middle of the forest by a torrent. It is surrounded on all sides by precipitous rocks, and the waterfall of the stream which forms it, falls into it on one side with perpetual dashing. Close to it, on top of the rocks, are alders, and above the great chestnut trees whose long and pointed leaves pierce the deep blue sky in strong relief; the water of this pool . . . is as transparent as the air, so that the stones and the

87

sand at the bottom seem as it were trembling in the light of noon-day. It is exceedingly cold also. My custom is to undress and sit on the rocks, reading Herodotus, until the perspiration has sub-sided, and then to leap from the edge of the rock into this fountain, a practice in the hot weather exceedingly refreshing. This torrent is composed, as it were, of a succession of pools and waterfalls up which I sometimes amuse myself by climbing when I bathe, and receiving the spray all over my body whilst I clamber up the moist crags with difficulty. . . .

In the solitude of a hidden pool, amid the peaceful pace of the village, Shelley returned to the poetry he had had so little time for in the past months. And for the moment he was pleased to reflect simply the lyrical loveliness of the new world around him:

> Listen, listen, Mary mine,
> To the whisper of the Apennine,
> It bursts on the roof like the thunder's roar,
> Or like the sea on a northern shore,
> Heard in its raging ebb and flow
> By the captives pent in the cave below.
> The Apennine in the light of day
> Is a mighty mountain dim and grey,
> Which between the earth and sky doth lay;
> But when night comes, a chaos dread
> On the dim starlight then is spread,
> And the Apennine walks abroad with the storm.[25]

It was a pleasant summer idyll for everyone but Claire. Try as she would, she could not recover from the loss of her daughter. The hope of seeing Allegra again only made her worry more as she brooded on Byron's attitude and considered how difficult it would be to persuade him to give up the child even for a short time. And now she was receiving disturbing

88

letters from the nurse Elise. Lord Byron, the letters reported, was living a life of utter depravity. A succession of mistresses, loose-moraled Venetians and plain harlots moved in and out of the Palazzo Mocenigo. Then came a letter with the news that so licentious had the atmosphere at the palazzo become that Byron had agreed to let Allegra move out, to the home of the British consul in Venice.

That was enough for Claire. Allegra was receiving neither motherly nor fatherly affection. Claire had given up her daughter only because she felt that the girl's father could give her a better home. Obviously he had no such intention. Claire decided to go to Venice and "rescue" Allegra.

Shelley pleaded with her to be patient. Claire would not listen. Shelley argued that Claire could not get away with her desperate plan, that Byron would stop her, and that his angry reaction would only make things worse in the end. Claire replied that she was leaving for Venice. Shelley decided that he had better go along. On August 17, 1818, Mary reported in a letter: "Shelley and Clare are gone (they went today) to Venice on important business and I am left to take care of the house."

An August thunderstorm came crashing down on Venice. Sheets of rain swept across the lagoon and gusts of wind set the gondolas tossing in the Grand Canal. Crouched in the enclosed gondola, Claire shuddered as each flash of lightning lit the roiling waters. Shelley tried to comfort her, still wishing he had been able to talk her into staying behind in Padua while he reconnoitered. The ceaseless gabble of the gondolier was not reassuring. The man could talk of little else besides the tales told all over Venice of the strange Englishman who lived in the great palazzo on the Grand Canal. Only the onrushing

storm interrupted the gondolier's tale, in halting English, of
the eccentric nobleman: he kept a zoo in his palazzo; he turned
night into day, and there was hardly a whore in all Venice who
had not visited him; he paid well for his pleasures, they said,
and the gondolier who could bring him a new and interesting
companion for the night could expect a handsome tip. When the
stravagante inglese did not have someone brought to him, he
would go out in his gondola, rowed by his own giant gondolier,
Tita, to call on a lady of his choice—often swimming home,
fully clothed, in the early light of dawn.

As the storm subsided, the gondolier took up his theme again,
and Shelley and Claire were vastly relieved when finally they
came to a pitching halt at the entrance to their inn. But as they
tried to refresh themselves with some supper, their waiter hung
over the table confiding that as *inglesi* they might be interested
in hearing about the escapades of a profligate English lord who
had rented the Palazzo Mocenigo.

Edward Hoppner, the British consul in Venice, was a son
of the famous portrait painter and an amateur artist himself.
His wife was a staid and motherly Swiss woman with a son of
her own and she had, in her opinion, rescued Allegra from a
horrible fate in the Palazzo Mocenigo. The day after their
arrival, as soon as they felt it was proper, Shelley and Claire
called on the Hoppners. They were welcomed, and after a few
minutes, Allegra was brought into the parlor.

She scarcely recognized her mother and the man who had
so often held her in his lap. She had grown taller and thinner.
"She is pale and has lost a good deal of her liveliness," Shelley
wrote Mary, "but is as beautiful as ever, though more mild."
Shelley watched Claire with her child for a few minutes, and
then left to call on Byron.

He was surprised at the joyful welcome he received. He

would have preferred sitting in the palazzo and talking, instead of riding out to the Lido and pounding along the beach on horseback, as Byron insisted. But Shelley was pleased when Byron suggested that the Shelleys and Claire take Allegra with them to visit I Cappucini, a villa in the Euganean Hills which Byron had rented but had not used. Shelley readily accepted. And shortly Byron was writing his sister: "Allegra is well, but her mother (whom the Devil confound) came prancing the other day over the Apennines—to see her *shild*. . . . I got her to the Euganean Hills, where she & the child are now. . . ."

Shelley might have been distressed by his friend's callous attitude, but Claire was in no mood to inquire into the cause of her good fortune. She decided to take advantage of it before the quixotic Byron changed his mind. So Claire, Shelley and Allegra took off for Este and I Cappucini. And Shelley sent an eager message to Mary, still waiting at Bagni di Lucca. Could she come to Este with William and Clara?

Mary Shelley must have felt the contagion of Shelley's enthusiasm as she read his letter. In a torrent of words he set down the detailed instructions: she should pack for a long visit; she should leave in three days and take the early post to Lucca and the carriage to Florence, which she should reach that evening. From Florence to Este should take about three days, and she should be careful of the inns; he and Claire had found many of them impossible. In particular she should avoid the Tre Mori in Bologna; the beds were absolutely filthy. Fifty pounds was enclosed. "Kiss the blue-eyed darlings for me, and do not let William forget me," he wrote.

> Mary dear, come to me soon,
> I am not well whilst thou art far; . . .
> O Mary dear, that you were here;
> The Castle echo whispers "Here!"[26]

91

Shelley did not know that their friends the Gisbornes, whom they had urged to visit them at Bagni di Lucca, had finally come; and that the Shelleys' daughter, one-year-old Clara, was ill. Nevertheless Mary hurried to get ready. On August 29 she only had time to write in her diary the single, eloquent word "Bustle." The next day was her birthday. It was all but forgotten in the confusion, and again the diary shows the single entry: "Packing." Next day, Mary, Clara and little William were on their way.

The roads were dusty and tortuous. The weather was hot. In Florence there was a problem over their passports, which delayed them an entire day. It was six days later before they finally reached Este—hot, dust-covered and exhausted. And by that time little Clara was running a high fever. A local doctor diagnosed it as dysentery. He also treated Shelley, who was suffering from food poisoning, apparently contracted from eating some Italian cakes. Altogether it was a miserable start to their reunion at Este.

Gradually the soothing beauty of the villa and the surrounding countryside had its effect. Shelley recovered. Mary concentrated on translating Monti's *Cajo Gracco*. Claire reveled in companionship with Allegra, even though the little girl showed signs of having been spoiled by her father. Allegra and William renewed their friendship, chasing each other about the villa. And Shelley, in a summerhouse looking out across the plains to the Adriatic, wrote some of the first lines of his epic verse play, *Prometheus Unbound*.

> From the ends of the earth, from the ends of the earth,
> Where the night has its grave and the morning its birth,
> Come, come, come!
> Oh, ye who shake hills with the scream of your mirth,
> When cities sink howling in ruin; and ye

Who with wingless footsteps trample the sea,
And close upon Shipwreck and Famine's track,
Sit chattering with joy on the foodless wreck;
Come, come, come![27]

But as the days went by, Clara grew worse. Unable to hold food long enough for nourishment, she lost weight until she began to resemble a skeleton more than the fat, healthy baby she had been. Mary became impatient with the doctor at Este; a better one was summoned from nearby Padua. His ministrations seemed to help, and Clara showed some signs of improvement. But she did not recover fast enough. Shelley decided that they must take the baby to Venice, where a famous doctor, Francesco Aglietti, who was Byron's friend, could examine her. Both Shelley and Mary knew that in that part of the world dysentery was too often a fatal disease with small children.

It is only forty miles from Este to Venice. But the trip was too much for the weakened Clara. She grew rapidly worse on the way. By the time they had reached Fusina, across the lagoon from Venice, she was having convulsions. At Fusina, soldiers stopped them and asked them for their passports. Shelley searched frantically but could not find them. In horror he realized that they had left them back at the villa.

But the sight of the frantic parents and the deathly ill child touched even the hearts of the customs officials, who let them pass without their papers.

As they crossed the lagoon, Clara went into a coma. In Venice Shelley left Mary and Clara at the landing, rushing off to find Aglietti while Mary took the baby to the inn. But Aglietti was nowhere to be found. Shelley left an urgent message for him and raced back to the inn. What he found he described in a letter to Claire some days later:

93

"When I returned I found Mary in the hall of the inn in the most dreadful distress. Worse symptoms had appeared. Another physician had arrived. He told me there was no hope. In about an hour—how shall I tell you—she died. . . ."

Again Shelley rode a gondola out to the lonely Lido. This time he was accompanied only by the tiny coffin of Clara. Mary could not face the ordeal. In a little cemetery on the deserted beach, to the sound of waves and the cry of sea birds, one-year-old Clara was buried in the sands. And Shelley returned alone.

> Those who inflict must suffer, for they see
> The work of their own hearts, and this must be
> Our chastisement or recompense. O child!
> I would that thine were like to be more mild
> For both our wretched sakes—for thine the most
> Who feelest already all that thou hast lost
> Without the power to wish it thine again;
> And as slow years pass, a funereal train,
> Each with the gist of some lost hope or friend
> Following it like its shadow, wilt thou bend
> No thought on my dead memory?[28]

In his letter to Claire, Shelley concluded: "All this is miserable enough—is it not? but must be borne." And then he added something, thought about it again, and erased it.

As soon as the Hoppners heard what had happened, they went to the inn and asked the Shelleys to come to their home. Shelley was reluctant; they scarcely knew the Hoppners, and this seemed hardly the time to be sociable with anyone. But the Hoppners were insistent, and Mary was ready to seize at anything that would take her away from the scene of the tragedy. They moved in with the Hoppners. For the next five days their hosts tried their best to divert the Shelleys' minds, with hectically planned activities, and with Byron's help. Shelley and Mary were taken on the rounds—to the Doge's Palace, the shops on the Rialto Bridge, the Bridge of Sighs and the Palazzo Mocenigo. Byron did his best to entertain them, including a gathering in which Shelley read aloud the fourth canto of *Childe Harold*. Byron also thought of asking Mary if she would like to do some transcribing, giving her his new *Mazeppa* and his *Ode to Venice* when she eagerly agreed. But their tours of Venice also included a trip out to the lonely Lido, now Clara's burial place. And Mary recorded her grief with the laconic entry: "This is the Journal of misfortunes. . . ."

Finally, on September 29, they turned back toward Este, to little William and to Allegra. In the long silences of the lonely ride, Shelley worried about Mary's state of mind. She seemed unable to keep from dwelling on the past few weeks. They had been so content at Bagni di Lucca, before Shelley went rushing off to Venice, before his urgent letter for her to come to Este, before the harrowing ride to Este with the children, before the days and nights of anxiety over their daughter, before the scenes in the gondola and the inn which she could see so clearly, before that last morning when Shelley rode away from the inn with the tiny coffin. Shelley could only sit quietly beside her in the carriage, deep in his own remorse and feeling hers all the more.

> The colour from the flower is gone,
>   Which like thy sweet eyes smiled on me:
> The odour from the flower is flown,
>   Which breathed of thee and only thee!
>
> A withered, lifeless, vacant form,
>   It lies on my abandoned breast,
> And mocks the heart which yet is warm
>   With cold and silent rest.

> I weep—my tears revive it not.
> I sigh—it breathes no more on me;
> Its mute and uncomplaining lot
> Is such as mine should be.[29]

I Cappucini, the villa in Este that Byron had rented but had never occupied, had once been a Capuchin convent. It perched on the edge of a hill, but there was room for a garden and a trellised path to the summerhouse where Shelley did his writing. Across a ravine loomed the spectacular ruins of the ancient castle of Este, and at night Shelley and Mary could listen to the echoes from its walls and watch the owls and bats flit in and out among the crenellated walls and crevices of the dark towers. By day the aspect was more pleasant, with the Apennines rising in the distance beyond the poplar-lined plains. The beauty of the scene gradually softened the misery of the recent past. And, little by little, Shelley's remorse took on a faint tinge of hope.

> Many a green isle needs must be
> In the deep wide sea of Misery,
> Or the mariner, worn and wan,
> Never thus could voyage on—
> Day and night, and night and day,
> Drifting on his weary way,
> With the solid darkness black
> Closing round his vessel's track;
> Whilst above, the sunless sky,
> Big with clouds, hangs heavily,
> And behind, the tempest fleet
> Hurries on with lightning feet,
> Riving sail, and cord, and plank,
> Till the ship has almost drank
> Death from the o'er-brimming deep;
> And sinks down, down, like that sleep

When the dreamer seems to be
Weltering through eternity . . .

Other flowering isles must be
In the sea of Life and Agony:
Other spirits float and flee
O'er that gulf; even now, perhaps,
On some rock the wild wave wraps,
With folding wings they waiting sit
For my bark, to pilot it
To some calm and blooming cove,
Where for me, and those I love,
May a windless bower be built,
Far from passion, pain, and guilt,
In a dell mid lawny hills,
Which the wild sea-murmur fills,
And soft sunshine, and the sound
Of old forests echoing round,
And the light and smell divine
Of all flowers that breathe and shine. . . .[30]

Mary tried. She tended the garden. She transcribed the stanzas Byron had given her. She read. She cooked. She let the beauty of the sweeping hills and green plains soothe her soul. Most of all, she concentrated her affection on William and on Allegra, who played together like brother and sister. But the anguish of remembrance would return whenever she came upon one of Clara's toys, or her empty cot, or a dress of hers. And over the scene hung the dread of the day when Allegra too would have to leave. Mary, and Claire even more, felt their hearts sink each morning when Allegra, as she woke and stood still for her dress to be whisked over her head, asked: "Where is Papa?"

Watching William and Allegra together—and their effect on Mary—Shelley made one of his impulsive decisions. Now Allegra was even more important to Mary than to Claire.

More than two months ago they had decided to head south for the winter, to Rome and Naples and perhaps even farther. But could they do it now, leaving Allegra behind in Venice? Shelley decided to return to Venice, with Mary, and plead with Byron to let them take Allegra with them. He would take Mary along to help make his case; hadn't Byron been more than generous and thoughtful with her after Clara's death? Shelley broached the subject to Mary, who agreed. So on October 11, 1818, they returned to Venice. They realized how strongly Byron felt about Allegra spending too much time with Claire, and they knew how he would react, at first, to the proposition that his daughter be taken hundreds of miles away from him. But Shelley also knew that a great wound had been made in their marriage, and that it might be healed by the presence of Allegra.

This was Shelley's third visit to Byron in Venice. He had made the first one with misgivings and had been happily surprised by his friend's generosity. After the tragedy of the second visit Byron had done his best to rally Shelley's spirits and take Mary's mind off her misery. On his return to Este Shelley had written a friend: ". . . he is changed into the liveliest and happiest looking man I ever met." But now, on the third visit, Shelley was appalled. As he wrote later to his same friend, he was shocked by Byron's "obstinate and self-willed folly . . ."

Nearly every evening of the Shelleys' ten-day visit was spent dining with the Hoppners. The English consul had to some extent replaced Hobhouse in Byron's affections, and the horseback rides on the Lido were now taken with Hoppner. But the Hoppners seemed to have no compunctions about freely reporting all the gossip about Byron to the Shelleys. There was plenty of gossip—about the procession of grasping prostitutes, the thieving servants, the unsavory male companions, the midnight seductions, the battling mistresses and, finally, the dominance of the human tigress called La Fornarina. Mary Shelley saw this brazenly beautiful, illiterate woman, and was not favorably impressed. Shelley deplored the whole spectacle. As he described Byron's behavior: "He allows fathers and mothers to bargain with him for their daughters. He associates with wretches who seem almost to have lost the gate and physiognomy of man, and who do not scruple to avow practices which are not only not named, but I believe seldom even conceived in England." To another friend Shelley reported: "Our poor friend Lord Byron is quite corrupted by living among these people. . . ."

Shelley was genuinely afraid that a great talent might be going into decay. He argued that Byron's degradation could affect the spirit of his poetry: "Nothing can be less sublime than the true source of these expressions of contempt and desperation." And yet, reading the fourth canto of *Childe Harold*, Shelley had to admit that the sheer strength of the poetic talent was still there.

> I stood in Venice, on the "Bridge of Sighs";
> A palace and a prison on each hand:
> I saw from out the wave her structures rise
> As from the stroke of the Enchanter's wand:
> A thousand Years their cloudy wings expand
> Around me, and a dying Glory smiles
> O'er the far times, when many a subject land
> Looked to the winged Lion's marble piles,
> Where Venice sate in state, throned on her hundred isles!

Shelley promptly got to the point of his visit, pleading with Byron to let Allegra stay with them a while longer. It was not for Claire alone. In fact, if Byron insisted, they could even ask Claire to leave their household and take a position somewhere as a governess. They could simply take Allegra in as if she were their own, in place of Clara Shelley. Now that Clara was gone, little William would be alone without Allegra. William Shelley was three. In the past year he had had to leave the familiar associations of his home in England, to travel through France and Italy, to be uprooted again after settling down at Bagni di Lucca. Far worse, he had been separated from Allegra once before, and then had lost his sister, Clara. Now, in the gardens at Este, William and Allegra had begun again to enjoy each other's companionship. They were inseparable. Whatever Byron's feelings still might be toward Claire, at least he must be able to see what it would do to little William Shelley to have his devoted playmate suddenly taken away from him again; it could have a crushing effect on him. And it could be even worse for Mary.

Byron listened to and understood Shelley's pleas. But to him there were other considerations, not all of which he felt free to discuss with his friend. There seemed little point in repeating his reasons for despising Claire Clairmont. He had not been the one to precipitate that affair; to Byron she was no better than all the other round-heeled simpletons who had hounded him wherever he went. Claire Clairmont had certainly understood his feelings toward her when she had pleaded with him to be her lover. Now she acted the injured lady, and in Byron's opinion she was obviously trying to use her daughter to worm her way back into his good graces. Once he had been indifferent to Claire; now he hated her. And he could think of few influences worse for Allegra than that of an overly sentimental, deceitful and slightly aging woman of easy virtue.

As for his friend Shelley, his wife and their son, Byron felt that the greatest kindness he could do them would be not to tell them how he felt. To him the death of Clara had been clear proof of the error of Shelley's ways. While Shelley condemned Byron's dissolute behavior in Venice, Byron was equally contemptuous of Shelley's way of life. He little doubted what had caused Clara's death—the sickly diet which the Shelleys compelled her to follow. No meat; green vegetables, often eaten raw and unwashed; and not enough even of that to keep a growing child robust. The Shelleys, Byron was convinced, had no conception of the proper nourishment for children in this land of pestilence and poor sanitation. It was not Byron's fault that Shelley's own restlessness had continually uprooted his family, to travel all about Europe. These aimless wanderings and a diet confined to fresh fruit and vegetables might not endanger the life of a child in England; but they could be the death of one in Italy. They just had.

Nor were the Shelleys, in Byron's opinion, a very much better influence on a young girl than Claire Clairmont. Byron could hardly be called religious, but he scorned Shelley's proclaimed atheism. It ill behooved the Shelleys to look disapprovingly on Byron's behavior. Shelley had left his wife to run off with Mary, in company with Claire, who, Byron was convinced, also shared Shelley's bed. For Shelley to argue that this itinerant, unhealthy, atheistic, immoral household was a better atmosphere for Allegra than the Palazzo Mocenigo seemed to Byron rather sanctimonious, if not presumptuous.

And besides, Byron admitted to himself, he had become rather fond of Allegra.

This last, and his opinion of Claire, were the only arguments he could offer in answer to Shelley's pleas. So the friendship between the two men was considerably strained when Shelley finally surrendered to what he regarded as Byron's stubbornness and sadly left Venice to break the news to Claire.

He did not have to tell her; she could read it on his face. On

October 29, Shelley and Allegra traveled alone together to Venice, where he delivered her over to her father. Mary, who had waited in Venice, now left with Shelley for the lonely return trip to Este. As Shelley wrote: "You may think how unwillingly I have left my little favorite in a situation where she might fall again under his authority. But . . . I have no longer any right." They could only hope that Byron would again agree to let Allegra live with the Hoppners, though they must have known that the Hoppners were growing tired of Allegra's spoiled manners. The girl "was not by any means an amiable child," Hoppner wrote, "nor was Mrs. Hoppner or I particularly fond of her. . . ."

On November 5, the Shelleys left Este and Venice behind, heading south for Rome and Naples, where they hoped to find a healthier winter climate. And Allegra was left to Byron.

[VI]

Autumn storms drenched and chilled the Shelleys as they headed south. The dirt roads turned to clay, which engulfed and sucked at the carriage wheels. William complained at the long, jolting journey. Everywhere there were reminders: the packing case that had been Clara's, the sight of Claire brooding at the rain-smeared carriage window, the moments when little William asked for Clara or Allegra. Mary maintained her cold silence, answering only when spoken to. Paolo, the coachman, cursed at the horses and the mud. Elise, now William's nurse, occasionally forgot herself and made some remark about Allegra.

Shelley's spirits lightened a little at Ferrara as he studied the beautifully illuminated manuscripts in the big library, and the armchair and inkstand once used by Ariosto. But he was repelled by the damp and dark little cell where Tasso had been imprisoned; as he called it: "a horrible abode for the coarsest and meanest thing that ever wore the shape of man, much more for one of delicate sensibilities and elevated fancies."

Breaking the tedium of the journey, they stayed two days in the next town, Bologna, visiting the churches and art galleries. And for the next six days they enjoyed some of Italy's most impressive and pleasant countryside. The plains of Forlì gave way to the foothills rising to the sky-piercing summit of San Marino, dropping off abruptly to the long wide beaches of Rimini, shimmering under a November sun. Turning west, the Shelleys followed the Flaminian Way, noting in a tunnel the chisel marks that had been made by the Romans. Shelley thought Spoleto, with its soaring castle, "the most romantic city I ever saw." And the great waterfall of the Velino at Terni led him to write: "You see the ever moving water stream down. It comes in thick and tawny folds, flaking off like solid snow gliding down a mountain. . . . The very imagination is bewildered in it." Soon they were crossing the flat campagna outside Rome.

As they approached the city, Mary was struck by the sight of a solitary hawk "sailing in the air for prey." It was a rainy evening as they entered Rome, and in the rain they went from inn to inn looking for rooms at reasonable rates—"cheating innkeepers," Mary complained. "We at length get settled in a comfortable hotel."

But the stay in Rome was a short one. Like tourists they went to see St. Peter's, the Vatican, the Colosseum, the Forum, the Pantheon. They went to an opera ("the worst I ever saw," noted Mary). And after a week, Shelley left for Naples, going on ahead of the rest to look for lodgings.

The way led through some of the worst badlands of Italy,

and Shelley carried a gun, to the horror of a priest who rode in the carriage with him. It was Shelley's turn to be horrified as they were entering Naples: before the eyes of the travelers a young man came running out of a shop, pursued by a man with a knife and a woman with a bludgeon. The man caught up with his quarry and with one blow of his knife killed him. Shelley's reaction was accentuated when the priest only laughed at his concern.

Shelley did find a pleasant apartment at 250 Riviera di Chiaia, near the Royal Gardens. Mary, Claire and William arrived three days later, and the family settled down for three months of warm weather, attractive surroundings and a chance to forget. Shelley and Mary took walks in the Royal Gardens, looking out across the famous bay at Capri and Ischia and smoking Vesuvius. Shelley bought some carriage horses, and they took rides down the rugged, beautiful coastline south of Naples, gazing out across the blue Mediterranean and up the towering mountains alongside, with the houses, vineyards and whole villages perched on endless terraces. He bought a boat, and they sailed along rocky bluffs and inlets where the blue lights danced in the grottoes and the sea fans waved on the clear ocean floor while above them the jagged mountains plunged into the sea.

> The sun is warm, the sky is clear,
> The waves are dancing fast and bright;
> Blue isles and snowy mountains wear
> The purple noon's transparent might;
> The breath of the moist earth is light,
> Around its unexpanded buds;
> Like many a voice of one delight,
> The winds, the birds, the ocean floods,
> The City's voice itself is soft like Solitude's.

I see the Deep's untrampled floor
  With green and purple sea-weeds strown;
I see the waves upon the shore,
  Like light dissolved in star-showers, thrown;
    I sit upon the sands alone—
  The lightning of the noontide ocean
    Is flashing round me, and a tone
  Arises from its measured motion,
How sweet! did any heart now share in my emotion. . . .[31]

For all the delights of climate and beauty of the countryside, Naples was a trial for the Shelleys. Mary missed company; though Shelley did not much care for the type of visiting Englishman one encountered in Italy, Mary felt the lack of someone to speak to and she found the southern Italians less interesting and worse conversationalists than those of Pisa, Milan and Venice. Her few friends in Italy were around Pisa, far to the north, and she found Naples a lonely place, particularly at this time while she was still recovering from the loss of Clara. As for Shelley, he suffered from pains in the side. An English doctor diagnosed them as symptoms of liver trouble; his prescription of mercury and Cheltenham salts helped a little, but the pains persisted, occasionally to such an extent that he could not leave the house.

There was one trip to Vesuvius which ended in an eerie torchlighted procession down the steep mountainside, with the volcano belching and sending fire and sulphurous smoke up behind them while the guides, evidently drunk, sang wild songs and threatened to desert them on the mountainside. Amidst all this Shelley was seized with uncontrollable pain and had to be taken to a shelter to lie down until he could walk again. The pain, the people, the fierceness of much of the countryside, all contributed to an unhappy stay in Naples.

> . . . Alas! I have nor hope nor health,
>   Nor peace within nor calm around,
> Nor that content surpassing wealth
>   The sage in meditation found,
>   And walked with inward glory crowned—
> Nor fame, nor power, nor love, nor leisure.
>   Others I see whom these surround—
> Smiling they live, and call life pleasure;
> To me that cup has been dealt in another measure.
>
>   Yet now despair itself is mild,
>   Even as the winds and waters are;
> I could lie down like a tired child,
>   And weep away the life of care
>   Which I have borne and yet must bear,
> Till death like sleep might steal on me,
>   And I might feel in the warm air
> My cheek grow cold, and hear the sea
> Breathe o'er my dying brain its last monotony. . . .[32]

Still Shelley went to the current tourist attractions of the area—Virgil's tomb, Herculaneum, the wildfowl preserve at Lago d'Agnano, the hunting preserve at Caccia d'Ischieri (where they saw King Ferdinand sitting in the royal shooting box waiting for wild boars), and the Grotto del Cane (where they decided against watching the performance put on for tourists: the slow asphyxiation of dogs by volcanic gas). They also went to the opera and visited some museums, but most of the time they stayed in their lodgings, Shelley and Mary reading Dante's *Inferno* aloud to each other, Mary reading Montaigne and Virgil's *Georgics* and Shelley studying Euripides and Plutarch. And their letters to England reflected such a state of boredom that their friend Leigh Hunt pledged himself to write them once a week, to help cheer them up. Then the

Shelleys' visit to Naples was suddenly dramatized by one of the weirdest and still most mysterious events in their lives.

The official records in Naples show that on February 27, 1819, Percy Shelley appeared before a Neapolitan magistrate, with two witnesses and an infant, to sign a statement attesting that the infant was Elena Adelaide Shelley, daughter of himself and Mary Shelley. On that same day the baby was baptized at the parish of St. Joseph. This is the bare and tantalizing record; the only other reliable reference to the little girl appeared in one or two of Shelley's letters, in which he called her his "ward" and a "Neapolitan." Beyond that there is only conjecture, and what appears to be a conspiracy of silence. All that is certainly known is that there was a baby girl, that she was registered as Elena Adelaide Shelley, that she was left in a foster home when the Shelleys went north again and that she died of a fever on June 9, 1820. But in the years since then there have been countless speculative theories.

One theory holds that an unknown Englishwoman, a friend of Shelley's, came to him in Naples with an illegitimate child and pleaded with him to adopt it. According to this theory, Shelley may even have been the father of the little girl. He is supposed to have adopted the child and the mother is supposed to have returned to England, forever keeping her secret. There is, however, no concrete evidence that such a woman existed, and Shelley's reference to the child as a "Neapolitan" would tend to weaken this theory.

Another, perhaps more logical, theory is that Shelley looked for and located a little Italian girl to adopt in hopes of thus taking Mary's mind off the loss of Clara. Shelley's attempt to help fill the void with Allegra had failed when Byron had refused to cooperate. No doubt little William continued to complain about having no playmate and Shelley, with his love of children and his impulsive hospitality, may suddenly have made this desperate gamble and failed. For there is nothing in Mary's journal or correspondence to indicate that she ever set eyes on the child, and certainly Mary would have referred to the baby if she had taken her in, if only for a while. If indeed Shelley adopted the child in hopes of filling Mary's empty heart, he apparently succeeded only in adding to her anguish. This theory is more credible than the proposition of the mysterious Englishwoman. But there is nothing concrete to support it either, and it is difficult to understand why, if this is what happened, Shelley never explained it to any of his friends and instead preferred to keep silent.

A third theory is the most scandalous of all. During the Shelleys' stay in Naples, it was discovered that their coachman, Paolo, and the nurse Elise had, in Mary's delicate phrase, "formed a connection." Shelley fired Paolo, first insisting on his marrying Elise to legitimize the unborn child. Paolo and Elise—and their unborn child—went their way. But later Paolo, knowing of the Neapolitan ward and perhaps of some guilty feelings in connection with it—tried to blackmail Shelley, without success. Months later Elise and Paolo turned up in Venice, where Elise told Mrs. Hoppner, the wife of Byron's friend and the sometime foster mother of Allegra, a story of Shelley and Claire having a baby without Mary's knowledge, spiriting it from their lodgings and Shelley adopting it. Certain factors tended to support this tale—Claire's previous immorality, the fact that she had been feeling ill during the Naples visit, the rift between Mary and Shelley. But other factors make it virtually impossible. Claire could never have hidden so advanced a pregnancy in such close quarters, nor would she have tried to if this had been the case; she would simply have stayed in Rome, or gone off somewhere else with funds provided by Shelley. And no one who knew

Claire could picture her leaving a second child behind when they returned to Rome—after her experience with Allegra. Certainly she would have held onto this baby, or stayed behind with it in Naples. She did neither.

When Elise's tale was later related to Byron by the Hoppners, he put it directly to Shelley, whereupon both Shelley and Mary denied it with enough surprise and horror to lend credibility to the denial. Yet in a long letter Mary wrote to Mrs. Hoppner protesting her certain knowledge that Shelley had not had an affair with Claire and that Claire could not possibly have produced a child at this time, Mary Shelley makes no reference to the child herself. So the little Neapolitan girl remains one of the most enigmatic figures in the story of Byron and Shelley. She would come into their lives once again, to play a momentary part in the gathering tragedy.

Before the Shelleys left Naples there was a last visit to Pompeii. At the Royal Bourbon Museum Shelley had met a young Englishman, Charles MacFarlane, and together next day they took off toward Pompeii, jolting down the road in a *calesse* behind two fiery black horses. They enjoyed the exhilaration of the drive, and then, suddenly, they were in the moody silence of the dead city. After hours of walking among the echoing walls and along the worn, cobbled streets, they rested on a lava rock overlooking the blue Mediterranean far below. MacFarlane tried to make conversation, but Shelley was utterly lost in thought.

> I stood within the city disinterred;
> And heard the autumnal leaves like light footfalls
> Of spirits passing through the streets; and heard
> The Mountain's slumberous voice at intervals
> Thrill through those roofless halls;

The oracular thunder penetrating shook
   The listening soul in my suspended blood;
I felt that Earth out of her deep heart spoke—
   I felt, but heard not: through white columns glowed
     The isle-sustaining Ocean-flood,
A plane of light between two heavens of azure!
Around me gleamed many a bright sepulchre
Of whose pure beauty, Time, as if his pleasure
   Were to spare Death, had never made erasure;
     But every living lineament was clear
     As in the sculptor's thought; and there
The wreaths of stony myrtle, ivy, and pine,
   Like winter leave o'ergrown by moulded snow,
     Seemed only not to move and grow
Because the crystal silence of the air
   Weighed on their life; even as the Power divine
   Which then lulled all things, brooded upon mine. . . .[33]

Shelley recovered during the trip back to Naples, to the extent that when some beggars wheedled a few coins from him, and MacFarlane pitied them as "poor creatures," Shelley responded: "Not a bit of it; they are happier than I—I dare say they are happier than you."

The Shelleys had planned to return to Venice in the spring. But the more they thought about Rome the more it appealed to them. So Rome was the decision. And on the same day that Shelley was registering Elena before the Neapolitan magistrate, Mary was in their lodgings writing in her diary, as she had before the fatal trip to Este, the one word "Pack."

Elena was left behind, and the day after the adoption the Shelleys and Claire were heading north, drawn by the horses Shelley had bought and driven by a new coachman named Vicenzo. They traveled slowly, stopping the first night in Capua and then swinging back along the coast to Gaeta, where

Cicero had once owned a villa. Here they found an inn built where his villa had been; the ruins of the original structure still, wrote Shelley, "overhang the sea, and are scattered among the orange-groves." They paused to rest and enjoy the beauty of the place—behind them the steeply rising rows of olive and orange trees, "starred with innumerable globes of their ripening fruit" against the deep green of the foliage, and before them the sparkling sea. Next day they followed a route along the coast, still enjoying the "sublime character" of the richly fruitful mountains rising out of the sea. They turned inland again, to find near Albano "arches after arches in unending lines stretching across the uninhabited wilderness, the blue defined line of the mountains seen between them; masses of nameless ruin standing like rocks out of the plain; and the plain itself, with its billowy and unequal surface, announced the neighborhood of Rome."

Venice had been a tragedy. Naples had been a disappointment. But now Rome was better. Here was ancient history come alive. The Colosseum, which they visited by day, by dark and by moonlight, whispered with the ghosts of ancient Rome. In St. Peter's they attended Mass and, Mary wrote, "saw Pope Pius VII, a poor old man upon the brink of the Grave, and many Cardinals almost as old and trembling"—all representing the latest chapter in the eternal history of the Church. And as often as he could, in whatever weather, Shelley strolled ruminatively through the ruins of the Capitol and the Forum. Coming in from such a walk one night he sat down and wrote:

I walk forth in the purple and golden light of an Italian evening, and return by star or moonlight, through this scene. The elms are just budding, and the warm spring winds bring unknown odours, all sweet from the country. I see the radiant Orion through the mighty columns of the temple of Concord, and the mellow fading light softens down the modern buildings of the Capitol, the only ones that interfere with the sublime desolation of the scene. . . . What shall I say of the modern city? Rome is yet the capital of the world.

Rome did something for Shelley's health too. He felt better than he had in years. So did Mary, who began to forget the monosyllabic reticence she had adopted after Clara's death; she expanded in the new atmosphere, and even started taking painting and drawing lessons. Claire matched her with singing lessons. Finally, after the long months of bereavement, the little group began to recover a measure of equanimity and happiness. And in the jagged, dramatic ruins of the Baths of Caracalla, "among the flowery glades and thickets of odoriferous blossoming trees," Shelley sat and wrote the second and third acts of one of his greatest works, *Prometheus Unbound*.

> My soul is an enchanted boat,
> Which, like a sleeping swan, doth float
> Upon the silver waves of thy sweet singing;
> And thine doth like an angel sit
> Beside a helm conducting it,
> Whilst all the winds with melody are ringing.
> It seems to float ever, for ever,
> Upon that many-winding river,
> Between mountains, woods, abysses,
> A paradise of wildernesses!
> Till, like one in slumber bound,
> Borne to the ocean, I float down, around,
> Into a sea profound, of ever-spreading sound.[34]

Rome, Shelley's better health, the drawing lessons and the singing lessons—all tended to soften the pain of the recent months, so much that even the latest report on Allegra did not disturb them overly. Mrs. Hoppner wrote from Venice that Allegra was still living with the Hoppners while her father continued to live *"dans une débauche affreuse."* The Venetian climate was far from healthy, but warm weather would no doubt be more salutary. Meanwhile, she reported, Allegra *"est devenue tranquille et sérieuse comme une petite vieille. . . ."* For a while the pain cut into Claire's heart, but soon the sunny atmosphere of Rome helped her to accept what she knew must be, at least for now.

A chance encounter with an old friend from home, Amelia Curran, not only offered companionship but also provided paintings of Shelley, Mary, Claire and little William, since Miss Curran was an artist of some ability. Winter turned to spring, and Mary was pleased to discover that she was pregnant again. They had thought of returning to Naples, but all went so well in Rome that they decided that they were at last enjoying themselves and that it would be unwise to tempt fate by heading south again. Then, on May 25, William Shelley complained of feeling ill.

After a couple of days he seemed to recover. But then he turned sick again, this time much worse. For sixty hours at a stretch, without sleep, William's father sat at his bedside, holding the tiny hot hand, trying to cool William's brow and watching helplessy while the boy grew weaker. Mary wrote: "We do not quite despair, yet we have the least possible reason to hope. . . . The hopes of my life are bound up in him. . . ." On June 7, at noon, William died.

Sitting at his desk, Shelley wrote about "Willmouse," as he had called his son. The boy had lived only three and a half years. And, Shelley wrote, "it was impossible to find a creature more gentle and intelligent. His health and strength appeared to be perfect, and his beauty, the silken fineness of his hair, the transperance of his complexion, the animation and deep blue colour of his eyes, were the astonishment of everyone. The Italian women used to bring each other to look at him when he was asleep."

But writing about it, Shelley found, was too painful. "You will be kind enough to tell all my friends," he wrote to one of them. "It is a great exertion to me to write this, and it seems to me as if, haunted by calamity as I have been, that I should never recover any cheerfulness again. . . ." And to another friend he added: "Mary bears it, as you may naturally imagine, worse than I do."

All the gain of Rome was gone. Shelley accompanied the small coffin to its burial place—this time in the Protestant Cemetery in Rome.

> My lost William, thou in whom
> Some bright spirit lived, and did
> That decaying robe consume
> Which its lustre faintly hid—
> Here its ashes find a tomb,
> But beneath this pyramid
> Thou art not—if a thing divine
> Like thee can die, thy funeral shrine
> Is thy mother's grief and mine. . . .[35]

Three days after William's death the Shelleys were on the road to Leghorn. And as they rode away from the most recent scene of their Italian tragedy, Shelley wondered why, amidst all the sympathetic messages he had received from his friends, there was no word from Byron.

It happened that at this particular time Lord Byron was attempting to cope with one of the great crises of his life.

There could scarcely be a sharper contrast than that of the Shelleys' life at the time and that of Byron. He was still the most extravagant figure in Venice. Visitors were rowed past the Palazzo Mocenigo to stare at his blue-and-white gondolas and listen to the noises of his dogs, his monkeys and his birds and to see if they could spot the great man himself at his door or on his balcony. Sometimes tourists even bribed servants to get them into the palazzo. By night the windows glowed with light and rang with noise as Byron's women and other hangers-on caroused through the late hours, often while he was off at the hideaway where he had his secret meetings with his more interesting conquests. But as each amour seemed to bore him more than the last, and he gradually lengthened the late hours over his desk in his solitary, private world of poetic creation, the paramours and parasites were sent on their way.

The hardest part was breaking off with La Fornarina. He did not want to, but she had become so dominating that he had to. At first he tried to tell her, gently but firmly, that she must go. She did not believe him. Then he summoned up his courage and ordered her to leave. To his astonishment, she consented meekly.

It seemed too easy; it was. He was carving the roast one day when a commotion on the stairs was followed by a dramatic entrance. It was La Fornarina; a servant had tried to close a door in her face and she had simply broken it down. She strode into the dining room and to the head of the table, where she tried to seize the carving knife. Cutting himself in the process, Byron managed to wrest it away from her. The two faced each other in silence, La Fornarina panting and flashing her fiery defiance. Byron broke the silence to tell her that she must leave. She seemed to crumple. Without a word, all defiance evidently gone, she turned and walked out. Byron wrapped a napkin over his bleeding hand and resumed carving.

There was another commotion, this one noisier than the last. A servant staggered into the room carrying the dripping body of La Fornarina. She had thrown herself into the canal.

But she was too tough to die. Byron had her put to bed, and she quickly recovered. Then, quietly and patiently, he told her again. It was all over. She must leave.

This time she accepted it. She walked down the wide steps of the Palazzo Mocenigo for the last time, and never approached Byron again. With her departure a phase of Byron's life in Venice was finished.

Now he devoted more of his time to the other pleasures of Venice, to the opera and the theater and to the salons of Mmes. Albrizzi and Benzoni. Countess Marina Queroni Benzoni became his favorite. She had long been a famous character on the Venetian scene. At the time of the French Revolution the countess had joined the dancing around a hastily constructed Liberty Tree, dressed in an Athenian tunic which exposed her above the waist. Now, at sixty, her figure had gone to fat, but she had lost none of her youthful gaiety. At her *conversazioni* and everywhere else she was attended by her faithful *cavalier servente*, the Cavalier Giuseppe Rangone, a Venetian diplomat who had forsaken his career to devote himself to the countess. Beppe, as she called him, was her companion for thirty years, and married her at last when she was approaching seventy. The countess had a voice like a foghorn, a robust sense of humor and the nickname El Fumente, coined by the gondoliers, who noticed the steam arising from the hot garlic rolls which she stuffed in her bosom as she rode from party to party. The countess was unperturbed by any sense of moral principles; at the sight of Byron she set out to seduce him. Whether she did or not is questionable, but many were the comments on the attention she paid him whenever he attended her salons. It was at one of these salons, on a night in early April, 1819, that Byron and his friend Alexander Scott stopped in for a few minutes that were to change Byron's life.

It was a cold, stormy night, and the tossing canals were deserted. There would be scarcely anybody at Countess Benzoni's salon on a night like this; but Byron was not yet ready to return to his empty study and his solitary struggle with the pen. The countess was gushing as usual; the refreshments were no better than usual. Byron and Scott escaped from the countess for a moment and seated themselves on a sofa facing the door. They had not been there long when the countess was upon them again. She took Byron by the hand and asked him to come and meet a charming young countess who had only just arrived in Venice. Byron demurred. He had had enough of charming new countesses. Hadn't he told Countess Benzoni that he was bored with all this? "You know that I do not wish to meet any more ladies; if they are ugly because they are ugly and if they are pretty because they are pretty." His hostess protested that he must make an exception in this case; here was one of the most beautiful young visitors to come to her salon. Scott interjected a note that perhaps did not delight his hostess: surely Byron should make an exception in a salon where beauty was an exception. Byron shrugged, rose and followed Countess Benzoni's urging hand. And as he limped across the salon his eye caught that of a golden-haired, white-shouldered young lady, and he realized that it was she who was to be introduced to him.

Teresa Guiccioli had not wanted to go to Casa Benzoni that evening. She had a headache, but at her husband's insistence she had gone to the theater; Count Alessandro Guiccioli could not get enough of the theater. When he proposed a visit to Countess Benzoni's salon, Teresa asked if she could go back to the hotel instead. But Count Guiccioli insisted, and his wife had no choice.

The count was accustomed to having his own way; he had thoroughly dominated two previous wives, and in the one year of his marriage to Teresa he had firmly established his authority. Count Guiccioli was fifty-eight; and his relationship with his nineteen-year-old wife was more like that of father and daughter than husband and wife.

So on this April evening, despite her headache, Teresa had obeyed, in return for the promise that they would only stay a few minutes at the Countess Benzoni's salon. Through the raw night, with the gondola rocking and the canals surging and sucking at the buildings, they had ridden to Casa Benzoni. And as they had been ushered into the chandeliered drawing room, Teresa had briefly noticed the bored expression on the face of a handsome young Englishman sitting near the door.

Now she looked up expectantly as the same young Englishman came limping toward her. As for Byron, his first impression was of a profusion of auburn hair, cream-white shoulders, full bust and warmly appraising eyes. Countess Benzoni was burbling something about England's greatest poet, but neither Teresa nor Byron was listening. Flashing one of his calculated smiles, Byron sat on the sofa beside her. She knew no English, but his Italian was fluent by now. The small talk about Venice changed to small talk about Ravenna, which Byron claimed he wanted to visit because it was the site of Dante's tomb. His interest quickened when Teresa demonstrated her familiarity with Dante and Petrarch. Rapidly the conversation became more personal and more intimate. Byron was pleased to find the old magic working—the aura of romance and impulse that infected nearly all women in his presence. He asked if he could see her next day, alone. She agreed, "on condition," she later wrote, "that he would respect my honor." Now he knew: they always talked of "honor" when they had already decided to surrender it. He set the hour, and then Teresa quickly changed the subject.

Count Alessandro Guiccioli stood before them. He bowed correctly and asked if the countess realized that the few minutes she had insisted upon had long since elapsed. Teresa "rose to leave as if in a dream," as she remembered it. Byron was smiling with the quickened interest of another passing conquest. It would not be long before he realized how wrong he was.

Next day, at the hour during which Count Guiccioli always took his nap, Teresa waited at the steps to their palazzo. A nondescript gondola sidled up to the steps and the gondolier handed over a note to one of the Guiccioli servants, who brought it to the countess. The note was from Byron. Teresa slipped out the door and into the gondola, which swung quickly away and down the canal. Shortly the gondola rode alongside another, and Teresa was handed into it. There, waiting for her, was Byron. Swiftly his gondola rode away down the canal, around the sharp corners and through the narrow passageways to St. Maria Zobenigo and Byron's secret casino.

Byron was no doubt surprised, and probably intrigued all the more, when Teresa was, as she put it later, "strong enough to resist at that first encounter." But she consented to another meeting next day. And next day she arrived with a companion. She introduced her as Fanny Silvestrini, a former governess who was helping Teresa learn French. Byron was taken aback, but only momentarily. For while Fanny Silvestrini waited outside in the gondola, Teresa joined him in his casino. And, as she described it later, "my strength gave way."

It was dusk before Teresa went gliding home, languorously tingling from Byron's lovemaking and, in her characteristic manner, already making excuses to her conscience. It was an old tradition in Italian marriages of convenience for the wife to have a *cavalier servente*, a formally recognized escort-lover. In fact, this was often included in the marriage contract itself. It was not included in hers, she knew, but nothing could be more of a marriage of convenience than hers, and certainly her fifty-eight-year-old husband must expect her to find romance outside her marriage. Only now did she fully realize this, as she rode home from her afternoon with Byron.

And only now did Byron himself begin to sense that this would be more than an ordinary affair. As the next day and the next brought their secret meetings at the casino, while Teresa's *confidante* watched and waited in the gondola outside, the troubling truth began to dawn on him. There was the complete abandon with which she gave herself to him, more than any of the others and more than physically. There was her naïve assumption that he too was surrendering himself wholly, an attitude that at first amused but then dismayed him, particularly when Teresa, in Countess Benzoni's crowded salon a few nights later, openly called him *"mio Beeron,"* to the consternation of the other ladies, who knew that this went beyond the rules of the *cavalier servente*. But more than all this was the strangely growing attraction which was infecting him. And then came the incident that decided it.

Count Guiccioli concluded that he must take his countess away from Venice. When Teresa told him the dreadful news, she was taken aback at Byron's reaction: he urged her to do her husband's bidding, evidently grasping at this opportunity to break off the affair before it was too late. Playing a game that would become more apparent later, the count cordially invited Byron to come and visit them in Ravenna. Byron handed Teresa into her gondola as they departed, promising her that he would follow her to Ravenna—and promising himself that he would not.

Then she was gone. And he tried to forget her as he turned to his work, to the theater, to Countess Benzoni's salon, even to a young girl named Angelina. But he found he could not forget. Teresa did her part to keep him from forgetting: through the helpful, secret offices of Fanny Silvestrini, she wrote him her ingenuous love letters, also telling him that the count had taken her to one of his other estates, Ca Zen, on the River Po. Sitting at his desk in the big empty room of the Palazzo Mocenigo, Byron discovered that he could not compose the cynical stanzas of *Don Juan,* but instead wrote, "in *red-hot* earnest," his famous *Stanzas to the Po:*

> River, that rollest by the ancient walls,
> Where dwells the Lady of my love, when she
> Walks by thy brink, and there, perchance, recalls
> A faint and fleeting memory of me:
>
> What if thy deep and ample stream should be
> A mirror of my heart, where she may read
> The thousand thoughts I now betray to thee,
> Wild as thy wave, and headlong as thy speed!
>
> What do I say—a mirror of my heart?
> Are not thy waters sweeping, dark, and strong?
> Such as my feelings were and are, thou art;
> And such as thou art were my passions long.
>
> Time may have somewhat tamed them—not for ever;
> Thou overflow'st thy banks, and not for aye
> Thy bosom overboils, congenial river!
> Thy floods subside, and mine have sunk away:
>
> But left long wrecks behind, and now again,
> Borne in our old unchanged career, we move:
> Thou tendest wildly onwards to the main,
> And I—to loving *one* I should not love.

The current I behold will sweep beneath
   Her native walls, and murmur at her feet;
Her eyes will look on thee, when she shall breathe
   The twilight air, unharmed by summer's heat.

She will look on thee—I have looked on thee,
   Full of that thought: and, from that moment, ne'er
Thy waters could I dream of, name, or see,
   Without the inseparable sigh for her! . . .

A stranger loves the Lady of the land,
   Born far beyond the mountains, but his blood
Is all meridian, as if never fanned
   By the black wind that chills the polar flood.

My blood is all meridian; were it not,
   I had not left my clime, nor should I be,
In spite of tortures, ne'er to be forgot,
   A slave again of love—at least of thee. . . .

April wore into May, and the heat of summer permeated
Venice. Byron tried to concentrate on Angelina and on the sport
of escaping the watchful eyes of her "flinty-hearted father."
But his mind would not leave off the memory of the golden
hair, the snapping eyes, the white shoulders, the whispering
surrender of Teresa. More letters told him that the count had
taken her on to visit another of his many estates, this one a big,
damp, abandoned abbey set among the marshes. Then came the
news that Teresa had been pregnant when they had met in
Venice—and the news that she had come down with a fever
and had had a miscarriage. Now she was in Ravenna, apparently recovering. Byron waited for further word. Un-
satisfied by what he heard and suspicious that he was not being
told everything, he decided to take the chance: he would go
to see her. He did not believe for a minute that Count Guic-

cioli had meant his invitation, but whether the count did or not, Byron could no longer sit in Venice. Again Allegra moved in with the Hoppners, her father promising that he would be back within a month. A business agent was put in charge of the Palazzo Mocenigo and all its servants and menagerie. And on June 1, Lord Byron rode across Venice's canals and climbed into his carriage, to roll through the hot, parched countryside toward Padua, Bologna and Ravenna.

The June days were stifling and the road was a bumpy inferno. The first night out, Byron wrote to Allegra and the Hoppners: "I should now be swimming from the Lido, instead of smoking in the dust of Padua." It took him five days to reach Bologna, where he had asked Teresa to send him a letter. But when he reached the Pellegrino Inn, there was no letter.

Harassed by the heat, sick of the dusty countryside and angry at the lack of word from Teresa, Byron suddenly decided to turn back. He wrote Hoppner to say that he had changed his mind and that he would be back in Venice by the eleventh at the latest. But even as he determined to return, he knew he could not. For three days he waited in Bologna for news and for some sign that he could go on to Ravenna without a dangerous confrontation with Count Guiccioli. Finally he could stand it no longer. Off his carriage rattled across the Romagnese plains.

The roads were abominable and the dust and heat were almost more than Byron could bear. It was two days before the welcome buildings of Ravenna came into view. Then, just as he entered the main section of the town, his carriage came to a halt. A town official, no doubt enjoying the privilege of halting so grand a carriage, announced that it could proceed no farther. This was June 10, the festival day of Corpus Christi, and the streets of Ravenna were being kept clear for the procession to the cathedral. Climbing down from the carriage, Byron saw the streets strewn with flower petals, the buildings festooned with tapestries and holy pictures. Everywhere there was the spirit of a holy day.

At first annoyed but then resigned and mildly interested, Byron waited until the procession had passed by. Then his carriage rumbled slowly down the narrow, awninged streets to the Albergo Imperiale, where he moved in and planned his next step.

First he dashed off a message, in his workable Italian, to Teresa and sent it by a trusted messenger, a priest who had entry to Teresa's boudoir. Then Byron sent another message, this one to Count Giuseppe Alborghetti, one of Ravenna's first citizens, to whom Byron had foresightedly arranged a letter of introduction. Count Alborghetti immediately responded with an invitation to join him in his box at the theater that evening. Byron accepted.

Count Alborghetti was delighted to be entertaining so distinguished a visitor. Receiving his guest with cordiality, he plied Lord Byron with questions. To what did Ravenna owe the pleasure of his lordship's visit? Yes, the great Dante was worth a pilgrimage by even so worthy a literary descendant as Lord Byron. Had his lordship yet visited Dante's tomb? He must permit the count to show it to him tomorrow. Perhaps his lordship had had a tiresome trip? The Romagnese plain was not at its most attractive at this time of year. Were the rooms at the Albergo Imperiale comfortable? It was too bad that Ravenna could not offer something worthier of so distinguished a visitor. Did his lordship by chance know anyone else in Ravenna?

Byron, answering his host's questions absent-mindedly, was surveying the theater. Count Guiccioli was famous for his consuming love of the theater; if Teresa were at all recovered, the count would have her here with him. If not, the count might be here alone. As he looked about, Byron absently replied to his host's question. Yes, he was acquainted with Count and Countess Guiccioli. And then he spotted Count Guiccioli. He was alone. Evidently the count had seen Byron, because he was looking in the direction of Alborghetti's box and making his way toward it, when Byron heard his host say: "Alas, you will not be able to see the young lady. They say she is at death's door."

Teresa, it happened, was recovering. She sat in bed writing a letter to Byron—asking him to be patient and to stay away from Ravenna for a while, at least until she was better and until her husband overcame his suspicions—when one of her closest friends, Signora Geltrude Vicari, burst in upon her with the breathless news that her lover was here. Signora Vicari had not been introduced to him, but she had seen his enormous, colorful carriage when it had been halted at the Porta Sisi, and there could be no doubt in her mind that the handsome young Englishman in the coach with the armorial crest was the great poet whose love Teresa had confessed to her friend.

As Teresa was considering this news, her husband was himself greeting Lord Byron in Count Alborghetti's box at the theater. Count Guiccioli's manner was most cordial. His smile was hospitable, and masked his surprise. He reassured Byron: Teresa's health was improved. Byron could not put down the feeling that there was something sly, perhaps menacing, in Count Guiccioli's exaggerated hospitality. That night, before climbing into the lumpy, lonely bed in the Imperiale, Byron wrote Teresa again, more passionately in Italian than he might have in English: "My Love: I have been to the theater without finding you. . . . Your husband came to see me in the box and replied courteously to the few inquiries I dared to make at the moment. . . . My sweetest Soul—believe that I live for you alone—and do not doubt me. I shall stay here until I know what your wishes really are. . . . I beseech you to command me as entirely and eternally yours. . . . I kiss you a thousand thousand times with all my soul. . . ."

Next day, to Byron's surprise, Count Guiccioli called at the inn and asked if his lordship would care to come to the palazzo and see the countess. Byron seized the opportunity. But the reunion, after so long a separation, was anticlimactic. Teresa lay in her great bed, surrounded by relatives and visitors. She could only grip Byron's hand in a feverish grasp and flush at the sight of him. They talked innocent pleasantries as if he were another well-wisher, and Byron could almost feel the keen gaze of the count behind his back. Byron broke away as soon as he politely could, went back to his inn and sat down to tell Teresa in a letter what he could not in person.

My love: Pray instruct me how I am to behave in these circumstances. . . . I have no life now, except in you. My peace is lost in any case—but I should prefer death to this uncertainty. . . . I do see you—but how?—in what a state? . . .

It is impossible for me to live long in this state of torment— I am writing to you in tears—and I am not a man who cries easily. When I cry my tears come from the heart, and are of blood. . . .

If you knew what it costs me to control myself in your presence! But I will not say more— . . .

I embrace you—I kiss you a thousand thousand times. . . .

For nearly a week it went on like this—the strained visits to the bedside, always in the presence of other callers and the watchful count; the secret letters; and the increasingly curious behavior of Count Guiccioli, who regularly called on Byron to ask if he would like to ride about the town. "I can't make him out at all," Byron wrote Hoppner. "He visits me frequently and takes me out (like Whittington, the Lord Mayor) in a coach and *six* horses." But the visits to Ravenna's few points of interest, even Dante's tomb, were halfhearted. To Byron, more and more as each day went by, his world depended, nearly as much as he told her in his love letters, upon the frail figure in the big bed at the Palazzo Guiccioli.

And then Teresa's doctor informed her that she could get up and about. In fact, the doctor said, a ride in the countryside might do her good. On June 15 Teresa and Byron at last found themselves alone, in her closed carriage, riding out through the dark-green pine forest down toward the sea. It was sunset as they came in sight of the Adriatic. Soft red tints colored the little pools under the green, umbrella-shaped pine trees. Crickets sounded, and now and then the shrill call of a nightingale echoed through the grove. They paused in the softness of the twilight, but not for long. Behind them rode Count Guiccioli in his carriage, with some of his friends. As the two lovers rocked together in the jolting carriage on the road back to Ravenna, Teresa asked Byron to write a poem for her alone. From the Palazzo Guiccioli he returned to his desk at the inn.

> Lady! if for the cold and cloudy clime
>> Where I was born, but where I would not die,
>> Of the great Poet-Sire of Italy
> I dare to build the imitative rhyme,
> Harsh Runic copy of the South's sublime,
>> Thou art the cause; and howsoever I
>> Fall short of this immortal harmony,
> Thy gentle heart will pardon me the crime.
> Thou, in the pride of Beauty and of Youth,
>> Spak'st; and for thee to speak and be obeyed

Are one; but only in the sunny South
　Such sounds are uttered, and such charms displayed,
So sweet a language from so fair a mouth—
　Ah! to what effort would it not persuade?[36]

Teresa continued to recover, but too slowly for Byron. He worried about her fevers and her cough. He wrote Hoppner: "I greatly fear the Guiccioli is going into a consumption. . . . Thus it is with every thing and every body for whom I feel any thing like a real attachment. . . . I never even could keep alive a dog that I liked or that liked me." He sent an appeal to the great Aglietti, the doctor whom Shelley had pursued so madly and in vain the night his daughter died. Aglietti did not like to leave Venice, but for his friend Byron he came to Ravenna. He prescribed little the other doctors had not, wisely noticing that Teresa's best medicine was already being administered.

For Byron and Teresa were lovers again. And under the influence of their renewed relationship Teresa rapidly regained her health. Byron had sent for his horses, which were stabled in Ravenna, and the two rode through the *pineta*, Ravenna's pine forest, every late afternoon, Teresa letting her horse run wild. Byron recalled it with amusement: "he runs after mine— and tries to bite him—and then she begins screaming in a high hat and Sky-blue riding habit—making a most absurd figure." At other times she guided him around Ravenna, to the church with the Byzantine mosaics, to the ancient, high-ceilinged and impressive library, and to Dante's tomb. And in the Palazzo Guiccioli, while the count slept away the afternoon and a black-faced groom stood watch at their parlor door, they made love. ". . . (no *bolts* and be d——d to them) and we run great risks . . . so that if I come away with a Stiletto in my gizzard some fine afternoon—I shall not be astonished."

But he realized that he was serious, and to Hoppner he voiced his newly reflective frame of mind: "If any thing happens to my present *Amica*, I have done with the passion for ever—it is my *last* love. As to libertinism, I have sickened myself of that, as was natural in the way I went on, and I have at least derived that advantage from vice, to *love* in the better sense of the word. *This* will be my last adventure." He knew he had left Venice forever. The time had come for Allegra to join him in Ravenna.

Count Guiccioli unexpectedly changed Byron's plans. Now that Teresa had recovered from her illness, the count whisked her off to Bologna. Among his many properties was a palazzo in Bologna, and a number of farms in the area, which he had decided to visit. Byron put off his decision on Allegra. Quickly following Teresa and her husband, he arrived in Bologna the day after they had.

Pretending no surprise at Byron's following him and his wife, the count asked Byron to accompany them to the theater. He took Byron for more rides in his impressive coach. He invited Byron to dinner at his massive Bologna palazzo. And then one evening, over the brandy and cigars, the count showed his hand.

Byron had by now learned most of the count's story. The Cavalier Commendatore Alessandro Guiccioli had for some years demonstrated his skill at walking the political tightrope. When Napoleon's army had invaded the Romagna, Count Guiccioli had been a local political leader; a few years later, after Napoleon's fall, the count had been in equally good favor with the Papal government's representatives replacing those of Napoleon. The count's rapid rise in wealth and influence had been helped by an advantageous marriage. His first countess, much older than he, had brought him a large dowry which he had invested well. At her death he had married one of the Guiccioli maids, thus legitimizing six children she had borne him during a long and open relationship. She too had died in a few years.

Teresa was the third Countess Guiccioli—to a large degree because, as the most attractive of the five daughters of Count Ruggero Gamba, she had been the one expected to marry well enough to restore the Gambas' sinking fortunes. Count Guiccioli had by this time become one of the wealthiest men in Italy. But his financial rise had not been uninterrupted. On one unhappy occasion the count had overextended his finances and had been sued by a creditor, a wealthy landowner named Dominico Manzoni, with the result that Count Guiccioli had even gone to debtors' prison for a few months. Recovering quickly from this temporary disgrace, Guiccioli had recouped his fortune— and Dominico Manzoni, perhaps not incidentally, had been mysteriously murdered; the case was never solved, and rumors of Guiccioli's possible involvement had even reached Byron's ears.

As Byron listened to the genial count, he did not have to be reminded of Guiccioli's ability to keep on the right side of the Romagna's political scene. At the moment, the count pointed out, he and Byron were on the same side—in sympathy with the rebellious Italian patriots meeting secretly to plot for the day when they could rise against the Romagna's Austrian rulers. No doubt their motives were dissimilar—Byron's an idealistic hope for Italian freedom and the count's a determination to have the right friends if the present government should indeed be overthrown. Nevertheless, as the count saw it, they were in the same boat. But it was safer for Byron: as an Englishman he was virtually immune from danger. They might ask him to leave the principality, or even arrest him for a few hours. But nothing serious could befall so distinguished a representative of so powerful a nation as his. It was a different matter for the count. Of course, he was powerful in the Romagna at present. But who knew how long the *status quo* would last?

Count Guiccioli's vast holdings could disappear overnight if there were severe political troubles. Obviously the count had realized that if, on the one hand, he did not side with those who opposed the Austrians, he stood to lose out if and when the Austrians were overthrown. But, on the other hand, if he sided with the rebels and they were put down, he stood to lose even more.

There was, however, an interesting possibility for improving this awkward situation. Count Guiccioli had noticed that in many parts of the world the British had appointed local men of distinction as consuls, vice consuls and the like. If he were in so fortunate a position, wouldn't the rebels, or even the Austrians for that matter, think more than twice before they trampled on the rights of an official personage of the mighty British government?

Byron was obviously delighted. What a simple explanation for the count's puzzling behavior. And what a happy solution to the growing problem of his relations with his *amica*'s husband. Off went a letter to his publisher, Murray:

Will you get a favour done for me? *You* can, by your Government friends, Croker, Canning, or my old Schoolfellow Peel, and I can't. Here it is. Will you ask them to appoint (*without salary or emolument*) a noble Italian (whom I will name afterwards) Consul or Vice-Consul for Ravenna? He is a man of very large property—noble too; but he wishes to have a British protection in case of changes. . . . That his office might be useful, I know; as I lately sent off from Ravenna to Trieste a poor devil of an English sailor, who had remained there sick, sorry and pennyless (having been set ashore in 1814,) from the want of any accredited agent able or willing to help him homewards. . . . I know that in the Levant you make consuls and Vice-Consuls, perpetually, of foreigners. This man is a Patrician, and has twelve thousand a year. . . .

And while he waited for the business to be arranged, he relaxed and enjoyed Bologna and the presence of his love. He rented the Palazzo Merendoni, only a few doors away from the Guicciolis' Palazzo Savioli, and as his visits to Teresa's apartment grew more and more routine he realized that he was becoming inextricably bound to her.

But the count took her away again; he was off for a few days to inspect his properties between Bologna and Ferrara, and Teresa dutifully accompanied him, though not before she had slipped Byron a key to the Palazzo Savioli and instructed the servants that he would be calling often to visit her rooms and walk in the gardens.

Wondering when she would return, Byron finally began to accept fully his new existence. In a letter to Hobhouse he revealed a sense of the struggle: "I feel—and I feel it bitterly —that a man should not consume his life at the side and on the bosom of a woman, and a stranger; that even the recompense, and it is much, is not enough, and that this Ciscisbean existence is to be condemned. But I have neither the strength of mind to break my chain, nor the insensibility which would deaden its weight." Then, while walking in Teresa's garden, after noticing one of Teresa's books, Byron wrote his final confession.

The book was, he knew, one of her favorites—Mme. de Staël's *Corinne*, a small, thick volume bound in purple plush. Byron had often teased her about her fondness for this sentimental novel. He spotted it as it lay on a table in her sitting room, neglected by her but a memento of her. He scooped it up and took it with him as he limped along the garden paths. And sitting in the shade of a tree, he opened it and wrote in the margin.

My dear Teresa, . . . You will not understand these English words, and *others* will not understand them—which is the reason I have not scrawled them in Italian. But you will recognise the handwriting of him who passionately loved you, and you will divine that, over a book which was yours, he could only think of love. In that word, beautiful in all languages, but most so in yours —*Amor mio*—is comprised my existence here and hereafter . . . my destiny rests with you. . . .

There was no more reason for Allegra to stay behind in Venice. Byron sent for her, and a few days later she and her nurse climbed down from the coach in Bologna. Byron found that her hair was becoming darker. She had grown a dimple on her chin, and had developed a "particular liking of Music— and of her own way in everything—is not that B. all over?" he wrote his half-sister Augusta. Byron was a bit disturbed that this little "English" girl could speak "nothing but Venetian. Bon di, papa &c." But Allegra's arrival signified her father's break with the past, of his move from the Venice of his earlier profligate life to the Bologna and Ravenna of his new domestic life. And now Teresa returned to Bologna too.

She had, it developed, made good use of the time alone with her husband, who had long since learned that she was more than just a pretty, placid young girl. At the convent school she had attended before her marriage, Teresa had been a star pupil who had thrived under a curriculum that had gone far beyond that normally provided for young girls of the time, so far that the Church had closed down the school a few years later on the charge that it was dangerous to teach young women so much. By the time of her marriage she was an accomplished student of eloquence and rhetoric, composition and literature and the rudiments of philosophy. Behind her demure prettiness lay a will of iron. She had a whimsical turn and a sense of the ridiculous; but always she knew what she wanted, and how to get it. What she wanted this time was agreement from her husband that she was entitled to a *cavalier servente*. Not only did the count agree, but he even invited Byron to move into the unoccupied ground floor of the Palazzo Savioli. Now the lovers could be alone together even more than before; Teresa could spend more time petting and spoiling Allegra; and, Byron discovered, Count Guiccioli could corner him for more talks about their immediate future.

In answer to the count's question, Byron had to admit that he had not heard from England in the matter of the consulship for Ravenna. But the count had a further proposition: his inspection of his estates indicated that certain expenditures were advisable; and at the moment it happened that his fortune, despite its size, was tied up. Byron would not mind loaning the count a substantial sum just for immediate uses, would he? Byron certainly would not.

However, Byron's Italian banker knew Count Guiccioli and the count's business affairs better than Byron did. And he warned Byron that, judging by past performance, he should not expect repayment. Byron was not that wealthy. He explained to the count that, to his surprise, his banker reported that *his* funds were tied up too, and that he could not make the loan right away.

Before the count could respond by cutting short his hospitality, Teresa checked his move: she was taken ill again. Was this a coincidence, or was she virtually able to become sick at will? Whatever the case, Teresa's illness was convincing. And after a few days she even managed to persuade her husband that she needed the attention of the doctor who had cured her before: Aglietti of Venice.

Thereupon followed one of the most Italianate episodes of Byron's Italian adventure. Count Guiccioli knew very well that Teresa would ask for Byron as her escort to Venice. And he knew that if he proposed to accompany her himself, she probably would not go and would continue to languish in ill health until he gave in. So, no doubt priding himself on his little scheme, he readily agreed to Byron as an escort, insisting that Teresa also be accompanied by Lega, the count's personal manservant. And Lega was carefully instructed by his master to watch the couple like a hawk and report everything he saw. Count Guiccioli recognized that Teresa was entitled to a *cavalier servente*. But he was shrewd enough also to know the axiom that the most immoral codes of conduct usually have the most rigid rules of their own. This was the case with the nineteenth-century Italian code of the marriage of convenience and the *cavalier servente:* it did not include cross-country journeys *à deux* from hotel room to hotel room. While the matter of the consulship hung fire, and while there might still be a chance for a loan, the count was in no hurry to make a final move. But when he *was* ready, he wanted to have convincing evidence at hand.

What the count, as an Italian aristocrat, should have realized, however, was that he was dealing with Italians. And while his manservant Lega promised to act as his spy, Lega neglected to mention that Fanny Silvestrini, Teresa's conspiratorial maidservant, was his mistress. And so, when the count agreed to let Byron escort Teresa to Venice for her diagnosis by Aglietti on condition that Lega go along, Teresa happily consented.

Teresa remembered it later as one of the most idyllic periods of her life. The Guiccioli coach and six rattled north through the Euganean Hills, followed by Lord Byron's green-crested carriage. At the first hotel Lega was easily lured away from his appointed duty by his mistress. During the second day the carriages made a diversion to visit Arquà and the home and the burial place of Petrarch, more a favorite of Teresa than of Byron; but he dutifully limped up the steep hill to Petrarch's house and signed his name after hers in the visitors' book. Their stop that night, at an inn in Padua, was particularly emotional; it happened that Byron had helped the innkeeper with a loan the year before, and their host showed his gratitude with a memorable meal and a serenade from the next room. Next day they were off to Byron's villa at La Mira, to pause for refreshment before gliding into Venice by gondola, leaving Allegra at the villa. And in Venice, despite Lega's orders and Teresa's promise to move into another palace, Teresa went to the Palazzo Mocenigo with Byron.

The great doctor Aglietti may have been baffled by Countess Guiccioli's ill health, but whether for medical or diplomatic reasons he prescribed a "change of air." Teresa so informed her husband in a letter which proposed her journeying to Lakes Garda and Como, and which also included a calculated note: "Byron greets you and charges me to tell you that the English friend to whom he wrote about the Vice Consulate, etc., has answered him and that he will send in a petition at once and do everything possible to attain it." With that, Teresa and Byron moved out to La Mira.

No wonder that the count quickly wrote Lega asking him what was up. But the ever-watchful Fanny was on hand. "The Cavaliere has written to Lega," she informed Teresa in a quick note from Venice to La Mira, "asking him to keep him *informed* about his wife. He asks him to give more detailed news of you, which he is awaiting impatiently. In answer," Fanny continued soothingly, "Lega will write to him in the most appropriate manner." And Teresa could rest assured that Fanny would see to it that the appropriate answer was the least incriminating one.

So came the most romantic interlude since the evening when Byron had been led across the salon to meet the new young countess. There was no one to interrupt them; there were no restrictions or conventions to set the hours when they could meet. They walked in the gardens, rode along the sunset-tinged Brenta, made love through the evening and separated only in the early hours of the morning, when Teresa slept while Byron sat at his desk writing the newest verses of his newest work, *Don Juan*.

> She loved and was beloved—she adored,
> And she was worshipped; after Nature's fashion,
> Their intense souls, into each other poured,
> If souls could die, had perished in that passion—
> But by degrees their senses were restored,
> Again to be o'ercome, again to dash on;
> And, beating 'gainst *his* bosom, Haidée's heart
> Felt as if never more to beat apart.[37]

Adoration, passion—but also an ever-growing domesticity, long after adoration had gone and passion had cooled with other women. A measure of what had come over Byron was indicated on the arrival of his old friend from London, the poet Tom Moore. For three days Byron delightedly showed Moore around Venice. But only on the third night did Byron announce "with all the glee of a schoolboy who had just been granted a holiday," as Moore described it, "that, as this was my last evening, the Contessa had given him leave to 'make a night of it. . . .' " It was 3 A.M. the next morning before Byron bade his drinking companions good night and returned to La Mira and Teresa. And when Moore called on them to say good-bye next day, the sight of Byron, Teresa and Allegra was enough to make one forget that Teresa was married to another man and that little Allegra was Byron's daughter by another woman.

But as October wore on, the news of this arrangement reached ears that had not heard of it before. Count Ruggero Gamba, Teresa's father, got word of where his daughter was and with whom, and took off like a shot for Bologna to see his son-in-law.

What in the name of God, Count Gamba wanted to know, was Guiccioli thinking of? Didn't he know Lord Byron's reputation? Even if he didn't, couldn't he see that Byron was "too gifted, too seductive not to trouble the heart of a young woman and not to excite the observation of the public?" The tradition of the *cavalier servente* was one thing; open adultery was another.

Count Guiccioli had known all this, of course. But his impulse to do something about it had been tempered by his plans for making some personal gain from the situation. He listened to Count Gamba, and promised that he would put a stop to it, as soon as he could get away.

It developed that he could not get away for a couple of weeks. But when he finally took off for Venice, he descended on the errant couple with a proper vengeance. He found them in what seemed to be a compromising situation: they were both in the Palazzo Mocenigo. As always, there were extenuating circumstances: Byron had come down with a raging fever, and Teresa had come in from La Mira to help care for him. But Count Guiccioli was taking no chances. With his son and several servants, all uninvited, he too moved into the Palazzo Mocenigo.

There was an excruciating series of emotional scenes. Alternating between his resolve to break up the affair and his temptation to encourage it and make something out of it, Count Guiccioli berated Byron one day and flattered him the next. One day he was explaining that while he personally understood the tradition of the *cavalier servente* and indeed would welcome Byron back to Ravenna, the objections raised by Teresa's father were so strong that it would be better if Byron did not come back—and, for obvious reasons, it would be better not to tell Teresa of this decision right away. Shortly thereafter the count, reduced to tears in an argument with Teresa, was begging Byron to help him explain to her why she should choose her husband and renounce her lover. Byron's reply was that he would do no such thing, that if it was her choice to return to her husband, he would abide by the decision and "repass the Alps," but if not, he would take her away with him; in any case, he would not try to persuade her to leave him.

Many years later, Teresa's version of this dispute was that her husband forced her to decide between him and Byron, and she chose Byron. But Byron's version of it, in an unguarded moment, was that he was the one who insisted on a clear decision by Count Guiccioli that he be accepted openly as Teresa's lover or be asked to leave her forever, and that the count accepted him. What is certain is that these were emotional, bitter, sometimes hysterical days, full of hot Italian temperament and glacial British stubbornness. When it was over, Byron was emotionally exhausted. And, despite the outcome of his argument with the count, he had made an agonizing decision.

Teresa had reluctantly returned to Ravenna with her husband, convinced that Byron would soon follow. But Byron's mind was made up. Left alone in the Palazzo Mocenigo, he wrote his friend Hobhouse: "She agreed to go back to him; but *I* feel so wretched and low, and lonely, that I will leave the country. . . ." To another friend he wrote: "I have done my duty, but the country has become sad to me; I feel alone in it; and as I left England on account of my own wife, I now quit Italy for the wife of another."

But how could he break the news to Teresa? At first his letters were equivocal; he assured her of his love, he bemoaned her absence, he complained that the big palazzo was empty without her. But he mentioned neither a return to Ravenna nor his decision to leave Italy. Somehow, though, Teresa could sense the truth. Her letters to him became more frantic, imploring him for assurance that he would come. Still he did not commit himself.

One reason was that he could not leave immediately anyway. The damp, chill autumn in Venice had brought on its annual sickness, and soon half a dozen of the Palazzo Mocenigo's inhabitants, including Allegra, were down with the fever. Weeks went by while Aglietti made his regular visits, diagnosed "tertian fever" and prescribed bark. Byron too felt ill. "I cured myself without bark, but all the others are taking it like trees," he wrote. At long last, on November 25, 1819, Aglietti decided that Allegra had recovered enough to travel. It was time to go. Byron sat at his big desk and painfully wrote his letter of farewell.

"You are, and ever will be, my first thought. . . . I pray of you, I implore you, to be comforted, and to believe that I cannot cease to love you but with my life. . . . I go to save you, and leave a country insupportable to me without you. . . . Farewell! in that one word is comprised the death of my happiness."

He set about selecting what he would take with him. The

first leg of the journey would be north over the Alps and across the Continent to England. After that, he was undecided. He might go to South America, where the people were rebelling against their Spanish oppressors, and where the colorful figure of Simón Bolívar had caught his fancy. Byron wrote to England, warning his half-sister Augusta that he should be there soon, after three years. He referred to Teresa in the past tense; for him it was all over. "You must not dislike *her*, for she was a great admirer of *you*, and used to collect and seal up all *your letters* to me as they came that they might not be lost. . . ."

He also wrote a farewell poem.

> Could Love for ever
> Run like a river,
> And Time's endeavour
>   Be tried in vain—
> No other pleasure
> With this could measure;
> And as a treasure
>   We'd hug the chain.
> But since our sighing
> Ends not in dying,
> And, formed for flying,
>   Love plumes his wing;
> Then for this reason
> Let's love a season;
> But let that season be only Spring.
>
> When lovers parted
> Feel broken-hearted,
> And, all hopes thwarted,
>   Expect to die;
> A few years older,
> Ah! how much colder

> They might behold her
>   For whom they sigh!
> When linked together,
> In every weather,
> They pluck Love's feather
>   From out his wing—
> He'll sadly shiver
> And droop for ever
> Shorn of the plumage which sped his Spring.[38]

But as he read it and reread it, he did not have the heart to send it to her.

One reason was that, with the same providential timing as before, Teresa became ill again. Her father wrote Byron that she begged him to come and see her. Byron continued his packing for England. By December all was ready. One morning he supervised the loading of the gondolas. He donned his cap and gloves and took up his cane. It was nearly 1 P.M. before all was ready. Allegra sat waiting in her gondola. Everything was loaded except for Byron's last possessions, his ever-present swords and pistols. Looking at the packed gondolas, at Allegra in her fur coat and cap, and at the looming façade of the Palazzo Mocenigo before him, Byron made one of his dramatic gestures. If, he announced, his last possessions were not packed in the gondola before the clock towers struck one, he would stay.

He knew they could not. The bells in Venice's campanile tolled. Byron called to Allegra. Fate, he said, had decided for them. They would not leave Italy after all.

He knew it was not fate, nor the weather, nor Allegra's sickness. He had tried his best to make the break, and he had found he could not. A few days later, his letter arrived in Ravenna with the words that ended Teresa's anxiety: "Love has won." And a few days after that, Byron and Allegra arrived in Ravenna themselves. It was Christmas Eve. The Palazzo Guiccioli rang with the rejoicing.

And in Venice Mrs. Hoppner quickly passed along the news in a letter to Claire Clairmont in Pisa.

1. BYRON'S MOTHER. Catherine Gordon's plainness and plumpness were more than compensated for, in Captain Jack Byron's eyes, by the Gordon fortune.

2. AUGUSTA LEIGH. Byron's half-sister looked fashionable and candid in this miniature by James Holmes. "Gussie," as Byron affectionately called her, was his confidante even in his college days.

3. NEWSTEAD ABBEY. The Priory (above) had tumbled into disrepair, through the neglect of the Fifth Lord Byron, but there were still 3,200 acres and many buildings.

4. THOMAS MOORE. Nearly as famous a poet in his own right at the time, Tom Moore was a close friend of Byron's, visited him in Venice, and was involved in the famous burning of Byron's memoirs.

5. JOHN CAM HOBHOUSE. Byron's closest friend for the longest period, "Hobbie" accompanied him to Italy. Later Lord Broughton, he is reported to have coined the phrase: "His Majesty's Opposition."

6. LADY CAROLINE LAMB. A tomboy as a girl, Caroline kept her eccentric ways after marrying William Lamb. Byron wrote that "Her figure, though genteel, was too thin to be good. . . ."

7. ANNABELLA MILBANKE. At the time she met Byron, Annabella had what he called "the fairest skin imaginable." He was also struck by "a simplicity, a retired modesty about her. . . ."

8. BYRON IN ALBANIAN DRESS. So affected was he by his journey to Albania that Byron had Thomas Phillips paint him in this Albanian attire. He even grew a mustache during this period.

9. CLAIRE CLAIRMONT. Her full name was Mary Jane Clairmont, but she preferred the name Clare, which she later changed to Claire. Byron was not at first attracted to her, but her persistence won out.

10. PERCY SHELLEY. The ethereal quality of Shelley's appearance, especially in pictures of him, was deceptive, as Byron discovered. Shelley was tough and strong willed, though often absentminded.

11. MARY SHELLEY. The daughter of Mary Wollstonecraft looked her best when portrayed at her desk. She wrote other novels besides *Frankenstein*, and edited volumes of Shelley's works after his death.

12. VILLA DIODATI. Byron's vacation retreat in Switzerland stood on a hill with a sweeping view of Lake Geneva. At first Byron thought it was too small and too expensive. But he moved in after Shelley found a villa ten minutes away.

13. LORD BYRON AT THE VILLA DIODATI. The poet is depicted on the terrace of the Villa Diodati by an unknown artist who was unfamiliar with Byron's daily habits. A late riser, in good weather he usually went boating with Shelley on Lake Geneva, and did most of his writing after midnight.

14. MARGARITA COGNI. Byron's mistress in Venice managed to look wistful and meek in this portrait, a far cry from the leonine figure Byron described as "fit to breed gladiators from."

15. BYRON IN VENICE. The Byron of 1818 who lorded it over his Venetian neighbors in his Palazzo Mocenigo had developed this arrogant, sensual profile, meanwhile fighting off encroaching fat.

16. TERESA GUICCIOLI. Byron's last and greatest love (as drawn in 1818) attracted him as much by her intelligence as her beauty. And, as he said, "What shall I do? I am in love, and tired of promiscuous concubinage. . . ."

PALAZZO MOCENIGO. Far more pretentious
 the Villa Diodati, Byron's residence in
ice looked out on the Grand Canal near
 Rialto Bridge and the Piazza San Marco.
on lived in the upper floors, filling the
nd floor with his menagerie.

18. ALLEGRA. The daughter of Byron and Claire Clairmont already looked like a little adult in this miniature of her painted in Venice when she was not yet two.

19. THE PINES NEAR RAVENNA. Through pine forests like these Byron and Teresa often rode to escape the prying eyes of Count Guiccioli.

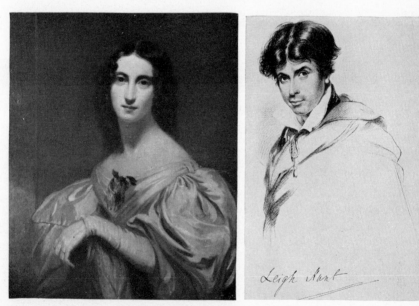

20. JANE WILLIAMS. Plain but soulful, she appealed to Shelley, who found her more restful than Mary. She and Edward Williams and their children shared the house at Lerici with the Shelleys.

21. LEIGH HUNT. In this drawing by John Hayter, Hunt looked the proper young poet. His willingness to live on others' bounty and his inability to provide for himself enraged Byron.

22. TRELAWNY. The romantic, bearded and hawk-nosed appearance of Trelawny impressed Mary Shelley, who said that his extravagance was "partly perhaps put on, but it suits him well."

23. "TITA." Even more impressive a figure than Trelawny, Giovanni Battista Falcieri, nicknamed "Tita," was Byron's colorful Venetian gondolier. He was still with Byron at the end in Greece.

24. LERICI. In a sketch by Captain Roberts, Shelley's last house (right) is shown at the head of the then quiet bay as *Ariel*, the yacht in which Shelley met his death, lies calmly at anchor.

25. THE FINALE ON THE BEACH. Artist Louis Edouard Fournier used his imagination well in this depiction of the cremation of Shelley on the beach at Viareggio. The painting follows many of the actual details with the exception of the facts that Shelley's body was not so well

[VII]

When Mrs. Hoppner's letter reached Claire, she made an acidulous entry in her journal: "The Hero has gone to Ravenna." By any previous standards Claire should have regarded it as good news. It meant a break with what Mrs. Hoppner had called Byron's *débauche affreuse* in Venice. It signified a semi-permanent arrangement with another woman, but Claire had long since given up hope of restoring any connection with Byron—in fact, nothing would have embarrassed her more, so bitter had she become. Her reaction to *Don Juan,* for example, which she recorded a few days later, took the sarcastic form of notes for a satire: "Hints for Don J—which appears to me a soliloquy upon his own ill-luck—ungrateful & selfish—like a beggar hawking his own sores about and which create disgust instead of pity." . . .

Claire should have been in better humor. She and the

145

Shelleys had at length found some respite from the doom that had seemed to dog them. In Leghorn, after William Shelley's death and the flight from Rome, they had located a pleasant villa outside the city, on a lane in an open field with a sweeping view of the sea. It was a quiet place, far from anything that could remind them of their loss. Grapes, cabbages and green pines grew in the red earth. And the sound of peasants singing in the fields and cicadas rasping in the trees could be heard in the soft evening air.

> . . . If I were a dead leaf thou mightest bear;
> If I were a swift cloud to fly with thee;
> A wave to pant beneath thy power, and share
>
> The impulse of thy strength, only less free
> Than thou, O uncontrollable! If even
> I were as in my boyhood, and could be
>
> The comrade of thy wanderings over Heaven,
> As then, when to outstrip thy skiey speed
> Scarce seemed a vision; I would ne'er have striven
>
> As thus with thee in prayer in my sore need.
> Oh, lift me as a wave, a leaf, a cloud!
> I fall upon the thorns of life! I bleed!
>
> A heavy weight of hours has chained and bowed
> One too like thee! tameless, and swift, and proud. . . .[39]

But Mary, as Shelley had written, was hurt even more deeply than he, and she recovered more slowly. More than two weeks after they had arrived in Leghorn, she wrote to Miss Curran, her friend back in Rome: "I no sooner take up my pen than my thoughts run away with me, and I cannot guide it except about *one* subject, and that I must avoid. . . . I never shall recover that blow; I feel it more now than at Rome. . . ." At William's death she had given up her daily journal. Now she tried to resume it. On Shelley's twenty-seventh birthday, Wednesday, August 4, 1819, she wrote: "We have now lived five years together; and if all the events of the five years were blotted out, I might be happy. . . ."

But time was, as always, the healer for both. For Shelley—time and hard work. For Mary—time and the hope of the future. As the summer wore on she could take some comfort in the fact that she was pregnant again. Plans were made to go to Florence in the fall, so as to be near her favorite, Dr. Bell, when her time came. These plans for the future, combined with the soft lassitude of the Villa Valsovano, slowly tempered her grief. And this time, instead of being pulled apart by their tragedy, the Shelleys were drawn together.

What Shelley was writing at this time tended to fit Mary's mood. It was a tragedy based on one of the saddest events in Italian history. They had heard the story during their visit to Rome: a beautiful young girl, Beatrice Cenci, had been so abused, and in fact seduced, by her evil father that she had in desperation plotted with her brother to murder him. The outcome could only be execution, which Beatrice faced with the equanimity of one who knew that she had done what must be done. From this story Shelley fashioned his eloquent *The Cenci*, on which Mary helped him daily as he wrote. And the mood which still gripped them both could be seen in the somber portrait of Beatrice Cenci, in the sweeping tragedy that engulfed her and, finally, in the poignant last words of Beatrice as the Lord Cardinal comes to lead her to the execution.

> Give yourself no unnecessary pain,
> My dear Lord Cardinal. Here, Mother, tie
> My girdle for me, and bind up this hair

In any simple knot; ay, that does well.
And yours I see is coming down. How often
Have we done this for one another; now
We shall not do it any more. My Lord,
We are quite ready. Well, 'tis very well.

Gradually the summer days in the villa outside Leghorn
fell into a pleasant pattern. Shelley rose at seven, ate one of his
frugal breakfasts and climbed to his "tower" study where he
spent the morning writing and looking out over the Mediterranean. By two he was ready for dinner with Mary, followed
by joint readings of Dante and perhaps a walk in the surrounding countryside. In the evenings there might be visits with
their friends the Gisbornes. But long before midnight Shelley
would have retired, to listen to the far-off sounds of the sea
or to be lulled by the call of the nightingale and to dream
through the soft summer night.

> I arise from dreams of thee
> In the first sweet sleep of night,
> When the winds are breathing low,
> And the stars are shining bright:
> I arise from dreams of thee,
> And a spirit in my feet
> Hath led me—who knows how?
> To thy chamber window, Sweet!
>
> The wandering airs they faint
> On the dark, the silent stream—
> And the Champak odours fail
> Like sweet thoughts in a dream;
> The nightingale's complaint,
> It dies upon her heart;
> As I must die on thine,
> Oh! beloved as thou art!

148

> Oh, lift me from the grass!
> I die! I faint! I fail!
> Let thy love in kisses rain
> On my lips and eyelids pale.
> My cheek is cold and white, alas!
> My heart beats loud and fast;
> Oh, press it to thine own again,
> Where it will break at last.[40]

By early October the birth of Mary's baby was approaching, and the Shelleys moved into an apartment in Florence. And on November 12, in the morning after only two hours of labor, Mary gave birth to another boy. He was christened Percy Florence Shelley, and his arrival on the scene did more than anything else to alleviate the sense of doom that had built up around the Shelleys.

During this time Shelley was cheered by the visit of two visitors from home. One was Sophia Stacey, the ward of Shelley's uncle Robert Parker, and she brought along a companion with whom she was touring Italy. They wasted no time in calling on the Shelleys, and with his heedless generosity Shelley invited the girls to move in with them. Sophia was taken with Shelley; her adjectives for him were "mysterious" and "interesting." Shelley in turn found himself charmed by the young girl, whom he squired to the art galleries and took strolling in Florence's Cascine Forest.

But after Christmas, when Sophia Stacey had said good-bye and headed for Rome, the cold weather began to tell on the Shelleys and Claire. Finally they agreed that Florence in the winter was no place for them. On the morning of January 26 they boarded a boat and floated down the Arno to Empoli, sixteen miles away. There a carriage was waiting for them, and by evening they were settled in temporary quarters in Pisa, where the softer, warmer air from the Mediterranean, a dozen miles away, made life a great deal more comfortable. It was five weeks after Byron and Allegra had left Venice to move to Ravenna.

Troubles did not leave the Shelleys behind in Pisa. With the baby, his nurse and Claire, they were crowded in their first quarters and even in the apartment which they found a few days later. It was a month after their arrival when they moved to the top floor of the Casa Frasi on the Arno, where Shelley could have the luxury of his own study. Even in these larger quarters Mary and Claire began to get on each other's nerves. Claire wrote in her journal in February: "A Greek author says 'A bad wife is like Winter in the house.'" And Mary recorded: "A better day than most days, and good reason for it, though Shelley is not well. Clare away at Pugnano."

Percy Florence came down with measles in March. Shelley had not fully overcome the effects of Florence's cold winter. As late as April, when he heard that his cousin, Tom Medwin, was coming to Pisa, Shelley wrote: "You will find me a wretched invalid unless a great change should take place." But by May he could report that "I am now recovering." And with the warmer weather of spring, he finally began to feel healthy again. A resident of Pisa was the famous Dr. Vacca Berlinghieri, who diagnosed Shelley's trouble as largely due to nerves. And this diagnosis was supported, for example, by the bad days that Shelley tended to have when he heard from his father-in-law back in London.

William Godwin was continuing his profligate, arrogant ways. For Mary's sake, and because of his still-lingering respect for the once-great philosopher, Shelley tried to help him. But every dispatch of money to England only led to more appeals, and recriminations when Shelley demurred. The pleading letters became frantic, with the old man claiming that he faced utter ruin if he could not have £500 at once. Mary worried so much that it affected her milk, and for the baby's sake Shelley refused to let her read any more of her father's letters. Then came news which struck with an even greater blow.

The first indication came at the end of June, in a message from Naples concerning the "Neapolitan ward" Shelley had left behind. As he wrote in a letter, Shelley accepted it with sorrowful resignation. "My poor Neapolitan, I hear has a severe fever of dentition. I suppose she will die and leave another memory to these which already torture me. I am waiting for the next post with anxiety but without much hope. . . ." Shortly he had the answer: "My Neapolitan charge is dead. It seems as if the destruction that is consuming me were as an atmosphere which wrapt and *infected* everything connected with me."

But summer brought the pervading warmth Shelley needed. As his strength returned, he and Mary were able to take walks again, and Shelley discovered the beauty and peace of the pine groves between Pisa and the sea. The best time was near dusk, when he and Mary could walk alone through the pine-sheltered paths and along the golden Arno, breathing the blossom-scented air and listening to the evening calls of the birds wheeling in high circles above the *pineta*.

> Hail to thee, blithe Spirit!
>   Bird thou never wert,
> That from Heaven, or near it,
>   Pourest thy full heart
> In profuse strains of unpremeditated art.
>
>   Higher still and higher
>   From the earth thou springest

Like a cloud of fire;
   The blue deep thou wingest,
And singing still dost soar, and soaring ever singest.

In the golden lightning
   Of the sunken sun,
O'er which clouds are brightening,
   Thou dost float and run;
Like an unbodied joy whose race is just begun.

The pale purple even
   Melts around thy flight;
Like a star of Heaven,
   In the broad daylight
Thou art unseen, but yet I hear thy shrill delight . . .

Better than all measures
   Of delightful sound,
Better than all treasures
   That in books are found,
Thy skill to poet were, thou scorner of the ground!

Teach me half the gladness
   That thy brain must know,
Such harmonious madness
   From my lips would flow
The world should listen then—as I am listening now.[41]

July's heat grew more intense, and August promised to be hotter. Mary remembered Clara and William and began to worry about little Percy Florence. So Shelley rode out in the country to a village called Bagni di San Giuliano, at the foot of San Giuliano Mountain. There he found a "pleasant and spacious" set of rooms in the Casa Prinni, which he rented for three months. By August 5, the Shelleys, with Claire still along, settled into their summer quarters.

They strolled through the busy little village square; they

walked the quiet country roads; they even climbed Mount San Pellegrino. They read—Virgil's *Georgics*, Plato's *Republic*, Byron's *Don Juan* and Keats's *Hyperion*. Shelley wrote to Keats, urging him to come to Italy and visit them. He had heard that Keats was ill, and he recommended Italy's climate as salubrious. Keats replied in an appreciative but evasive letter, indicating that he was thinking of Italy, but not promising to visit Shelley. Claire left them for a while, to go down to Leghorn and enjoy the sea bathing. And in October she went to Florence to try a job as a governess.

The Shelleys' vacation ended abruptly when on October 25 a long rain raised the nearby rivers to such levels that the Casa Prinni was flooded and the Shelleys had to be evacuated from the second floor. Four days later they were back in Pisa, moving into larger quarters, in the Palazzo Galetti, overlooking the Arno. And as they prepared for another autumn and winter, they enlarged their circle of acquaintances among the odd assortment of Pisa's inhabitants.

There was one raffish character who would have appealed more to Byron than to Shelley. Professor Francesco Pacchiani was a former canon who had not been unfrocked but who should have been. Tall, dark and devilish, he was in fact sometimes called "Il Diavolo Pacchiani" because of his unorthodox behavior. He scoffed at the precepts of priesthood. Halted and questioned one night by the watch, he responded with a riposte which became a local legend: "I am a public man, in a public street, with a public woman." Pacchiani was a physicist who had developed a method of producing muriatic acid, and who had angered everyone at the University of Pisa, where he was Professor of Physical Chemistry, by his laziness and neglect of his duties. He was a poet, a wit, a charmer and a cheerful liar. It was a mark of Pacchiani's character—and a revealing example of the difference between the characters of Shelley and Byron—that Shelley decided he did not like the professor very much after Pacchiani tried to tell him a dirty joke.

And it was Pacchiani who, all innocently, precipitated one of the crises in the Shelleys' life by introducing them to a beautiful young girl who almost became Shelley's Teresa.

Emilia Viviani was the nineteen-year-old daughter of the Governor of Pisa; her father had packed her off to a convent school until he could find a proper husband for her. Her real name, it has since been learned, also was Teresa; but she preferred the name Emilia. She was bright and perceptive, affectionate and sentimental—which may be why her father, Niccolò Viviani, had sent her to the convent for safekeeping. On November 29, 1820, Professor Pacchiani, who had been Emilia's tutor when she had been living at home, took Mary and Claire to meet the young girl at the convent. The ladies were impressed by Emilia's plight, and they promised to visit her frequently to cheer her up. On one of their visits they brought Shelley along.

The high walls, barred windows and barren cells of the Convent of St. Anna appalled Shelley from the moment he entered it. Walking slowly down the echoing corridors, he entered a visitors' room and was introduced to Emilia.

She had the sharp, clean, perfectly proportioned features of the Greeks. Her long black hair fell below her shoulders, accenting the milk-white complexion and the slender young body. Her effect on Shelley was instantaneous; so was the effect of his pallid, intellectual features, his other-worldly expression and his high, soft voice on Emilia.

Mary Shelley was quick to spot this. From then on her "sisterly affection" for Emilia cooled, and in fact she began to make remarks about Emilia's excessive sentimentality and suggest that the girl might be a bit unbalanced. Shelley was captivated. For the next ten months he visited the convent, going for walks in the garden with Emilia, listening to bits of poetry she had written, commiserating with her on her "imprisonment" and listening happily to her professions of affection for Claire and Mary and especially him. He tried to influence Emilia's father to release her from the convent, without success. Shelley wrote snatches of poetry to her:

> Thy gentle voice, Emilia dear,
>   At night seems hovering o'er mine.
> I feel thy trembling lips—I hear
>   The murmurs of thy voice divine. . . .

To such outpourings Emilia replied, perhaps with an unappreciated sagacity: "Call me always, if you like, your Sister . . . and I too will always call you my dear Brother." She was careful also to write to Mary, calling her "one of the loveliest of God's or Nature's creatures." And to both she bemoaned her lot: "I am indeed unhappy! What a fate! I suffer heavily, and am the cause of a thousand griefs to others. O God! Were it not better that I should die? Then I should cease to suffer, or at least to make others suffer. . . . It would be better if you had never known me!" Shelley reacted with physical sickness at the thought of this lovely creature imprisoned by a willful father, and at his own helplessness. Their meetings were only at the convent, and most of them with Mary along—no doubt by Mary's design. But at one point Shelley wrote Byron about Emilia, adding that it would be wise not to mention the letter to Mary. Then Emilia asked Shelley if he would write a poem just for her. The answer was *Epipsychidion*.

> Sweet Spirit! Sister of that orphan one,
> Whose empire is the name thou weepest on,

In my heart's temple I suspend to thee
These votive wreaths of withered memory.

Poor captive bird! who, from thy narrow cage,
Pourest such music, that it might assuage
The rugged hearts of those who prisoned thee,
Were they not deaf to all sweet melody;
This song shall be thy rose: its petals pale
Are dead, indeed, my adored Nightingale!
But soft and fragrant is the faded blossom,
And it has no thorn left to wound thy bosom.

High, spirit-winged Heart! who dost for ever
Beat thine unfeeling bars with vain endeavour,
Till those bright plumes of thought, in which arrayed
It over-soared this low and worldly shade,
Lie shattered; and thy panting, wounded breast
Stains with dear blood its unmaternal nest!
I weep vain tears: blood would less bitter be,
Yet poured forth gladlier, could it profit thee. . . .

I never thought before my death to see
Youth's vision thus made perfect. Emily,
I love thee; though the world by no thin name
Will hide that love from its unvalued shame. . . .

Spouse! Sister! Angel! Pilot of the Fate
Whose course has been so starless! O too late
Beloved! O too soon adored, by me!
For in the fields of Immortality
My spirit should at first have worshipped thine,
A divine presence in a place divine;
Or should have moved beside it on this earth,
A shadow of that substance, from its birth;
But not as now: I love thee . . .

A ship is floating in the harbour now,
A wind is hovering o'er the mountain's brow;

There is a path on the sea's azure floor,
No keel has ever ploughed that path before;
The halcyons brood around the foamless isles;
The treacherous Ocean has forsworn its wiles;
The merry mariners are bold and free:
Say, my heart's sister, wilt thou sail with me? . . .

Here, perhaps more than at any other time in his life, Shelley felt he had found his ideal spiritual companion, the apotheosis of feminine loveliness with whom he could experience platonic love verging on, but not attaining, the physical. To her he could sing his ethereal songs of love, even dream of luring her away across "the sea's azure floor," while all the time the high walls and barred windows of a convent protected him from having to suit action to words. And so in *Epipsychidion* he crooned his hymn to Emilia's beauty, in spirit and in substance. And he was nearly finished with his hymn of love when he learned that Emilia had got married.

Mary could be excused for the tinge of exulting sarcasm in her letters recounting this news to the Shelleys' friends. In the months that followed, Shelley too began to see the Emilia Viviani episode in a somewhat harsher light. She had not, after all, been the only young Italian girl to be sent to a convent school until a husband could be found. But she had done nothing to dampen Shelley's ardor. She had encouraged him to plead with her father, to use his influence to get her released from the school. In fact, she had even tried at one point to borrow money from him. And then, after her marriage, she sweetly asked Shelley for a last favor: would he see what he could do to explain things to one Signor Danielli, whom Emilia had encouraged to think she might marry? Shelley obligingly did his best, and then ruefully told a friend how he had learned his lesson: "It seems that I am worthy to take my degree of M.A. in the art of Love. . . ." Later on, after *Epipsychidion* was published (anonymously, which led one critic to take it as a defense of marrying one's sister and attribute it to Byron), Shelley wrote to a friend: "I cannot look at my poem! The person whom it celebrates was a cloud instead of a Juno. . . . The error—and I confess it is not easy for spirits encased in flesh and blood to avoid it—consists in seeking in a mortal image the likeness of what is, perhaps, eternal."

Perhaps because of his infatuation with Emilia Viviani, or perhaps because of his natural blindness to such things, Shelley did not realize that at the same time Mary was more than mildly interested in another man. The same Professor Pacchiani who had introduced the Shelleys to Emilia had also introduced them to a dashing and romantic figure from the Middle East. Prince Mavrocordato was a Greek patriot who had fled from his homeland to escape the conquering Turks. He was short, but he flaunted bushy black mustachios and bound his flowing black hair in a turban. Mary was fascinated by him, and quickly agreed to take Greek lessons from him. To a friend she wrote: "Do you not envy my luck that, having begun Greek, an amiable, young, agreeable, and learned Greek Prince comes every morning to give me a lesson of an hour and a half?" Mary hung on his words, fluttered at his compliments and tried to teach him English in return for his Greek lessons. As for Shelley, he tolerated the man; he played a game or two of chess with him and read *Agamemnon* with him; but he disapproved of the prince's modern Greek accent. In any case, he was too lost in Emilia to care much. When, six months later, the Greeks revolted against the Turks, Prince Mavrocordato left to take part in the revolution, and Shelley wrote: "He is a great loss to Mary, and *therefore* to me . . . but not otherwise."

By that time Shelley had become entranced with a new friend, this time a male companion who shared many of his interests and activities. Edward Ellerker Williams had been at Eton at the same time as Shelley, though evidently they did not remember each other. Williams had gone to India as an army officer, where he had met a young army wife who had been deserted by her husband. She was now known as Jane Williams, though she had never been divorced from her first husband and had never married Williams. When they moved to Pisa, Shelley took to Williams immediately. Williams was a sometime poet and artist. But, more important, he shared Shelley's love for the simple beauty of the *pineta* outside Pisa, the lazy sweep of the Arno and the nearby Serchio, and the soft peacefulness of the seashore a few miles from Pisa. Williams had served in the Royal Navy before his army stint, and he delighted Shelley by constructing a tiny canvas-covered sail-boat, in which they ghosted down the river and along the shore. Shelley enjoyed nothing better than simply drifting wherever the boat would take him; he hated the interruption of having to handle oars or sails. Williams answered his need exactly; while Williams handled sheet and tiller, the little craft chuckled along as Shelley lay in the bottom, dreaming his daydreams and composing his poetry.

> Our boat is asleep on Serchio's stream,
> Its sails are folded like thoughts in a dream,
> The helm sways idly, hither and thither;
>   Dominic, the boatman, has brought the mast,
>   And the oars, and the sails; but 'tis sleeping fast,
> Like a beast, unconscious of its tether.
>
> The stars burnt out in the pale blue air,
> And the thin white moon lay withering there;
> To tower, and cavern, and rift, and tree,

The owl and the bat fled drowsily.
Day had kindled the dewy woods,
   And the rocks above and the stream below,
And the vapours in their multitudes,
   And the Apennine's shroud of summer snow,
And clothed with light of aëry gold
The mists in their eastern caves uprolled. . . .

    The Serchio, twisting forth
Between the marble barriers which it clove
At Ripafratta, leads through the dread chasm
The wave that died the death which lovers love,
   Living in what it sought; as if this spasm
Had not yet passed, the toppling mountains cling,
   But the clear stream in full enthusiasm
Pours itself on the plain, then wandering
   Down one clear path of effluence crystalline,
Sends its superfluous waves, that they may fling
   At Arno's feet tribute of corn and wine;
Then, through pestilential deserts wild
   Of tangled marsh and woods of stunted pine,
It rushes to the Ocean.[42]

One night Shelley and Williams decided to sail from Leg-horn to Pisa by moonlight through the canal. Fortunately Mrs. Gisborne talked them into taking her son-in-law along; she well knew how lackadaisical these two sailors were, and she knew also that Shelley could not swim, while her son-in-law, Henry Reveley, was a good swimmer. The sailing party had got halfway when Williams unexpectedly stood up, lost his balance, grabbed the tiny mast to steady himself and capsized the boat. Williams was a good enough swimmer to save him-self; but Shelley would have drowned if Reveley had not hauled him to shore.

Far from being bothered by such incidents, Shelley and

Williams wrote to their friends, asking them to come and join the fun. Williams had one friend in particular who he knew would be fascinated by Percy Shelley. To this friend he wrote: "Shelley is certainly a man of most astonishing genius, in appearance extraordinarily young, of manners mild and amiable, but withal full of life and fun. His wonderful command of language, and the ease with which he speaks on what are generally considered abstruse subjects, are striking; in short, his ordinary conversation is akin to poetry, for he sees things in the most singular and pleasing lights: if he wrote as he talks, he would be popular enough. Lord Byron and others think him by far the most imaginative poet of the day." Williams' friend, reading such eulogies, decided he must go to Pisa to meet this man. The friend's name was Edward Trelawny.

Shelley added his own urgings to other friends—to Leigh Hunt, who was making a hard time of it in England but who had continued his correspondence in hopes of cheering up his old companion of London days; and Shelley did not forget the friend who had now moved to Ravenna: to Byron he wrote a letter urging him to join the active, pleasant group gathering in Pisa.

Byron, it happened, had been getting regular reports—from Claire. Byron was fed up with letters from Claire. Month after month he had been receiving these letters—begging letters, pleading letters, even threatening letters. Still he refused to reply to her directly, instead writing to mutual friends whom he could count on to relay the message. To one plea by Claire that Allegra be sent to Pisa for a visit, Byron replied to the Hoppners:

About Allegra, I can only say to Claire—that I so totally disapprove of the mode of Children's treatment in their family, that

I should look upon the Child as going into a hospital. Is it not so? Have they *reared* one? Her health here has hitherto been *excellent*, and her temper not bad; she is sometimes vain and obstinate, but always clean and cheerful, and as, in a year or two, I shall either send her to England, or put her in a Convent for education, these defects will be remedied as far as they can in human nature. But the Child shall not quit me again to perish of Starvation, and green fruit, or to be taught to believe that there is no Deity. Whenever there is convenience of vicinity and access, her Mother can always have her with her; otherwise no. . . .

Mrs. Hoppner passed the letter on to Claire, who read it sadly and wrote in her journal: "A letter from Mad. Hoppner concerning green fruit and god—strange jumble . . ." Still she wrote Byron again and again. Byron continued to ignore the letters or respond through friends. In May, as Claire noted, there was "A Brutal letter." Finally Byron wrote Shelley, asking him to make Claire stop it. "I should prefer hearing from you," Byron wrote, "as I must decline all correspondence with Claire who merely tries to be as irrational and provoking as she can be—all of which shall not alter my regards to the Child—however much it contributes to confirm my opinion of the mother."

Shelley, as usual, tried to be the arbiter and peacemaker. Politely he replied:

I have no conception of what Claire's letters to you contain, and but an imperfect one on the subject of her correspondence with you at all. One or two of her letters, but not lately, I have indeed seen; but as I thought them extremely childish and absurd, I requested her not to send them, and she afterwards told me she had written and sent others in the place of them. I cannot tell if those which I saw on that occasion were sent you or not. I wonder, however, at your being provoked at what Claire writes, though that she should write what is provoking is very probable. You are conscious of performing your duty to Allegra, and your refusal to allow her to visit Claire at this distance you consider to be part of that duty. That Claire should wish to see her is natural. That her disappointment should vex her, and her vexation make her write absurdly is all in the usual order of things. But, poor thing, she is very unhappy and in bad health, and she ought to be treated with as much indulgence as possible. The weak and the foolish are in this respect the kings— they can do no wrong.

Byron was not impressed. And Shelley himself was taken aback when he received a wild and frightening letter from Florence, where Claire still held her governess job. The letter pleaded with the Shelleys to come and help her with a scheme which she had devised to kidnap Allegra. Shelley realized that it could not go on much longer like this. He was about to make a more serious plea to Byron for some kind of truce— when the news arrived that Byron had put Allegra in a convent.

[VIII]

I have just received the letter which announces the putting Allegra in a convent. Before I quitted Geneva you promised me—verbally it is true—that my child, whatever its sex, should never be away from its parents. . . . This promise is violated, not only slightly, but in a mode and by a conduct most intolerable to my feeling of love for Allegra. It has been my desire and my practice to interfere with you as little as possible; but were I silent now you would adopt this as an argument against me at some future period. I therefore represent to you that putting Allegra, at her years, into a convent, away from any relation, is to me a serious and deep affliction. . . . I have been at some pains to inquire into their system, and I find that the state of the children is nothing less than miserable. I see no reason to believe that convents are better regulated at Ravenna, a secondary, out-of-the-way town of the Roman States, than at Florence, the capital of Tuscany. Every traveller and

164

writer upon Italy joins in condemning them, which would alone be sufficient testimony without adverting to the state of ignorance and profligacy of the Italian women, all pupils of convents. They are bad wives, most unnatural mothers, licentious and ignorant; they are the dishonour and unhappiness of society. This then with every advantage in your power of wealth, of friends, is the education you have chosen for your daughter. . . .

CLAIRE

Byron did not answer.

Claire tried again. Byron did not answer.

Then Claire wrote a prophetic note: "Towards Wednesday morning I had a most distressing dream—that I received a letter which said that Allegra was ill, and not likely to live. . . ."

That did it. Byron wrote to Shelley: wasn't there *anything* he could do to make Claire stop it? As usual, Shelley tried to pacify him, by saying that perhaps the convent was a good idea after all. And so Byron could announce with satisfaction to his friend Hoppner: "It is some consolation that both Mr. and Mrs. Shelley have written to approve entirely my placing the child with the nuns for the present." Although Byron would not answer Claire, it was obvious that some of her thrusts had gone home; Byron's letter to Hoppner seemed to answer her point by point.

The people may say what they please, I must content myself with not deserving (in this instance) that they should speak ill. The place is a *country* town in a good air, where there is a large establishment for education, and many children, some of considerable rank, placed in it. As a *country* town, it is less liable to objections of every kind. It has always appeared to me, that the moral defect in Italy does *not* proceed from a *conventional* education,—because, to my certain knowledge, they come out of their convents innocent even to ignorance of moral evil,—but to the state of society into which they are directly plunged on coming out of it. It is like educating an infant on a mountain-top, and then taking him to the sea and throwing him into it and desiring him to swim.

He protested too much. He had done the right thing in sending Allegra away from the atmosphere which surrounded him; yet he realized that the atmosphere was largely his own fault. From the start, fifteen months ago when he and Allegra had arrived, in time for Christmas Eve, his life in Ravenna had become more and more unsuitable for a growing child.

Byron had known, as he made that last long ride from Venice, that his surrender had been complete. As he sat and watched the gay Christmas festivities and enjoyed the delight of Teresa at his arrival, he realized that the turning point had come. Right then, if he had been free and if divorce had been possible in Italy, he and Teresa would have married. Their relationship, he realized, would be similar to marriage from then on. It would take its own Italian form, since the rules called for him to be accepted as Teresa's *cavalier servente*. Already Byron's affection for Teresa was like that of a long-married husband—calmly, more or less contentedly in love, rather than passionately, eagerly, anxiously determined to make the most of each moment.

Byron's first lodgings, in the Albergo Imperiale, were cramped and uncomfortable; he had too large a collection of furniture, of servants and of animals for any small hotel apartment. And the business of going back and forth to the Palazzo Guiccioli was annoying. So he was as pleased as he was surprised by Count Guiccioli's offer of the second floor of the great palazzo, at what seemed a reasonable rent.

The Palazzo Guiccioli was one of the largest establishments in town. Set in the middle of one of Ravenna's high-walled streets, it extended an entire block through to the next street. The building, like so many palazzi of the time, was constructed in a square, around a large courtyard. The count and Teresa and their servants occupied only the ground floor of the big building, and evidently the count decided that he might as well make some money out of the floor above. Byron was well aware that there was more than money behind Count Guiccioli's smirking hospitality. Obviously the count still intended to gain concrete evidence, which he had not obtained so far, for use either in taking revenge against Byron or in separating from Teresa without having to pay any alimony or return her dowry. But Teresa herself was so urgent in her appeals that Byron consented. The old count's surprise must be imagined when he watched Byron move in with his daughter and all his baggage, furniture and his huge menagerie.

So began an odd and scandalous period in the relationship between Byron and Teresa, a sometimes pleasant, sometimes frustrating, openly adulterous interim. She was always there but not always available. They were free to meet for conversations or reading together, but their moments of love had to be stolen, either when the count was napping—and when Byron posted a guard at the stairs to warn them of the count's return —or when they could slip away in the late afternoon and ride out through the *pineta* near the sea.

> Ave Maria! 'tis the hour of prayer!
> Ave Maria! 'tis the hour of Love!
> Ave Maria! may our spirits dare
> Look up to thine and to thy Son's above!
> Ave Maria! oh that face so fair!
> Those downcast eyes beneath the Almighty Dove—

What though 'tis but a pictured image? strike—
That painting is no idol—'tis too like. . . .

Sweet Hour of Twilight! in the solitude
    Of the pine forest, and the silent shore
Which bounds Ravenna's immemorial wood,
    Rooted where once the Adrian wave flowed o'er,
To where the last Caesarean fortress stood,
    Evergreen forest! which Boccaccio's lore
And Dryden's lay made haunted ground to me,
How have I loved the twilight hour and thee![43]

It went on like this for five months, before the confrontation finally came.

It was a mid-May evening. The windows were open and a spring breeze moved the curtains. There was a rattling and rumbling as the carriage rolled down the high-walled street and swung into the palazzo's gate. The count came clumping up the steps, down the hall and into Teresa's sitting room.

Byron was there, as usual. Normally the count would nod gruffly to them both, Teresa would perhaps ask him if he had enjoyed the theater, he would grump a reply and go on down the hall to his rooms. But this time the atmosphere was different. There was a crackling expectancy in the air. Perhaps Teresa laughed or whispered something affectionate to Byron. Perhaps they did not expect the count to look in but instead to go on down the hall to his own rooms, and thus were surprised in an embrace; Byron later wrote a friend that the count had come upon them "*quasi* in the fact." Whatever the situation, the count angrily confronted Byron and announced that Byron's attentions to Teresa had gone on too long. The count had permitted them, he said, but now they were displeasing him greatly. He would thank Lord Byron to discontinue them.

Byron rose as the count spoke, and heard him out without

interrupting him. Teresa fluttered at his side, obviously fearful of Byron's fiery temper. But Byron said only that he would defer to his host in his own house, and—with a sarcastic smile—to his host's advanced age. He turned away and, without a glance at Teresa, limped out of the room to climb the stairs to his quarters.

And that night, in a violent battle which Byron must have heard a floor away even through the thick walls of the palazzo, Count Guiccioli and Teresa put an end to their marriage.

Next day Teresa's father received an urgent message to come to the Palazzo Guiccioli. There a weeping, nearly hysterical Teresa told him that she must leave her husband. Probably to her surprise, Count Gamba readily consented.

Divorce being impossible, Count Gamba's next move was to make a formal petition to Pope Pius VII:

Most Holy Father: Ruggero Gamba of the City of Ravenna, most humble petitioner of Your Holiness, with the most profound veneration states that in the past year, 1818, he gave his daughter Teresa in marriage to Signor Cavaliere Alessandro Guiccioli, of the same city. In the short space of one year the Cavaliere had behaved so strangely and heaped so many insults on his unhappy bride, that it has become wholly impossible for her to live any longer with so exacting a husband, and she is obliged, in the opinion of the whole city, to seek a complete separation. In this state of affairs the petitioner humbly appeals to Your Holiness, beseeching that the Cav. Guiccioli be ordered to pay a suitable allowance to his wife (the aforesaid daughter) in accordance with the position of her husband, in order that she may live suitably, as befits her birth and position.

This last was the key. Count Gamba knew his wily son-in-law well enough to realize that Guiccioli would attempt to escape paying any separation allowance to his estranged wife, even if it meant proving that he had been cuckolded. But Gamba had reason to believe that his "humble petition" would be received with perhaps more attention than a plea from Guiccioli. Pius VII was a close friend of Gamba's mother-in-law, Teresa's maternal grandmother. Before becoming Pope, when he had been Bishop of Imola, His Holiness had visited the family palazzo at Pesaro. He had even officiated at the wedding of Count and Countess Gamba.

But despite such favorable auspices matters like this moved slowly and uncertainly at the Vatican. It would be nearly two months before Teresa and her father knew the Pope's answer. Meanwhile she was forced to remain in her husband's palazzo; if she fled, Count Guiccioli could legally have her brought back. To Byron it seemed an insane situation: the estranged count and his countess living on one floor of the palazzo, while the countess' lover lived on the floor above. On the one main stairway they passed each other daily, the count and the lord ignoring each other's presence. Byron's menagerie continued to keep the nights alive with their screeching, clucking, barking and mewing; dogs, cranes and an occasional monkey roamed about the place. When the count could stand it no longer and escaped to his club or to the theater for a few hours, Byron again paid his secret calls on his mistress. When they could not meet, they exchanged love notes, carried up and down the stairs by their trusted servants. "My love . . . there is a mystery here that I do not understand, and prefer not to understand. Is it only now that he knows of your infidelity? What can he have thought—that we are made of stone—or that I am *more* or *less* than a man?" And meanwhile their servants were being spied upon by the count's servants, including the majordomo, the cook, the maids, the coachman, an accountant and even two blacksmiths and carpenters—eighteen in all—so that Guiccioli could assemble his counterintelligence to combat Count Gamba's petition.

Then, as if to heighten the ludicrousness of the situation, Guiccioli sent a note to Byron "requesting an interview." Byron granted it. Again the count repeated his demand that Byron move out. Again Byron refused. The count asked for a loan. Byron was infuriated, and refused, without this time attempting to make any excuse. The count stalked back down the stairs, no doubt giving a wide berth to the bulldog at the door.

Like Byron, Count Gamba began to realize that Guiccioli's main motive was avarice more than shame. In an additional plea, this time to the Papal Legate in Ravenna, Teresa's father hinted openly at his newly conceived suspicions, protesting that "if I wished, by words, deeds or writings, to prove how he attempted, for vile financial considerations, to prostitute, sell and disgrace my daughter and make her unhappy, I could show it with the greatest clearness; but the extremely delicate nature of the subject obliges me to keep silent, avoiding the scandal of public controversy." So outraged was Teresa's father as he thought about it that he even challenged Guiccioli to a duel. Guiccioli ignored him. Amid tension and tears, the suspense dragged on as everyone waited for the decision from Rome.

After seven weeks Byron had had enough. A letter from Hobhouse, urging him to come home to England for a visit, or at least to meet him for a holiday in Switzerland, was almost too much to resist. He replied that he had decided to leave Ravenna if Teresa's separation decree was not granted. But, he wrote: "When the *Pope* has decided on Madame Guiccioli's business . . . I will tell you whether I can come to England (via Switzerland) or not. . . . I can't settle anything till I know the result."

It happened that on that day, July 6, 1820, the Pope handed down his decision. He agreed that it was "no longer possible for [Teresa] to live in peace and safety with her husband," and that she should be permitted to leave her husband's home and return to that of her father, "in such laudable manner as befits a respectable and noble Lady separated from her Husband." Furthermore, Count Guiccioli was directed to pay a separation allowance of 100 scudi (which Byron estimated as equal to £1,000 a year in England, but which Shelley later characterized as "a miserable pittance" for one of Count Guiccioli's means) in order that Teresa could continue to live in the manner to which she had become accustomed.

The news reached Teresa through her friends on July 13, two days before official notification was delivered to Count Guiccioli. Taking advantage of the time lag, Count Gamba told his daughter to be ready to leave immediately on July 14. Guiccioli still did not know the news, but something in his wife's flustered manner made him suspicious, and he left orders, before taking his afternoon siesta, that no one should put a Guiccioli horse to carriage. But at four o'clock in the afternoon a servant faithful to Teresa either took a Guiccioli horse and carriage or hired one, and Teresa slipped away quietly, evidently without even bidding Byron good-bye. The carriage rushed through the city to the outskirts, where another carriage waited. In it was Count Gamba, who took his daughter into his arms and comforted her through the rest of the drive to his villa at Filetto, fifteen miles away.

It was a month before Byron saw Teresa again. Despite the fact that she had moved from the Palazzo Guiccioli—and despite the angry count's insistence that Byron move out also—Byron still refused to leave. But as the summer's heat brought fevers to the city, he began to consider where to send Allegra.

At first he decided against a convent school. He started a search for a villa near Filetto, and Teresa. He realized that his relationship with Teresa had entered a delicate new phase. In the Italy of 1820 it was one thing to become the *cavalier servente* of a married woman; it was quite another to be the lover of a wife who had left her husband. Count Gamba had not only the ordinary incentive to guard his daughter from philandering Englishman but a newly important monetary consideration as well: odd as it might sound, adultery between Teresa and Byron could be tolerated while she lived with her husband; but it could lead, once she was separated, to a reversal of the Pope's decree and to the loss of her alimony.

So the two lovers exchanged passionate notes while Byron waited to find out what role Teresa's father would play. Finally, after a frustrating month, Byron climbed into his traveling coach and, escorted in full style by two postilions, rode out to Filetto for a sunny August afternoon.

The Villa Gamba stood on a plain looking out on a sloping lawn framed by olive trees. The river Montone flowed slowly down through the pine forest to the sea. Ducks whirred in and out of the river, and herons stalked through the nearby marshes. Byron and Teresa spent the afternoon walking along the river and listening to the sea wind hum through the pines. Then, as he made ready to ride back to Ravenna, a summer thunderstorm rumbled up the coast. With lightning flashing around the villa and the rain turning the road to quagmire, Byron had no choice but to stay for the night.

After a few more trips to Filetto, Byron found and rented the Villa Bacinetti, about nine miles from the Villa Gamba. Allegra had been made ill by Ravenna's heat, but at Filetto she soon began to recover. With Allegra as his excuse, Byron spent more time in the area, making frequent visits to the

Villa Gamba. More and more he came to like the Gamba family and its easygoing life. The gathering place of the villa was the big salon, with a ceiling rising to the roof and a balcony leading to bedrooms which were partitioned off but open above so the cool night breezes could circulate through the house. At night the villa buzzed with the conversation of the Gamba family as its members talked to each other over the partitions before finally dropping off to sleep.

But summer turned to damp fall, when the feeble fire could not warm or even dry out the high-ceilinged salon. Both the Gambas' and Byron's villas became unbearably cold. Byron brought Allegra back to the Palazzo Guiccioli, still grandly ignoring its affronted owner. And the Gambas, including Teresa, also moved back into their town house.

The winter was colder and more unpleasant than usual, and it grew on Byron's nerves. On January 4, 1821, he wrote in his diary: "This morning I gat me up late, as usual—weather bad—bad as England—worse. The snow of last week melting to the sirocco of today, so that there were two damned things at once. Could not even get to ride on horseback in the forest. Stayed at home all morning—looked at the fire—wondered when the post would come. . . . I was out of spirits—read the papers. . . . Wrote five letters in about half an hour, short and savage, to all my rascally correspondents. . . . Carriage at 8 or so—went to visit La Contessa G.—found her playing on the pianoforte. . . ." On January 22, his thirty-third birthday, he wrote: " 'Tis the middle of the night by the castle-clock, and I am now thirty-three! . . . I go to my bed, with a heaviness of heart at having lived so long, and to so little purpose."

At least there were the evenings with Teresa. But still Byron had to leave for home at the evening's end. "Came home *solus,"* he wrote one night, "very high wind—lightning—moonshine—solitary stragglers muffled in cloaks—women in masks—white houses—clouds hurrying over the sky, like spilt milk blown out of the pail—altogether very poetical. It is still blowing hard—the tiles flying, and the house rocking—rain splashing—lightning flashing—quite a fine Swiss Alpine evening, and the sea roaring in the distance."

And as he listened to the wild night sounds, Byron sat at his big desk in the palazzo and worked away at *Don Juan* and *Marino Faliero* and *Sardanapalus.*

> The day at last has broken.
> What a night
> Hath ushered it! How beautiful in heaven!
> Though varied with a transitory storm,
> More beautiful in that variety!
> How hideous upon earth! where Peace and Hope,
> And Love and Revel, in an hour were trampled
> By human passions to a human chaos,
> Not yet resolved to separate elements—
> 'Tis warring still! And can the sun so rise,
> So bright, so rolling back the clouds into
> Vapours more lovely than the unclouded sky,
> With golden pinnacles, and snowy mountains,
> And billows purpler than the Ocean's, making
> In heaven a glorious mockery of the earth,
> So like we almost deem it permanent;
> So fleeting, we can scarcely call it aught
> Beyond a vision, 'tis so transiently
> Scattered along the eternal vault: and yet
> It dwells upon the soul, and soothes the soul,
> And blends itself into the soul, until
> Sunrise and sunset form the haunted epoch
> Of Sorrow and of Love . . .[44]

Often, above the moaning of the storm and the far-off thunder of the sea on the shore, Byron could hear in a nearby room the cough or feverish murmur of Allegra. The harsh winter had been difficult for her. This at last was the main reason why he decided to send her to the convent school.

There were other reasons. Allegra had become the spoiled darling of her father, of Teresa and of the servants. The "bluff little commodore," as Byron playfully called her, tended to think the world revolved around her. There had even been complaints that she had been telling lies. Besides, she needed some friends her own age; her only playmates were the animals in her father's menagerie. More than anything else, she needed to get started on her education; there was no one in the palazzo who could handle this assignment. Teresa took her for sleigh rides in Ravenna's *corso*, but Teresa was not interested in the dull routine of lessons.

Through his banker in Ravenna, Pellegrino Ghigi, Byron had heard of the convent school in Bagnacavallo, twelve miles inland from Ravenna; Ghigi's own daughter had entered the school the previous year. A convent school seemed in order partly because Byron felt that Allegra should be brought up as a Catholic. Why? Because she would almost certainly not return to England. In England she would never be able to overcome the stigma of illegitimacy, while in Italy she could be endowed with a fair income and thus attract a suitable Italian husband.

The town of Bagnacavallo had once been a Roman fortress. In the center of the town was the Camaldolese monastery, built as early as the fourteenth century and later abandoned. In 1817 it had been taken over by the Capuchin nuns. The Capuchin order was among the poorest and strictest in the Church. But the school in the monastery of San Giovanni Battista, as they called it, catered to the best families of the Romagna. Besides banker Ghigi's daughter, many future contessas and donnas were being educated there. Byron saw no need to inspect it; the place sounded like just what Allegra needed.

But all of the convent's students were older than Allegra. After some correspondence, and Byron's agreement to pay double fees for the special attention required for a younger student, Allegra was accepted.

March 1, 1821, was Allegra's fourth birthday. She was given the usual toys and some especially pretty dolls, and was led to the waiting carriage. She wore her new ermine coat. Her things were already packed—a few clothes, her dolls and a "going-away present": the silk peer's robes her father had worn in his first appearance in the House of Lords, now to be used for dresses for his daughter. Byron kissed her good-bye, and the carriage rolled away.

Byron's banker, Signor Ghigi, accompanied Allegra to the school. He reported that she was unawed by the tall, gloomy walls of Bagnacavallo and that she was polite when introduced to the Mother Superior and Sister Marianna, who was to be her special teacher. Her companion had already been selected for her: Isabella, daughter of the Marchese Ghislieri of Bologna. The little girl walked demurely down the echoing corridor to her cell, and was soon lost among the eighty other girls in the school.

Among Byron's reasons for sending Allegra away was the political situation in the Romagna; it was rapidly becoming ominous. The Romagnese were nearly at the point of actual revolt against their Austrian overlords. In fact, all Italy was stirring with the fever of revolution, and Byron could hardly be expected to sit idly by under such circumstances. Teresa's father and brother were deep in the plotting, and Byron joined them. Partly because of this and partly because a rich English exile was a suspicious character anyway, the police were keeping a close watch on the Palazzo Guiccioli. Byron was warned not to continue his rides in the *pineta;* some overenthusiastic loyalist might be tempted to take a shot at him. Byron continued the rides, but he went armed.

"We are in expectation of a *row* here in a short time," he wrote to England; in another letter he reported: ". . . there is THAT brewing in Italy which will speedily cut off all security communication, and set all your Anglo-travellers flying in every direction, with their usual fortitude in foreign tumults." Meanwhile he did everything he could to feed the fire. His servants, at his orders, ostentatiously marched about Ravenna heavily armed, in defiance of a city ordinance requiring a permit for any arms. Knowing his letters were opened and read by Austrian censors, Byron made sure to direct part of each message to them: "The police at present is under the Germans, or rather the Austrians, who do not merit the name of Germans, who open all letters it is supposed. I have no objection, so that they may see how I hate and utterly despise and detest those *Hun brutes,* and all they can do in their temporary wickedness, for Time and Opinion, and the vengeance of a roused-up people will at length manure Italy with their carcases." Then in another letter to Tom Moore Byron wrote of an incident which, as he said, "will show the state of this country better than I can."

The commandant of the troops is *now* lying *dead* in my house. He was shot at a little past eight o'clock, about two hundred paces from my door. I was putting on my great-coat to visit Madame la Contessa G. when I heard the shot. On coming into the hall, I found all my servants on the balcony, exclaiming that a man was murdered. I immediately ran down, calling on Tita (the bravest of them) to follow me. The rest wanted to hinder us from going, as it is the custom for every body here, it seems, to run away from "the stricken deer."

However, down we ran, and found him lying on his back, almost, if not quite, dead, with five wounds; one in the heart, two in the stomach, one in the finger, and the other in the arm. Some soldiers cocked their guns, and wanted to hinder me from passing. However, we passed, and I found Diego, the adjutant, crying over him like a child—a surgeon, who said nothing of his profession—a priest, sobbing a frightened prayer—and the commandant, all this time, on his back, on the hard, cold pavement, without light or assistance, or any thing around him but confusion and dismay.

As nobody could, or would, do any thing but howl and pray, and as no one would stir a finger to move him, for fear of consequences, I lost my patience—made my servant and a couple of the mob take up the body—sent off two soldiers to the guard—despatched Diego to the Cardinal with the news, and had the commandant carried upstairs into my own quarter. But it was too late, he was gone—not at all disfigured—bled inwardly—not above an ounce or two came out.

I had him partly stripped—made the surgeon examine him, and examined him myself. He had been shot by cut balls or slugs. I felt one of the slugs, which had gone through him, all but the skin. Everybody conjectures why he was killed, but no one knows how. The gun was found close by him—an old gun, half filed down.

He only said, *O Dio!* and *Gesu!* two or three times, and appeared to have suffered very little. Poor fellow! he was a brave officer, but had made himself much disliked by the people. I knew him personally, and had met with him often at conversazioni and elsewhere. My house is full of soldiers, dragoons, doctors, priests, and all kinds of persons,—though I have now cleared it, and clapt sentinels at the doors. To-morrow the body is to be moved. The town is in the greatest confusion, as you may suppose.

You are to know that, if I had not had the body moved, they would have left him there till morning in the street, for fear of

179

consequences. I would not choose to let even a dog die in such a manner, without succour:—and, as for consequences, I care for none in a duty.

Yours, etc.

P.S.—The Lieutenant on duty by the body is smoking his pipe with great composure.—A queer people this.

But finally the Romagnese's grand plan of revolt fizzled out. The climax came in the plain of Rieti, where the Romagnese general Pepe faced the Austrian army. Pepe's men fled with scarcely a shot fired. When the news came to Ravenna, Byron went to the Gambas' house. Teresa was at her harpsichord. As he told her, tears came to her eyes. "Alas," she said, "the Italians must now return to making operas."

"I fear," Byron replied, "that and macaroni are their forte."

Encouraged by the defeat of General Pepe, the Austrians set out to clean up the civilian pockets of resistance. For months their secret police in Ravenna had reported that nighttime meetings were being held in the English lord's rooms in the Palazzo Guiccioli, plotting God knew what. A simple and direct method for dealing with this menace would be to order Lord Byron to leave Ravenna. But the local officials were reluctant to make so bold a move; there was no way of telling what influence his lordship still had at home, and a move against him might precipitate an embarrassing confrontation with the British government itself. And there was an easier way. No one doubted the tie between Lord Byron and the beautiful daughter of Count Gamba, particularly now that she was separated from her elderly husband. So, the authorities reasoned, they could expel the Gamba family and Lord Byron would follow of his own choice.

That is why, on the night of July 10, 1821, as young Pietro Gamba, Teresa's brother, was returning from the theater, he was stopped in the street, taken into custody and immediately escorted to the frontier. He pretended innocence, but he was brusquely informed that he was accused of being a ringleader in fomenting a revolt against the state. Pietro somehow managed to get word to Teresa, who quickly searched his library and destroyed any documents that might be incriminating, just in time before the police arrived next morning for their search. They found nothing, but shortly they informed Count Gamba that he should prepare to leave the state also, taking his entire family with him.

The authorities were disconcerted by what followed. Count Gamba meekly obeyed their orders, packing up and moving to Bologna and then to Florence, where the local government granted him asylum. But Teresa did not leave with her father. For the time being, anyway, she convinced him that it was proper for her to remain in the family town house in Ravenna. On the day that her father consented to her plea, she sent a note to Byron: ". . . what a compensation to be able to stay here—where you are! This evening we shall see each other again."

But she and Byron reckoned without her husband. Whether prompted by the Austrian authorities or not, Count Guiccioli quickly petitioned the Pope. Did it not seem contrary to the spirit, if not the letter, of the separation contract for Signora Guiccioli to remain alone in her family's house in Ravenna, to receive her lover as she wished? Count Guiccioli proposed that his wife either be returned to him—or placed in a convent in order to make sure that this separation did not become a farce in which the countess mocked the intention of the agreement by living openly with her lover.

Teresa's first reaction was that this was only a threat. But Byron was convinced that the old count meant what he said, and that the Pope might well support his contention. After hours of hysterical pleading, Teresa agreed to go. Byron promised to follow as soon as he could pack up his cumbersome household. They would move to Switzerland, and all this unpleasantness would be left behind forever.

There was a last, fervent night on July 24, and with morning Teresa finally made her departure. But in Bologna she panicked. Somehow feeling that Byron never would follow her, she refused to go on, and in fact proposed to return to Ravenna. To her nearly incoherent message Byron replied:

"I love you and shall love you as I have always loved you— but I cannot encourage such fatal madness as your return here would be, the day after your departure. . . ." Still she refused to budge, until a second letter finally convinced her and, grudgingly, she made her way on to Florence to join her family.

Now Byron was alone in his echoing rooms, relieved that Teresa had escaped but already missing her, thinking too of Allegra, and reminded of his own untenable situation every time Count Guiccioli thumped around in his rooms on the floor below. But if only because of his innate stubbornness, Byron was in no hurry to fall in with the count's wishes and leave in the wake of his mistress. Again the count demanded that Byron pack up and move out. And again Byron refused.

Byron now decided to relieve his loneliness by inviting Shelley to come for a visit. His letter of invitation happened to be well-timed. Shelley had become increasingly worried about the effect on Claire of the news of Allegra's departure for the convent school, and of Byron's refusal to acknowledge Claire's letters. So on August 4, 1821, his twenty-ninth birthday, Shelley set out for Ravenna.

The journey took two long, jolting days. One leg, from

Bologna to Ravenna, took "all night, at the rate of two miles and a half an hour, in a little open carriage." On the last leg Shelley was thrown out of the chaise and over a hedge; but he was unhurt. It was 10 P.M. on August 6 when his carriage finally rattled down the echoing high-walled streets of Ravenna and up to the big gates of the Palazzo Guiccioli. Shelley was exhausted. But Byron refused to let him go to bed. All night, until dawn started to lighten the room at 5 A.M., he kept his guest in conversation.

He had not seen Shelley for so long, and there were so many things to tell him about—Allegra's school, Teresa's departure, his latest cantos of *Don Juan*. But first he had a tale that took Shelley's breath away.

Some months earlier Byron had received a letter from the Hoppners detailing what seemed a scandalous story, just the sort of gossip the sanctimonious Mrs. Hoppner loved to pass along. It was the story of Shelley's ward in Naples; the nurse-made Elise, who had tended Allegra and then William Shelley and who had been discharged by the Shelleys in Naples along with her lover Paolo, the Shelleys' groom, was now spreading the story in Venice that the Neapolitan baby was the illegitimate daughter of Shelley and Claire. The Hoppners passed the rumor on to Byron and asked him to keep it to himself. Byron promised that he would—and confronted Shelley with it on his first night.

Shelley, of course, was outraged. He was up before Byron next day to write a hurried letter to Mary, asking her to refute the story in a letter to the Hoppners. If she would send the letter to him at Ravenna, he would see that it was relayed to them in Venice. Still amazed at the accusation, he wrote: ". . . that I have committed such unutterable crimes as destroying or abandoning a child, and that my own—imagine

183

my despair of good, imagine how it is possible that one of so weak and sensitive a nature as mine can run further the gauntlet through this hellish society of men. . . ."

Mary promptly replied with a letter voicing her own dismay, and incidentally revealing how much she had changed from the young freethinker who had run off with Shelley seven years ago. "Before I speak of these falsehoods permit [me] to say a few words concerning this miserable girl. You well know that she formed an attachment with Paolo when we proceeded to Rome, and at Naples their marriage was talked of. We all tried to dissuade her; we knew Paolo to be a rascal, and we thought so well of her that we believed him to be unworthy of her. An accident led me to the knowledge that without marrying they had formed a connexion; she was ill, we sent for a doctor who said there was danger of a miscarriage. I would not turn the girl on the world without in some degree binding her to this man. We had them married . . ."

Mary rushed on to the accusation and her refutation: "I am perfectly convinced in my own mind that Shelley never had an improper connexion with Clare. . . . The malice of [Elise] is beyond all thought—I now remember that Clare did keep her bed there for two days—but I attended on her . . . Those who know me will believe my simple word . . . to you I swear —by all that I hold sacred upon heaven and earth by a vow which I should die to write if I affirmed a falsehood—I swear by the life of my child, by my blessed and beloved child, that I know these accusations to be false."

The letter went swiftly off to Shelley, who gave it to Byron to pass on to the Hoppners, after Byron pointed out that he had to explain to the Hoppners how Shelley had heard the accusation which Byron had agreed to keep secret. Byron promised to send the letter along immediately.

Later, after his death, the letter was found still among his papers.

But meanwhile there was so much else to occupy the two poets. They criticized each other's poetry; Shelley liked Byron's *Don Juan* better than his *Marino Faliero,* and Byron preferred Shelley's *Prometheus Unbound* to *The Cenci.* And then they turned to Keats. This had been a sore point.

While Shelley had been cultivating Keats's acquaintance, Byron had been making sarcastic references to him. Keats had had the audacity, in Byron's opinion, to lampoon Byron's idol, Alexander Pope. Byron had replied with a snarling reference to "Johnny Keats's *p-ss a bed* poetry." Keats was another one of those sickly sentimental lyrical poets like Wordsworth and the other "lakers"; "a tadpole of the lakes," Byron had also called him. To his publisher Byron had complained about a review praising "Jack Keats or Ketch, or whatever his names are: why, his is the Onanism of poetry. . . . I don't mean he is *indecent,* but viciously soliciting his own ideas into a state, which is neither poetry nor any thing else but a bedlam vision produced by raw pork and opium."

This was the same poet who had so inspired Shelley that he had tried to win his friendship in England and had then invited him to Italy. Keats had come to Italy, but not to visit Shelley. On February 23, 1821, in the now-famous little house by the Spanish Steps in Rome, Keats had died of consumption at the age of twenty-five. And Shelley, appalled at what he believed to be Keats's reaction to the cruel criticism of his work, wrote a tribute which has become one of the monuments of English poetry.

> I weep for Adonais—he is dead!
> O, weep for Adonais! though our tears

Thaw not the frost which binds so dear a head!
And thou, sad Hour, selected from all years
To mourn our loss, rouse thy obscure compeers,
And teach them thine own sorrow, say: "With me
Died Adonais; till the Future dares   . .
Forget the Past, his fate and fame shall be
An echo and a light unto eternity!" . . .

Peace, peace! he is not dead, he doth not sleep—
He hath awakened from the dream of life—
'Tis we, who lost in stormy visions, keep
With phantoms an unprofitable strife,
And in mad trance, strike with our spirit's knife
Invulnerable nothings. *We* decay
Like corpses in a charnel; fear and grief
Convulse us and consume us day by day,
And cold hopes swarm like worms within our living clay. . . .

The One remains, the many change and pass;
Heaven's light forever shines, Earth's shadows fly;
Life, like a dome of many-coloured glass,
Stains the white radiance of Eternity,
Until Death tramples it to fragments. Die,
If thou wouldst be with that which thou dost seek!
Follow where all is fled! Rome's azure sky,
Flowers, ruins, statues, music, words, are weak
The glory they transfuse with fitting truth to speak. . . .

The breath whose might I have invoked in song
Descends on me; my spirit's bark is driven,
Far from the shore, far from the trembling throng
Whose sails were never to the tempest given;
The massy earth and sphered skies are riven!
I am borne darkly, fearfully, afar;
Whilst, burning through the inmost veil of Heaven,
The soul of Adonais, like a star,
Beacons from the abode where the Eternal are.[45]

Shelley sent a copy of *Adonais* to Byron—and thereby accomplished the virtually impossible. Byron read the elegy and wrote his publisher a grudging letter: "You know very well that I did not approve of Keats's poetry, or principles of poetry, or of his abuse of Pope; but, as he is dead, omit *all* that is said *about him* in any MSS of mine, or publication. His *Hyperion* is a fine monument, and will keep his name." A few months later he could confess a bit more graciously for *Blackwood's Magazine*: "My indignation at Mr. Keats's depreciation of Pope has hardly permitted me to do justice to his own genius, which, malgre all the fantastic fopperies of his style, was undoubtedly of great promise. His fragment of *Hyperion* seems actually inspired by the Titans, and is as sublime as Aeschylus."

With the long, rambling talks about poetry and Italy and friends and lovers, Byron kept Shelley up every night until nearly dawn. But even then Shelley could not stay in bed until 2 P.M., as Byron did. Usually he was up by noon, to have a light breakfast and go off on a tour of the city or a visit to an art museum or library. His guide and manservant during his stay was the huge, bearded Tita, who had been Byron's colorful gondolier in Venice. "Tita is here," Shelley wrote Mary, "a fine fellow with a prodigious black beard, who has stabbed two or three people, and is the most good-natured fellow I ever saw." By midafternoon Shelley would be back in the big palazzo, in time to greet Byron, who had finally risen, bathed and was eating his breakfast of egg yolk and tea. There was more conversation before their daily ride in the *pineta*. At dusk they would swing onto the waiting horses and go thudding down the twisting trails under the umbrella-shaped pines, until they could hear the swish of the sea. After a brisk canter along the flat beach, they turned and headed back to the cobbled streets of the city. Refreshed by the cool evening air and the salty scent of the sea, their appetites whetted by the exercise, they dined at eight. And then they settled back in the big study overlooking the courtyard gardens and talked—and talked and talked until the black windows turned to gray and the cocks at the edge of town reminded them that dawn was coming. With such a routine Shelley could not find time to get away for the main purpose of his visit until eight days after his arrival.

But many of the long night hours were devoted to the subject of Allegra. Byron was profuse in his explanations of why he had sent her to the convent school, and Shelley listened patiently as Byron rambled on with his excuses. Ravenna, as Shelley could see, was a low-lying town, a bit too near the swamps along the Adriatic to be healthy. In a way Venice had been like that—cold and damp in winter and humid in summer —and Allegra had had two bad cases of what Aglietti called tertian fever. A higher, healthier situation would be better for her. And she badly needed discipline—and so on, went all the excuses. But Byron now encouraged Shelley to visit the convent and see for himself.

At Bagnacavallo Shelley found echoing, walled streets and arcaded walks leading to the bare façade of the Convent of San Giovanni Battista. He was greeted cordially by the nuns, who produced Allegra and left them alone. She had grown much taller and thinner than the girl he remembered from the peaceful days at Este that now seemed so long ago. Her hair was slightly darker and hung in curls around her shoulders. She was dressed, no doubt with the utmost care by the nuns, in white muslin with pantalets and a black apron. Her blue eyes regarded him gravely, with no sign of recognition at first. Shelley presented her with a little gold chain he had brought as a gift. She smiled at the sight of it and thanked him politely. Gradually she succumbed to his way with children and began to remember him.

Shortly she was leading him on a chase through the garden and down the corridors. She showed him the cart she and the other girls rode in, taking turns pulling it. She took him to her clean, bare little cell, to the long table where they ate their meals. Shelley wondered if her pale complexion was because of the food. She chattered away about Paradise and the *Bambino*, and Shelley the atheist thought to himself, as he later wrote: "The idea of bringing up so sweet a creature in the midst of such trash till sixteen!" He gave her another gift, a box of candy, and he noted with approval that she passed it around to her friends and to the nuns—something the selfish little girl who had lived with Byron had not done.

But her transformation was not quite complete. Shelley asked her if she had a message for her mother. Yes. And what would it be?

"Ask her to send me a kiss and a pretty dress."

"What must the dress be like?"

"All of silk and gold."

And did she have a message for *Papa?*

"Ask him to come and pay me a visit"—there it was again—and bring *mammina* with him."

Shelley did not note whether he realized that to four-and-a-half-year-old Allegra "*mammina*" was not Claire but Teresa.

Back in Ravenna Shelley freely admitted to Byron and wrote to Mary and Claire that, so far as he could see, the convent school was good for Allegra; his opinion of convent schools had changed since the days of his anguish over Emilia Viviani's "imprisonment." Now, having accomplished the purpose of his trip, he got ready to return to Pisa. But Byron pleaded with him to stay for a few more days.

Byron had come to love Ravenna. Here more than anywhere else he felt that he was in the heart of Italy. To Tom Moore he had written: "What do Englishmen know of Italians beyond their museums and saloons . . . Now, I have lived in the heart of their houses, in parts of Italy freshest and least influenced by strangers,—have seen and become (*pars magna fui*) a portion of their hopes, and fears, and passions, and am almost inoculated into a family. This is to see men and things as they are." And many Ravennati, largely because of his charities, had come to like Byron as much as he liked their city.

For a year and a half Byron had scarcely seen an Englishman or even spoken English. He found Shelley's visit a greater tonic than he had expected. To be able to talk of England, of mutual friends and, more important, of English poetry and to read *Don Juan* to someone who understood it—all this gave Byron a tremendous uplift. His plea was so earnest that Shelley agreed to stay a little longer. And so the odd routine went on— the talks until dawn, the breakfast at noon and the hour or two that Shelley had to himself, to marvel at his surroundings and to report on them to Mary and Claire.

What impressed him most was Byron's menagerie. At the moment, he wrote a friend, it consisted of "ten horses, eight enormous dogs, three monkeys, five cats, an eagle, a crow, and a falcon; and all these, except the horses, walk about the house, which every now and then resounds with their unarbitrated quarrels, as if they were the masters of it." In a footnote, he added: "I find that my enumeration of the animals in this Circean Palace was defective, and that in a material point. I have just met on the grand staircase five peacocks, two guinea hens, and an Egyptian crane." And he could not resist a Shelleyan afterthought: "I wonder who all these animals were, before they were changed into these shapes."

He had, of course, encountered Byron's love for animals before, in Venice. Perhaps now he noticed, in the same connection, that although Byron collected every type of gun and devoted many hours to marksmanship, he never went hunting. Teresa did note this when she later wrote about Byron; on one occasion at the Villa Gamba Byron happily joined in on a target shoot, but would have nothing to do with it when live birds were substituted. During Shelley's visit, many of their afternoon rides through the *pineta* included some target shooting, at pumpkins, and Shelley was pleased to discover that, although Byron was as good a shot as ever, Shelley did nearly as well.

Still Shelley realized that he must return to Pisa. And he now redoubled his efforts to urge Byron to come with him. It would enliven things at Pisa if Byron were to join the little group. But Shelley's main motive was Allegra. He had not forgotten, though Byron no doubt had, a line in one of Byron's letters: "Whenever there is convenience of vicinity and access, her Mother can always have her with her; otherwise no." Bagnacavallo was more than one hundred miles from Pisa, and despite Byron's seeming indifference to Allegra since she had entered the school, he could hardly come all the way across Italy and leave her that far away. So Shelley went to work on his friend to induce him to come to Pisa.

It was a quiet, pleasant town, he pointed out. It had little or none of the nerve-racking conflicts with the hated Austrians. Pisa was more attractive in many ways than Ravenna; there were few more beautiful sights in the world than the red-gold sunset coloring the gentle flow of the Arno as it rolled through the center of the town, cutting its path between the two tall rows of brown-fronted houses. And Pisa was a far healthier place than either Ravenna or Bagnacavallo; that was why Shelley himself had moved there from Florence, and his own health had recovered as a result.

As Shelley talked through the warm nights in the rooms overlooking the courtyard in Ravenna, Byron considered the notion, and the more he thought about it the more he liked it. He had already written to friends in Geneva, asking them to find a house for the Gambas and for himself, on the lake and with room enough for his menagerie and stables for eight horses. But he could always change those plans—if the Gambas would change theirs. He decided to put it as a challenge: if Shelley could convince the Gambas, or Teresa anyway, that Pisa was preferable to Switzerland, on which she now had her heart set, Byron would join them all in Pisa.

This seemed an odd task to Shelley. He had never met Teresa, and his persuasion would have to be done by letter. But by now he had himself become so caught up with the idea of luring Byron to Pisa that he undertook the assignment even before leaving Ravenna.

Pondering how best to frame his argument, Shelley thought back to those days when he and Mary and Byron and Claire had been together in Geneva, and to all the troubles which had started there and which now plagued them. (Which were more sanctimonious, he wondered, the British or the Swiss?) He wrote to Teresa in Italian:

Your circumstances present some analogy with those in which my family and Lord Byron found themselves, in the summer of 1816. Our houses were close together and, not seeking any other society, our mode of life was retired and tranquil; one could not imagine a simpler life than ours, or one less calculated to attract the calumnies that were aimed at us.

These calumnies were monstrous, and really too infamous to

leave us, their victims, even the refuge of contempt. The natives of Geneva and the English people who were living there did not hesitate to affirm that we were leading a life of the most unbridled libertinism. They said that we had formed a pact to outrage all that is regarded as most sacred in human society. . . .

Hardly any affliction was spared us. The inhabitants on the banks of the lake opposite Lord Byron's house used telescopes to spy upon his movements. One English lady fainted from horror (or pretended to!) on seeing him enter a drawing room. The most outrageous caricatures of him and his friends were daily spread about; and all this took place in the short space of three months. . . .

Do not delude yourself, Madame, with the idea that the English people—accepting Lord Byron as the greatest poet of our time—would on that account abstain from troubling him and from persecuting him in so far as they were able. Their admiration for his works is involuntary and they slander him in consequence of their immoderate prejudices, as much as they read him, for their pleasure. . . . I very much fear that similar causes would not fail to produce the same consequences.

. . . Accustomed as you are, Madame, to the gentle manner of Italy, you can hardly conceive what an intensity this social hatred has reached in less happy climes. I have had to experience this, I have seen all who were dearest to me inextricably entangled in these calumnies . . . and this is why I am eager to write you all this, to spare you all the evils which I have so fatally experienced.

A bitter dredging up of long-forgotten memories, a reminder of the unhappy beginnings of their tragedy, and also a plea that touched a nerve with Teresa Guiccioli—few prospects could horrify her more than that of neighbors spying with telescopes and passing moral judgment on her liaison with a famous figure of scandal. Teresa replied that Shelley had indeed convinced her of the undesirability of settling in Switzerland. She would take his advice and go to Pisa. But a small fear still lurked in the back of her mind; she ended her letter with a request: "Sir

—your kindness makes me dare to ask you a favor—will you grant it? Do not leave Ravenna without Milord."

Shelley did not share her concern. In fact, now that Teresa had agreed to come to Pisa, he felt that he had succeeded and that there was no question of Byron's coming and bringing Allegra with him. Just to make sure, Shelley urged Byron not to come alone; Claire would be living in Florence, he pointed out, where she had a position as a governess, so there was no possibility of embarrassing confrontations and arguments over Allegra. Byron's reply was equivocal, but it seemed to Shelley that all was finally settled. And meanwhile he was becoming anxious to return to Mary. As he had just written in answer to one of her pleading letters: "You would forgive me for my longer stay if you knew the fighting I have had to make it so short." So finally, without Milord but with his promise to follow, Shelley left Ravenna on August 17, 1821, to return to Pisa and help get things ready for his famous friend.

With Mary's help he located and rented the Palazzo Lanfranchi, an imposing structure across the Arno from his own palazzo. Mary supervised its renovation so as to have it ready for Byron to move in. The Gambas, with Teresa, arrived on September 1, and found a palazzo of their own. Teresa finally met Shelley, and wrote Byron: "Your friend pleases me very much. His countenance is full of goodness and talent. He came to see me twice, and I can assure you that he has been of great comfort to me. But his health seems to be very poor. When I first saw him, I thought he was having an attack of fever . . . how, dear friend, is it possible to be so thin, so worn out?" She considered taking English lessons from Shelley, but Byron wrote to dissuade her.

As they made ready for Byron's arrival, he lingered in Ravenna and procrastinated. There were quarrels with the servants.

Permits had to be obtained, and this involved endless red tape. He found the prices of Ravenna's movers exorbitant and wrote to ask Shelley if he could do better in Pisa. Somehow Teresa's brother Pietro got involved in the transaction, and Shelley discovered that he and Pietro had each sent eight moving wagons; but he was able to catch one of the caravans at Florence and bring it back, thus avoiding the spectacle of sixteen moving vans descending upon the Palazzo Guiccioli. It was September 17, half a month after the Gambas' arrival in Pisa, before the remaining eight wagons reached Ravenna.

Then came more delays. Not until September 23 did four of the wagons leave for Pisa, carrying furniture, books, saddles, dogs and some "nerve lotion" of Teresa's. Byron came down with a fever, further delaying things. Then came a rumor that political exiles might be permitted to return to Ravenna after all; Byron waited to see, even though his secretary was complaining: "Milord's house now seems a desert. I am sleeping on bare straw." By mid-October Byron was still packing, and still equivocating. Shelley wrote: "When may we expect you? The Countess G. is very patient, though sometimes she seems apprehensive that you will *never* leave Ravenna." Meanwhile Byron was writing Tom Moore: "I am all in the sweat, dust and blasphemy of an universal packing of all my things, furniture, etc., for Pisa. . . . It is awful work, this love, and prevents all a man's projects of good or glory. I wanted to go to Greece lately . . . But the tears of a woman who has left her husband for a man, and the weakness of one's own heart, are paramount to these projects, and I can hardly indulge them." Here was one of the earliest indications that Byron's attention was beginning to wander from Italy to Greece.

At last Byron told the servants to take away the bed and linen and pack them in one of the wagons; he was to leave in the morning, and he felt sure that if he went to bed that night he might not be able to get up in time for departure in the morning. He sat up all night, at the only remaining table, writing his poetry.

The morning of October 29 was dark and dismal. Byron no doubt bid a civil good-bye to Count Guiccioli, who must have been hard put to hide his delight at seeing the last of his marathon tenant. The crested carriage rattled through the gate of the Palazzo Guiccioli for the last time, and Byron set out for Florence and Pisa.

Out in the countryside the caravan threw up a cloud of dust. Beneath Byron's seat, squawking as they lurched in their crate inhaling the dust, rode four geese. Byron had bought them for a St. Michaelmas dinner and had fattened them up, and then had not the heart to kill them; so here they came with him to Pisa, complaining and fluttering all the way. Behind in the palazzo, until his banker Ghigi could find a place for them, stayed a few pitiful remnants of the menagerie: ". . . a goat with a broken leg, an ugly peasant's dog, a bird which would eat only fish, a badger on a chain and two ugly old monkeys."

In the convent school at Bagnacavallo, the Mother Superior, Marianna Fabri, had heard that Byron was leaving Ravenna. She had written him: "We have heard with sorrow of your approaching departure, which we have thought fit to keep a secret from my little lady. I cannot, however, conceal my more than common regret . . . not to have had the honour of meeting you personally, so that, if I did not feel that I was trespassing on your kindness, I would beg you to grant us that consolation and so satisfy the lively desire of your Allegrina, before you go, on which occasion you will have the opportunity of seeing where, and how, she is situated, and, let me say, too, how much she is loved for her good and unusual qualities." On the opposite side of the letter was a note from Allegra, in Italian and in a large, careful hand which followed the copybook lines ruled on the page by her teacher. "My dear papa—It being fair time, I should so much like a visit from my Papa, as I have many desires to satisfy; will you please your Allegrina who loves you so?" Byron passed the letter to Hoppner, with a comment that the appeal was obviously motivated by the desire for a gift. And as his carriage rolled west, Allegra stayed behind in the convent school.

On October 30 Byron reached Florence, where he delayed long enough for a tour of the museums. And on November 1 his carriage was rocking down the road to Pisa. Now, eager to be there, Byron sat in his lurching carriage and composed a poem, to the lilting rhythm of the carriage wheels, the creaking springs and the geese squawking below him.

Oh, talk not to me of a name great in story—
The days of our Youth are the days of our glory;
And the myrtle and ivy of sweet two-and-twenty
Are worth all your laurels, though ever so plenty.

What are garlands and crowns to the brow that is wrinkled?
'Tis but a dead flower with May-dew besprinkled:
Then away with all such from the head that is hoary,
What care I for the wreaths that can *only* give glory?

O Fame! if I e'er took delight in thy praises,
'Twas less for the sake of thy high-sounding phrases,
Than to see the bright eyes of the dear One discover,
She thought that I was not unworthy to love her.

There chiefly I sought thee, *there* only I found thee;
Her Glance was the best of the rays that surround thee,
When it sparkled o'er aught that was bright in my story,
I knew it was Love, and I felt it was Glory.[46]

At Empoli, sixteen miles outside Florence, Byron's caravan forced the regular stagecoach to the side of the road. Byron did not bother to study the coach, or he would have seen the angry face of Claire Clairmont, en route to her employer in Florence —watching with hatred as she saw that Byron was coming to Pisa without Allegra.[47]

[IX]

On November 30, 1821, Mary Shelley had recovered her spirits so much that she wrote to a friend: "We are a little nest of singing birds." The Shelleys were comfortably settled in the Tre Palazzi di Chiesa, across the Arno from Byron's Palazzo Lanfranchi. Shelley had decided that Pisa was his favorite Italian town. To a friend he reported that "our roots never struck so deeply as at Pisa." And about Pisa he wrote one of his most sentimental fragmentary poems.

> The sun is set; the swallows are asleep;
>   The bats are flitting fast in the grey air;
> The slow soft toads out of the damp corners creep,
>   And evening's breath, wandering here and there
> Over the quivering surface of the stream,
> Wakes not one ripple from its Summer dream.

199

There is no dew on the dry grass to-night,
  Nor damp within the shadow of the trees;
The wind is intermitting, dry, and light;
  And in the inconstant motion of the breeze
The dust and straws are driven up and down,
And whirled about the pavement of the town.

Within the surface of the fleeting river
  The wrinkled image of the city lay,
Immovably unquiet, and for ever
  It trembles, but it never fades away . . .[48]

Byron also found Pisa to his liking, more congenial than
Ravenna had been. The climate was far pleasanter, and the
Renaissance-style Palazzo Lanfranchi, built of weather-
browned Carrara marble, was roomier and brighter than the
gloomy palazzo of the grumpy old count in Ravenna. The windows looked out on the Arno, and in the back was a high-
walled but sunny garden, with palms, magnolias and orange
trees. Byron wrote Tom Moore: "I can walk down into my
garden, and pluck my own oranges—and, by the way, have got
a diarrhoea in consequence of indulging in this meridian luxury
of proprietorship." Byron enjoyed himself scouting the city,
showing off before Shelley's friends and paying his evening
calls on Teresa at the Gambas' Casa Parra, a few blocks up the
Arno.

Pisa was an odd nest of birds, however. Besides Shelley's
friend Edward Williams, his common-law wife, Jane, and
their two children, there were "Mr. and Mrs. Mason," actually
George Williams Tighe and Lady Mountcashell; she had left
the Earl of Mountcashell nearly a decade ago and had run away
from England with her lover; now they lived in unwedded bliss
like the Williamses. There was the raffish, often oafish "Count"
John Taffe, Jr., who had become an expatriate from Ireland

evidently by necessity after an unfortunate affair with a woman. Arriving in Genoa, Taffe had ingratiated himself with another woman, one Mme. Artemisia Castellini Regny, who had entrée into the best salons of Italy. So Taffe was firmly established in Pisan society when Byron arrived. Byron found him amusing (not always intentionally) and companionable. Taffe had a high opinion of himself, particularly of his horsemanship and his writing ability; Byron laughed at the one and encouraged him in the other, knowing that Taffe would always be Taffe and nothing more. One woman Taffe did not impress was Mary Shelley, who referred to him scathingly as "the Poet Laureate of Pisa."

But for the moment Pisa's birds flocked and sang together. They called themselves the Pisan Circle. The ladies walked and talked and had tea together. Mary Shelley and Teresa Guiccioli found that they enjoyed each other's company; Mary, who undoubtedly had expected another Fornarina, was happily surprised by Teresa, whom she described as "a nice pretty girl without pretensions, good-hearted and amiable." (Shelley's more pragmatic judgment on Teresa was: "a very pretty, sentimental, innocent, superficial Italian, who has sacrificed an immense fortune to live for Lord Byron; and who, if I know anything of my friend, of her, and of human nature, will hereafter have plenty of leisure and opportunity to repent her rashness.")

The men stuck together, playing billiards, riding horseback and engaging in target practice. Shelley was still as good a shot as Byron, and still surprised that he should be. Shelley and Williams still spent many of the warm days sailing on the Serchio. But Shelley also liked his solitude, and for his hours alone he found a refuge in the woods outside Pisa—a peaceful place hidden in the pine forest between the city and the sea. A brook ran through the forest, dropping down to a cool, shaded pool shielded by a fallen tree. There, during the warm days, as he had in the mountain stream at Bagni di Lucca, Shelley would strip off his clothes, plunge into the pool, shower himself under the waterfall and then climb out to dry in a patch of sunlight streaming through the branches, while composing poetry that reflected his mood.

> Swiftly walk o'er the western wave,
>   Spirit of Night!
> Out of the misty eastern cave,
> Where, all the long and lone daylight,
> Thou wovest dreams of joy and fear,
> Which make thee terrible and dear—
>   Swift be thy flight!
>
> Wrap thy form in a mantle grey,
>   Star-inwrought!
> Blind with thine hair the eyes of Day;
> Kiss her until she be wearied out,
> Then wander o'er city, and sea, and land,
> Touching all with thine opiate wand—
>   Come, long-sought!
>
> When I arose and saw the dawn,
>   I sighed for thee;
> When light rode high, and the dew was gone,
> And noon lay heavy on flower and tree,
> And the weary Day turned to his rest,
> Lingering like an unloved guest,
>   I sighed for thee. . . .[49]

One of the few men who appreciated what Percy Shelley was writing in his boat and in his wooded glade was Byron. It was Byron to whom Shelley first showed whatever he wrote at the time; it was Byron who enjoyed these poems and praised them, and wrote his friends about them. And it was Shelley to whom Byron turned with his own verse, asking Shelley's opinion as he did with no one else, arguing vehemently with him but nearly always accepting his advice. And, despite the worldwide fame of Byron, it was Shelley who attracted the newest visitor to Pisa, the one who would play the dominant, dramatic role in the climactic scenes of their Italian years.

Edward John Trelawny had been a rebel and a romanticist from the time he had run away from a tyrannical father at thirteen and had gone to sea. As a sailor in the Royal Navy and as a wanderer through India, Java, Madagascar and the Greek Islands, Trelawny claimed to have been seaman, skipper, privateer and pirate. The summer of 1820 found him in Lausanne, Switzerland, where he claimed to make the acquaintance of a bookseller who changed the course of Trelawny's wanderings. "Your modern poets, Byron, Scott and Moore, I can read and understand as I walk along," said Trelawny's friend. "But I have got hold of a book by one now that makes me stop to take breath and think." The book was *Queen Mab*, by Percy Shelley.

Trelawny had never heard of the man. But when the bookseller added that *Queen Mab* had moved a priest to shout: "Infidel! Jacobin! Leveller! Nothing can stop this spread of blasphemy but the stake and the faggot!" Trelawny could not wait to read it. One taste of Shelley led to another, and in a few days, when he found himself in the company of the poet William Wordsworth, Trelawny had already become a Shelley devotee.

So he could not resist asking "one of the veterans of the gentle craft" what he thought of Percy Shelley.

"Nothing," said Wordsworth.

As Trelawny gasped in surprise, Wordsworth added: "A poet who has not produced a good poem before he is twenty-five, we may conclude cannot and never will do so."

Trelawny persisted. Following the poet as he stumped out to his carriage, he asked: "*The Cenci?*"

Wordsworth shook his head. "Won't do." He scooped up a Scottie that had scrambled into the carriage with him. "This hairy fellow is our flea-trap," he said, and the carriage rolled off.

Then, after meeting Edward Williams, corresponding with him and hearing from him that Shelley was with Williams in Pisa, Trelawny decided to set out for Pisa. The opportunity of meeting Shelley, and Lord Byron as well, was more than he could resist.

In January of 1822 he arrived, and he wasted scarcely an hour in calling on Williams and his family, who were living in the same house with the Shelleys. Williams was delighted to see him. The tall, dark, hawk-nosed visitor was soon engaged in his lively and colorful reminiscences. Then Trelawny noticed, with a prickly sensation, that there was someone in the corridor just outside the door across from him. What struck him was the fact that he could not make out the figure of the person—only a pair of "glittering eyes fixed on mine," almost as if they were alight in the dark like those of a cat. As he paused, transfixed by the unbroken stare, Jane Williams noticed his expression, followed his gaze and called out: "Come in, Shelley!"

As Trelawny remembered it later, Shelley seemed to drift into the room and across to him. Trelawny could scarcely believe his eyes. Was this, he asked himself, the evil genius of *Queen Mab*, the blasphemous radical who had left his wife to run off and live in sin with another woman? Here instead, at least to Trelawny's rough sailor's eye, was a bashful aesthete, ill at ease at the sight of a stranger. But then Edward Williams asked what book it was Shelley carried in his hand. It was the Spanish dramatist Calderón, and at Jane Williams' urging Shelley started to read.

Even Trelawny was overwhelmed. "Shoved off from the shore of common-place incidents that could not interest him," Trelawny wrote later, "and fairly launched on a theme that did, he instantly became oblivious of everything but the book in his hand. The masterly manner in which he analyzed the genius of the author, his lucid interpretation of the story, and the ease with which he translated into our language the most subtle and imaginative passages of the Spanish poet, were marvellous, as was his command of the two languages. After this touch of his quality I no longer doubted his identity."

In fact, so lost was Trelawny in the translating of *El Mágico Prodigioso* that it was some time after Shelley had finished before his visitor looked up and realized that Shelley had ghosted out of the room. Trelawny asked: "Where is he?"

Jane Williams replied: "Shelley? Oh, he comes and goes like a spirit, no one knows when or where."

Shelley had gone to find his wife and bring her to meet the newcomer. Trelawny was impressed by Mary Shelley, mindful of her fame as the author of *Frankenstein*. What he liked most, after the session with Calderón, was the way Mary "brought us back from the ideal world Shelley had left us in, to the real one." Mary wanted to know all about "the news of London and Paris, the new books, operas, and bonnets, marriages, murders, and other marvels. The Poet vanished, and tea appeared." Now Trelawny could feel more at home.

And Mary Shelley could wallow in Trelawny's gossip. More than that, she found herself awed and fascinated by this "half-Arab Englishman . . . He is clever; for his moral qualities I am yet in the dark; he is a strange web which I am endeavoring to unravel. . . . He is six feet high, raven black hair, which curls thickly and shortly like a Moor's, dark grey expressive eyes, overhanging brows, upturned lips and a smile which expresses good nature and kindheartedness. . . . His company is delightful for he excites me to think. . . . He tells strange stories of himself, horrific ones, so that they harrow one up, while with his emphatic but unmodulated voice, his simple yet strong language, he portrays the most frightful situations; then all these adventures took place between the age of thirteen and twenty. I believe them now I see the man. . . ."

Byron was fascinated too, but in quite a different manner. On the first day that Shelley brought this outlandish character to the Palazzo Lanfranchi, Byron tried to entertain him with his usual anecdotes—of his accomplishments at riding horseback, his expertise at target shooting and his feat of swimming the Hellespont. But Trelawny seemed not to be impressed, and in fact preferred to talk about *his* exploits all over the world. Byron realized that he was confronted with his Corsair in real life, and resented the fact. That evening he told Teresa, "I have met today the personification of my Corsair."

Teresa showed more interest than he expected. "I feel curious to see him," she said.

"You will not like him," Byron replied quickly.

In fact, she did not. After her first meeting with Trelawny the next day, she complained of his "*étrange regard*," and asked Byron to have nothing more to do with him. Byron only laughed, with a note of relief.

But Trelawny quickly insinuated himself into the group. With Shelley and Byron he rode out of the city, to the Villa la Podera, where Byron had set up a shooting gallery after the local authorities had refused him permission to engage in target practice in the Palazzo Lanfranchi's garden. They also rode through the rolling fields around the city, to the *pineta* which stretched in sweeping lines of umbrella pines down to the sea. On one of these occasions Trelawny discovered Shelley's wooded refuge. Trelawny and Mary Shelley had gone riding outside Pisa, hoping to run across Shelley, who had disappeared on one of his wanderings. After some hours of riding and walking, Mary Shelley decided to rest under one of the pine trees while Trelawny walked on to see if he could find the poet.

He soon came to the edge of the sea. Warm from the exercise, he stripped and took a swim. After drying in the sun, he dressed and started back, this time through a thicker part of the forest. As he pushed through the underbrush, he kept calling Shelley's name; herons, ducks and other birds flapped noisily from nearby pools, but there was no sign of Shelley. Then Trelawny heard the braying of a jackass. It soon approached, led by an old man who was collecting pine cones. Trelawny asked him if he had seen a stranger in the area.

The old man immediately knew whom Trelawny meant. *"L'inglese malinconico* haunts the wood," he said. "I will show you his nest." They walked over a hill, down through a valley and over a few more small rises and the old man pointed. *"Eccolo."* Then he went on his way.

There was the shadowed pool and the fallen tree. A shaft of light was streaming through the high tops of the pines. Shelley was seated at the edge of the pool, lost in thought.

Trelawny noticed some books scattered at his feet. One was

a volume of Sophocles, another was Shakespeare. And among the litter of papers was a scrap with scrawled lines, which Trelawny picked up and read.

> Ariel to Miranda: Take
> This slave of Music, for the sake
> Of him who is the slave of thee,
> And teach it all the harmony
> In which thou canst, and only thou,
> Make the delighted spirit glow,
> Till joy denies itself again,
> And, too intense, is turned to pain . . .
>
> The artist wrought this loved Guitar,
> And taught it justly to reply,
> To all who question skilfully,
> In language gentle as thine own;
> Whispering in enamoured tone
> Sweet oracles of woods and dells,
> And summer winds in sylvan cells . . .
>
> But, sweetly as its answers will
> Flatter hands of perfect skill,
> It keeps its highest, holiest tone
> For our beloved Jane alone.[50]

Trelawny broke the silence. Shelley looked up.

"Hello. Come in."

Trelawny stepped over the fallen tree and perched on a stump.

"Is this your study?"

"Yes. And these trees are my books—they tell no lies. You are sitting on the stool of inspiration. In those three pines the weird sisters are imprisoned. And this," Shelley said, pointing to the deep pool, "is their cauldron of black broth. The Pythian priestesses uttered their oracles from below; now they are uttered from above. Listen to the solemn music in the pinetops—don't you hear the mournful murmurings of the sea?"

Trying to bring his friend back to earth, Trelawny reminded him of his wife: Mary was waiting for them at the edge of the wood. Shelley jumped up, gathering his scattered books and papers. "Poor Mary," he said. "Hers is a sad fate. Come along." And as they started back, he added thoughtfully: "She can't bear solitude, nor I society—the quick coupled with the dead."

Mary was still waiting for them, and she tried to put a cheerful face on it; she had long since resigned herself to such behavior. So had Trelawny; but another afternoon was enough to unnerve him.

They had been walking along the Arno, and Trelawny had again decided to take a quick swim. Showing off as usual, he amazed Shelley with his diving and underwater swimming —"aquatic gymnastics," as Trelawny called them, "learnt from the natives of the South Seas." Trelawny paused for breath, and Shelley asked: "Why can't I swim? It seems so easy."

"Because you think you can't," said Trelawny. "Take a header off this bank, and when you rise, turn over on your back; you will float like a duck."

Shelley promptly stripped to his underwear, plunged into the water—and sank like a stone. He lay on the bottom, as still as if drowned. Trelawny dived to the bottom and pulled him out.

Shelley coughed, spat, regained his breath and, characteristically, began to muse about the incident. "They say Truth lies at the bottom of the well," he said. "In another minute I should have found it, and you would have found an empty shell. It is an easy way of getting rid of the body."

Trelawny was appalled. "What would Mrs. Shelley have said to me if I had gone back with your empty cage?"

Shelley jumped. "Don't tell Mary," he said quickly. "Not a word!" He looked back into the water and his voice took on the same mystical inflection as he said: "But it's a great temptation. . . . In another minute I might have been in another planet. . . ."

What struck Trelawny most was the contrast between the two poets. Every Wednesday evening he could watch Byron and Shelley together, when Byron gave a lavish English-style weekly dinner for the men of the Pisan Circle. As the evening started, the two poets would engage in congenial discussion of the work of other English poets, and even their own work. Byron still listened thoughtfully to every criticism Shelley offered. But whenever it threatened to get too serious, in his contrary way—or perhaps because he was shrewd enough to avoid deep discussion with Shelley—Byron would throw the conversation off the track with a pun or a joke. Or he would bring his friend up sharp with a self-deprecating remark. On one occasion, as Shelley approvingly read some lines from *Childe Harold*, Byron broke in with: "Heavens, Shelley! What infinite nonsense are you quoting?" And though Shelley always spoke frankly on the subject, he also showed his high regard for Byron's work. As he wrote Leigh Hunt: "Certain it is that Lord Byron has made me bitterly feel the inferiority which the world has presumed to place between us and which subsists nowhere in reality but in our own talents." In one of his gloomier moments he went so far as to say: "I do not write—I have lived too long near Lord Byron, and the sun has extinguished the glow-worm."

But on these evenings, as the party progressed, poetic understanding gave way and the two men's interests diverged. Byron turned to the others present, indulging himself in their flattery, their small talk and their racy stories, while Shelley retired into himself, trying politely but in vain not to register his growing disapproval as he drank his water and watched the others "making themselves into vats of claret, etc., till three o'clock in the morning."

It was on one of these occasions that Byron had a unique idea: why didn't they put on a play? They could do *Othello*. Byron would play Iago; Trelawny would be Othello; Williams would be Cassio; Medwin, Roderigo; Mary Shelley, Desdemona. The idea was carried even to the point of a few rehearsals, until Teresa rebelled. She did not like her role, of Bianca, the harlot. Nor did she want Byron playing Iago. So she talked him out of the scheme.

Trelawny proposed another project: why didn't they form a summer colony somewhere beside the sea, and each build a boat? He had noticed that Shelley, "like the Italian palms . . . never flourished far from water. When compelled to take up his quarters in a town, he every morning with the instinct that guides the water birds, fled to the nearest lake, river or sea shore, and only returned to roost at night." And Byron, for all his superior attitude toward the newcomer, not only listened intently to Trelawny's tales of the sea but even fashioned a poem on one of Trelawny's favorite stories: William Bligh's account of the mutiny aboard his *Bounty*.

> The gallant Chief within his cabin slept,
> Secure in those by whom the watch was kept . . .
> Alas! his deck was trod by unwilling feet,
> And wilder hands would hold the vessel's sheet;
> Young hearts, which languished for some sunny isle,
> Where summer years and summer women smile;
> Men without country, who, too long estranged,

Had found no native home, or found it changed,
And, half civilised, preferred the cave
Of some soft savage to the uncertain wave . . .[51]

Both Byron and Shelley rose to Trelawny's idea. Off to
Genoa, to Captain Daniel Roberts, an old friend of Trelawny's,
went the specifications for Byron's yacht: an iron keel, a copper
bottom, a big cabin. And four guns, "as large as you think safe
—to make a hell of a noise." Shelley's plans were less am-
bitious: ". . . seventeen or eighteen feet . . . three lugs and
a jib." But Shelley was far more entranced with the idea than
Byron. "We used to draw plans on the sand of the Arno,"
Trelawny wrote. "With a real chart of the Mediterranean
spread out before them, and with faces as grave and anxious as
those of Columbus and his companions, they held councils as to
the islands to be visited, coasts explored, courses steered, the
amount of armament, stores, water and provisions which would
be necessary. . . . Byron, with the smile of a Mephistopheles
standing by, asked me the amount of salvage we, the salvors,
should be entitled to in the probable event of our picking up
and towing Shelley's water-logged craft into port."

In fact, Dan Roberts and Trelawny both questioned the design for Shelley's boat. But it was drawn up by Williams, Trelawny said, and Williams would not listen to his friends' objections. He had served in the Royal Navy, and he knew what
sort of boat would serve his and Shelley's needs. As for Shelley,
any design good enough for Edward was good enough for him.
So the two yachts were ordered—and Shelley dreamed of his
far-reaching voyages, while Byron eventually forgot about the
whole thing.

Ignoring the summer colony, he made his own arrangements

for a villa near Leghorn for himself and Teresa. Their affair had become as domestic as it had ever been in Ravenna. Indeed, Teresa had by now grown more accustomed to some of Byron's eccentricities. She may still have objected to his seeing himself as an Iago, but she had given up trying to reform him. Perhaps it was a sign of her sureness. At any rate, she now relented and reversed an earlier plea. Shocked at a French translation of *Don Juan,* she had made such a scene that Byron had agreed to drop the project. But now in Pisa she changed her mind; and Byron, who had faithfully held to his promise, happily took up his mock-heroic theme again.

"There is a tide in the affairs of men,
 Which, taken at the flood"—you know the rest,
And most of us have found it, now and then:
 At least we think so, though but few have guessed
The moment, till too late to come again. . . .

There is a tide in the affairs of women,
 Which, taken at the flood, leads—God knows where:
Those navigators must be able seamen
 Whose charts lay down its currents to a hair;
Not all the reveries of Jacob Behmen
 With its strange whirls and eddies can compare:
Men, with their heads, reflect on this and that—
But women, with their hearts, on Heaven knows what.

And yet a headlong, headstrong, downright She,
 Young, beautiful, and daring—who would risk
A throne—the world—the universe—to be
 Beloved in her own way—and rather whisk
The stars from out the sky, than not be free
 As are the billows when the breeze is brisk—
Though such a She's a devil (if there be one),
Yet she would make full many a Manichean.[52]

Byron's renewal of *Don Juan* and Shelley's reveries of exploration were interrupted by two comic-opera incidents which seemed anything but amusing to the two poets at the time. The first was precipitated by the news that at Lucca, a town ten miles from Pisa, an Italian was to be burned alive, for performing some sort of sacrilege. Byron shuddered and asked: "Can it be possible? Do we live in the nineteenth century? . . . We must endeavor to prevent this *auto da fe*." At this point Shelley burst in with the proposal that they arm themselves, ride to Lucca and free the victim by force if necessary. The idea appealed to Byron, and plans were made for the rescuing expedition. But shortly the deflating truth was heard: the story had been exaggerated and the man was to receive a far milder form of punishment. The brave rescue project was dropped as quickly as it had been conceived.

The second incident was more comic but had worse results. One Sunday afternoon in the spring of 1822, Byron, Shelley, Trelawny and some friends were riding back into town after a picnic when one Sergeant Major Masi, a mounted dragoon who had apparently drunk too much on a picnic of his own, galloped through the party, elbowing riders aside and flinging dust in their eyes. Unaccustomed to such treatment even by a dragoon, Byron spurred his horse and, followed by the rest of the men, raced after the dragoon; Teresa and Mary—and Count Taffe —stayed at a safe distance and watched the affair.

Surrounding the man, Byron and his friends demanded an apology. The dragoon cursed them and threatened to arrest them. Byron snorted. "Arrest, indeed!" Though the others wanted to tangle with the dragoon, Byron turned away haughtily and rode on toward the city gate. The dragoon, incensed at the arrogant attitude of the "*maledetti inglesi*," lost his temper and dashed between them and the city gate, calling on the guards at the gate to refuse them entry. Looking neither to right nor to left, Byron and young Count Gamba, Teresa's brother, rode on through the gate unmolested. But as Shelley tried to ride by, the dragoon swung on him with his sword and knocked him off his horse. One or two of the Englishmen converged on him, whereupon the dragoon turned and dashed through the gate. A few blocks inside the city he was met by Byron, who had galloped to his palazzo for a sword and was now racing back to re-enter the fray. With him were a couple of his servants, one of whom grabbed at the dragoon's bridle. Byron ordered the servant to let go, whereupon the dragoon got away.

But he made the mistake of galloping past the Palazzo Lanfranchi. There the rest of Byron's servants, up in arms at the sight of his lordship returning for a sword and dashing off to battle, were out in the street. When they saw the dragoon coming toward them alone, they concluded that he had struck down their master. Carried away by loyalty, one of the servants ducked into the dragoon's path and got him in the stomach with a pitchfork. The wounded man toppled from his horse, but was scooped up by other dragoons and rushed to the hospital.

The repercussions shook the city. Rumors were everywhere: the *inglesi* were arming the peasants to rise against the government; Lord Byron and his friend Shelley had been killed in a pitched battle; the Englishmen were holed up in the Palazzo Lanfranchi, defending themselves against the mob with pistols and Byron's bulldogs. Meanwhile the dragoon lingered near death while the famous surgeon Vacca worked over him. Vacca reported to his English friends that the dragoon said he would not have started the battle if one of the Englishmen had not struck him with a riding crop; one of the English party claimed that it had been Count Gamba, not an Englishman, who had wielded the crop; Vacca pointed out that Count Gamba was regarded as in the same class with the Englishmen, so far as the government was concerned. The Gambas had been forced to leave Ravenna because of their insurrectionary activities; the Austrians decided to exile the Gambas from Pisa also.

There were weeks of interrogations and form-filling and hemming and hawing. Byron's gondolier, Tita, was asked to leave Pisa. Byron fought to keep him; the pitchfork had been wielded by another servant, whom Byron refused to identify. But finally Byron became convinced that he was getting off easily, even though the dragoon now appeared to be recovering. With Byron's reluctant permission, Tita sadly went into exile. And meanwhile Count Taffe, who had watched most of the affair from a safe distance with the ladies, bragged so ceaselessly about his bravery that Jane Williams gave him a nickname which delighted Byron: "False-Taffe."

For those who might have believed in presentiments, Pisa's weather had been ominous throughout the year. In winter the snow piled up in the Apennines, sending floods down the Arno. By spring, the water was rising under the bridges of Pisa and the debris of the river was piling up against the balustrades. The wind howled down off the mountains and rain lashed at the leaded windows. Lightning struck the palazzo next to Byron's. In the Palazzo Lanfranchi itself the wind made noises around the eaves and corners and ghostly sounds were heard everywhere. Byron's valet, William Fletcher, who had been unaffected by the tribulations of Geneva and Venice and Ravenna, complained of the eerie sounds in his quarters and asked for a different room. Byron himself looked suspiciously at walls that might have served as unearthly burial places for unfortunate victims of the palazzo's previous owners. In summer and fall there were even more violent storms. Shelley suffered from what he called "depression of the spirits." Mary complained of "rheumatism of the head"; she could not sleep, and in her long, anxious periods of insomnia she wondered what evil betided.

And in the even worse weather of Florence, Claire Clairmont brooded about her daughter in the hilltop town of Bagnacavallo. Distrustful of Shelley's judgment, Claire had asked "Mr. Mason" to have a look at the convent school, and he had returned with a far less favorable report than Shelley had. The Capuchin order was a poor one, he pointed out, so there were few comforts in the convent. The building was unheated; there were not even fires during the winter. The food was scarce and unappetizing. Claire's worst fears were supported, and she worried to the point of nightmares. She returned to Pisa to badger Shelley again to help her. Shelley and Mary could only counsel patience. Wait, they told her. Who knew when Byron would suddenly grow tired of Italy and go home to England, or to South America or somewhere else? At that point they should be able to talk him into letting Allegra return to her mother. Meanwhile they could only wait and hope.

Perhaps, Claire replied. But the anxiety was becoming more than she could bear. She was even considering leaving Italy herself for a while, to take another job, in Vienna. Would Shelley help her make one last plea? Maybe, with the inducement of her leaving, Byron would relent and let her see her daughter once again for a little while. Shelley agreed to try. Claire wrote another of her pleading letters.

. . . I shall shortly leave Italy for a new country, to enter on a disagreeable and precarious course of life. . . . I leave my friends with regret, but indeed I cannot go without having first seen and embraced Allegra. Do not, I entreat you, refuse me this little but only consolation. . . . The when and where of our meeting shall be entirely according to your pleasure, and with every restriction and delicacy that you may think necessary for Allegra's sake. . . . My dear Friend, I do conjure you not to make the world dark to me as if my Allegra were dead. . . .

Byron's reaction was a shrug of the shoulders and a comment that women could not live without making scenes. Shelley persisted, arguing that Claire was so concerned over Allegra that she was becoming physically ill. Then, finally, he realized how far Byron's own psychopathic hatred for Claire had gone. At the mention that Claire was ill, "a gleam of malicious satisfaction" came over Byron's face. "I saw his look and understood its meaning," Shelley wrote, "and I came away."

Claire could only give up, for the time being. She put off the trip to Vienna. And then came the first report of an epidemic in the school at Bagnacavallo.

A "fever"—no one knew exactly what type—had come into the school, perhaps brought in by infected food. It was not particularly virulent, and most of the girls who had come down with it were already recovering. But when it hit Allegra, the nuns worried, and a messenger was sent to Pisa. Byron's answer was to send an immediate order to procure the best doctor in the area and make sure he took charge. A messenger was to wait and bring him news of any change.

The change was for the worse. Allegra, never robust, quickly weakened under the debilitating effect of the fever. She became consumptive, and could not seem to recover her strength. On April 20, 1822, at ten o'clock in the morning, Padre Vincenzo Fabbri, the convent's spiritual director, came running across the convent garden. When one of the nuns called to him, he answered: "I cannot wait!" He reached the little cell in time to baptize Allegra. The Mother Superior knelt by the bed. Clustered around the room, the other nuns wept and murmured their prayers, as five-year-old Allegra died.

Sister Marianna, Allegra's special teacher, collapsed and was put to bed. The other nuns made a wax statue of the little girl and dressed it in her red dress, with her fur tippet and a necklace of gold chain. And the messenger was sent racing to Pisa.

He arrived on April 22. He was met by Teresa, who listened somberly, thanked him and sent him off. Then she went to the Palazzo Lanfranchi. She knew where she would find Byron; he had not gone out since the first message had arrived. Slowly she climbed the wide staircase to his study.

It was nearing dusk. In the golden sunset reflected by the river through the windows, she could see Byron. He was seated in an armchair with a pad of paper. He looked up quickly and asked, before she could say anything, whether his messenger had come from Bagnacavallo. Quietly, gently, she told him.

Years later she recalled how he seemed to sink into his chair, how his face grew gray and old. He sat so still for so long that she began to think he had gone into shock. Considering his seeming recent neglect of Allegra, Teresa was surprised by the impact with which the news hit him. She tried to make a consoling remark, and finally he spoke. He wanted only to be left alone.

Teresa walked out of the study, down the stairs and along the Arno to Casa Parra, recalling her own memories of the little girl—sassing her father's animals, sleigh riding in Ravenna's *corso*, dancing in her new fur tippet just before she left for the convent school for the last time.

Next morning, when Teresa went to the Palazzo Lanfranchi to see how he was, Byron said: "She is more fortunate than we are. . . . It is God's will—let us mention it no more." And never again, Teresa claimed, did he mention Allegra's name to

her. But Byron did have to mention Allegra at least once again
—to Shelley. He sent a note: "The blow was stunning and unexpected . . . it is a moment when we are apt to think that,
if this or that had been done, such event might have been pre-
vented,—though every day and hour shows us that they are the
most natural and inevitable. I suppose Time will do his usual
work—Death has done his."

Shelley, Byron was sure, would pass the solemn news on to
Claire in Florence. He did not know that Claire had returned
to Pisa. Shelley moved fast. He knew that if Claire heard the
news while in Pisa, she might storm the Palazzo Lanfranchi
and kill Byron. Shelley turned to Trelawny for help.

The summer cottage on the coast had been Trelawny's idea.
The Williamses and Claire had done some searching and had
found a cottage in the village of San Terenzo, on the Bay of
Lerici. They had only just returned from their search when
Shelley received his note from Byron. He quickly asked Tre-
lawny to escort Claire and Mary to the cottage; Shelley and
Williams would stay behind to pack up and follow as soon as
they could.

Trelawny understood. Quickly he took Claire, Mary and
two-and-a-half-year-old Percy Florence Shelley and set off for
the Bay of Lerici. Watching them go, Shelley realized that the
carefree days of the Pisan Circle were over. The tragedy that
had seemed to stalk him through the years in Italy evidently now
stalked Byron too. It had been when his Naples foundling had
died that Shelley had written: "It seems as if the destruction
that is consuming me were as an atmosphere which wrapt and
infected everything connected with me"; but never could he
have felt this more than at the time when he and the Williamses
packed up and prepared to leave Pisa. Never before had it been
impressed so much upon him that the Italy which had inspired

him and Byron to such poetic heights had also brought them nearly unbearable grief. Shelley knew that no man can flee his fate. But still he nourished the hope that on a new stage his tragic drama might take a happier turn.

And, for a while, it did.

[X]

[X]

The world offers few places more beautiful than the Bay of
Lerici. Guarded at one end by an ancient fort and sheltered at
the other by three steep-walled islands in a line, the bay is a
wide carpet of blue. Shelley was intrigued by the legend that
Petrarch had stayed here, and that Dante had been imprisoned
in the fortress on the point. Another literary Englishman had
been here before Shelley: the eighteenth-century novelist and
naval officer Tobias Smollett had in fact recommended the bay
for a British naval station. The bay's tideless waters wash
quietly on the rocky shore. Fishermen row out in their dories,
spread their wide circles of net and slowly haul them in. At
Portovenere, where the bay meets the open sea, the sun glances
off the rippling blue and sets lights dancing along the black
cliffs, the multicolored boats at the piers and the faded pink
houses at the waterfront. In the deep cliffside caverns the

ocean's swells roll in and suck and hiss and gurgle. Far down through the clear water the tendrils of seaweed sweep back and forth with the sea's surge.

In good weather. But when the *ponènti*, the wild storms of the Mediterranean, come up the Italian coast, the bay scoops them in. The first signs are the haze and the rolling breakers. The shallows turn a turbid green. Then rolling mountains of water come marching in across the bay, to explode against the rocky shore. The islands are lost in the wind-driven mists. The Bay of Lerici is a place of sometimes idyllic—and sometimes deadly—beauty.

The little house on the beach seemed a part of the bay. When the storms blew and the surf thundered against the foundation and the spray wet the windows, it was more like a ship at sea than a house on land. Mary was appalled. Shelley found it wild and wonderful. And he could hardly wait for his new boat.

On May 12, as thunder rolled and distant lightning flashed, she came riding around Portovenere and into the bay. Her plans had been altered slightly in the building. She was twenty-four feet long and drew four feet of water, and she sailed smartly up to her mooring off Lerici, around the point from the house. At one time Byron had proposed that she be named *Don Juan*, and Shelley had agreed. But in the meantime Mary had suggested the name *Ariel*, which Shelley now preferred. But the boat arrived with the letters DON JUAN painted boldly across her mainsail. After twenty-one days of washing and scrubbing with water and turpentine and even wine, Shelley and Williams finally cut and patched the sail to remove the letters, and Shelley wrote: "The superscription of my poor boat's infamy is erased."[53]

There followed days and nights on the Bay of Lerici aboard *Ariel*, in the little boat from the Serchio and in a reed-and-canvas *sandolino* which Williams built on the beach. There was the day, after a storm, when they sailed wonderingly through a sea of nautiluses and the whole bay seemed to shimmer with purple magic. There was the day when they suddenly sighted what looked like a man-of-war sailing grandly down the coast; she turned out to be Byron's yacht, *Bolivar;* as the two craft met, Trelawny fired *Bolivar's* six guns in salute and they raced for a short distance until *Bolivar* proved her superiority. "She is the most beautiful craft I ever saw," wrote Williams. He and Shelley inspected her thoroughly before Trelawny took her on to Leghorn.

There was the day when *Ariel* sailed out past Portovenere to Palmaria and Tino Islands, and beyond to another they had not known. As they approached, the currents seemed to draw them toward the rocky outcropping, and when they wore off on the other tack an odd musical chord sounded all around them. Williams later found it to be a shroud set up too tight, but the sound inspired Shelley to name their discovery "Syren's Island."

There were evenings when they sailed under the moonlight, listening to the ripple of the bow wave and the soft music of Jane Williams' guitar. "Williams is captain," Shelley wrote in a letter, "and we drive along this delightful bay in the evening wind under the summer moon until earth appears another world. Jane brings her guitar, and if the past and future can be obliterated, the present would content me so well that I could say with Faust to the passing moment, 'Remain, thou art so beautiful. . . .'"

> . . . I sat and saw the vessels glide
> Over the ocean bright and wide,
> Like spirit-winged chariots sent

O'er some serenest element
For ministrations strange and far;
As if to some Elysian star
Sailed for drink to medicine
Such sweet and bitter pain as mine.
And the wind that winged their flight
From the land came fresh and light,
And the scent of winged flowers,
And the coolness of the hours
Of dew, and sweet warmth left by day,
Were scattered o'er the twinkling bay,
And the fisher with his lamp
And spear above the low rocks damp
Crept, and struck the fish which came
To worship the delusive flame.
Too happy they, whose pleasure sought
Extinguishes all sense and thought
Of the regret that pleasure leaves,
Destroying life alone, not peace![54]

But the Bay of Lerici was hardly Mary Shelley's idea of paradise. She was frightened by the ferocious storms and by the wild, chanting natives, depressed by the graveyard on the hill above the house, filled with countless gravestones of children. "I was not well in body or mind," she wrote later. "My nerves were wound up to the utmost irritation, and the sense of misfortune hung over my spirits. No words can tell you how much I hated our house and the country about it. Shelley reproached me for this. His health was good and the place was quite after his own heart. What could I answer? That the people were wild and hateful, that though the country was beautiful yet I liked a more countrified place, that there was great difficulty in living."

By any practical, housewifely standards, Mary was quite

right. The cottage was little more than a boathouse, its ground floor uninhabitable and sometimes washed by storm waves, its main floor merely one big room surrounded by closet-like bedrooms. Two of them looked out on the terrace and the bay; Shelley occupied one and Mary and little Percy the other. The Williamses, unsuccessful in their hopes of finding a house of their own, moved into the third bedroom with their children, two-year-old Edward Medwin and fourteen-month-old Rosalind. The servants lived in a cabin behind the house. On bad days everyone was crowded together in the main area, which also served as a dining room. Mary disliked sharing her housekeeping with Jane Williams. She was constantly annoyed by the crowded conditions. And she hated the savage Italians who came nearly every night to swim, sing and dance on the beach below the little house. Only *Ariel* helped to soothe her spirits—when, as she wrote, "lying down with my head on his knee, I shut my eyes and felt the wind and our swift motion alone."

As the weeks passed, the clouds of discontent gathered. On the second day the cottage was engulfed with storm and surf. The two couples went to the Williamses' room to discuss how to break the news that they had kept from Claire for so long. She walked into the room. The others fell silent. Shelley at last had to tell her. He wrote Byron: "I will not describe her grief to you; you have already suffered too much; and, indeed, the only object of this letter is to convey her last requests to you, which, melancholy as one of them is, I could not refuse to ask, and I am sure you will readily grant. She wishes to see the coffin before it is sent to England, and I have ventured to assure her that this consolation, since she thinks it such, will not be denied her. . . . She also wishes you would give her a portrait of Allegra, and if you have it, a lock of her hair, however small. . . ."

But Claire too wrote Byron, a final, slashing attack ("Murderer . . ."), which also helped to relieve some of her frustration and agony. Byron sent it to Shelley, who wrote in explanation: "I think I need not assure you that, whatever mine or Mary's ideas might have been respecting the system of education you intended to adopt, we sympathize too much in your loss, and appreciate too well your feelings, to have allowed such a letter to be sent to you had we suspected its contents." And he added the information that: "I have succeeded in dissuading Claire from the melancholy design of visiting the coffin at Leghorn." Byron did send a portrait and a lock of Allegra's hair. Gradually Claire recovered from her throbbing grief. But the crowded little house on the bay was too much for her, and she returned to Florence.

As for Byron, he ordered the small coffin sent to England, to be buried at his favorite Harrow church, with a small tablet inscribed:

IN MEMORY OF ALLEGRA
daughter of G. G. Lord Byron
who died at Bagnacavallo
in Italy, April 20th, 1822
Aged five years and three months.
I shall go to her but she shall not return to me.
2nd Samuel, XII, 23

And then he tried to put Allegra out of his mind. In fact, when the men delegated to take the coffin to Leghorn called on Byron in Pisa on their way back to Bagnacavallo, Byron could not face them, and sent them away. It did not enhance his reputation among those at the convent who had always wondered why the little girl's father had not once visited her school, even during her final sickness.

Shelley in the Bay of Lerici and Byron in Pisa continued to write to each other. And, in an odd way—uneasy and unfathomable—Allegra remained a bond between them. Her lingering influence at first took an eerie form. The weather had been stormy at Lerici, with that unceasing wind and punishing sea which stretched everyone's nerves to the breaking point. Through the night of May 4 the surf pounded "like artillery," as Williams described it, and no one slept. The next day Shelley and Williams tried to launch their little boat, were capsized and almost drowned. By Monday the sixth, the wind and sea moderated. By evening the moon was out, and Shelley and Williams walked on the balcony terrace of the house, watching the bay heave under the yellow light of the moon. Shelley complained of being restless. Then, as they paced back and forth, he stopped short and grasped Williams by the arm.

"There it is again," he said. "There!"

It took a while before Shelley could tell Williams what he had seen: the small form of Allegra, rising from the moonlit waves, smiling and beckoning to him as if inviting him to join her.

As the next days and nights passed, more visions plagued Shelley. Walking again on the terrace, this time alone, he was met by a ghostly apparition resembling himself, who said only: "How long do you mean to be content?" Weather and circumstance added to his mood as the late spring wore into summer. A stifling stillness settled on the bay. By day the sea was a coppery mirror and the air shimmered over the rocky beach. By night the thunderstorms rumbled up the coast and exploded across the bay. Mary, pregnant again, worried about a possible miscarriage. Young Percy Shelley and the Williams children were fretful. Even Jane's normal good humor was strained. Williams tried to take her out rowing, but ended up having to fish her from the surf when the boat capsized. Then Mary had the miscarriage she had feared.

"I was so ill," she remembered later, "that for seven hours I lay nearly lifeless, kept from fainting by brandy, vinegar, eau-de-Cologne, etc." Some ice was "brought to our solitude," but still there was no sign of the doctor who had been sent for. Shelley, at his nerves' end from the agony of waiting and doing nothing while his wife slowly weakened from loss of blood, made a desperate decision. Against the advice and the pleas of the others, he forced Mary to sit on the ice. Almost fainting from the torture, Mary complied. The hemorrhaging ceased. Hours later the doctor arrived, and complimented Shelley on saving the patient's life.

Brooding over why fate seemed to plague them, Shelley wrote Trelawny: ". . . should you meet with any scientific person capable of preparing the *Prussic Acid, or essential oil of bitter almonds,* I should regard it as a great kindness if you could procure me a small quantity. . . . I would give any price for this medicine. . . . I need not tell you I have no intention of suicide at present, but I confess it would be a comfort to me to hold in my possession that golden key to the chamber of perpetual rest. . . ."

Then Shelley had his worst nightmare. It was a wild and terrible night in which he dreamed that the house was flooding, and he ran screaming into Mary's room and almost throttled her before he woke. Next day, shaking at the thought of it, Shelley began to wonder if he really was cracking up.

Williams had a further worry. *Ariel* sailed well in light airs, and he recorded that "she fetches whatever she looks at." But in a fresh breeze she heeled dangerously and shipped water. Despite Trelawny's continuing sarcasm, Williams remained

convinced that he knew all he needed to know about seaman-
ship. As for Shelley, he cared for nothing but the sense of being
on the water; Williams tried to teach him the rudiments of
helmsmanship, but Shelley would not put down his book, and
when *Ariel* came about, the boom nearly knocked him into the
sea. Each time, he went back to his reading and composing.
Williams shrugged and took over the helm. A young hand
named Charles Vivian, who had helped sail the vessel down
from Genoa and had been hired by Shelley, was of some help,
but Trelawny suggested that they take on at least one more
capable Genoese hand. To this Williams responded indig-
nantly: ". . . as if we three seasoned salts were not enough to
manage an open boat!" Trelawny forecast dire things for such
a ship with such a landlubberly crew. "If we had been in a
squall today," he said, "with the main sheet jammed, and the
tiller put starboard instead of port, we should have had to
swim for it."

"Not I," replied Shelley, glancing at the pig-iron ballast in
the bilges. "I should have gone down with the rest of the pigs
in the bottom of the boat."

On June 19 Williams hauled the boat out and went to work
on her. A new framework was built up on her stern. Her hull
was cleaned and greased. Most important, more pig-iron ballast
was stowed in her hold to bring her down to her bearings and
make her steadier in a breeze. And while Williams worked,
Shelley planned their first voyage down the coast. He had received news that his old friend Leigh Hunt had arrived in
Italy. Shelley had earlier persuaded Byron to let Hunt come
and move into the Palazzo Lanfranchi, to join them in producing a new literary magazine. Now he proposed that he and
Williams should sail the fifty miles down to Leghorn, where

Hunt and his family would debark. Shelley could go with them to Pisa, only a few miles inland, and help them settle in the apartment Byron had provided in his palazzo. Shelley and Williams would then sail back to Lerici.

The days that followed were wrapped in baking heat. Mary still lay in her sickbed, too weak to be up and about. Shelley and Williams tried sailing in the little *sandolino* but were becalmed in a long, sickening ground swell. One sweltering evening, despite the lack of wind, high seas upset the *sandolino* and Shelley had to be rescued. The sea that night, as if cheated of its victim, mounted the rocks and wall and sent its spray over the roof while Shelley sat in his room and tried to compose his poetic thoughts.

> Rough wind, that moanest loud
> Grief too sad for song;
> Wild wind, when sullen cloud
> Knells all the night long;
> Sad storm, whose tears are vain,
> Bare woods, whose branches strain,
> Deep caves, and dreary main—
> Wail, for the world's wrong![55]

On Monday, July 1, there was a little breeze at dawn. By midday it was blowing strong from the west, the best slant for a sail to Leghorn. Mary had reluctantly agreed to go along when the voyage had first been planned. But now, after her nearly fatal miscarriage, the exertion was out of the question. She called Shelley back three times, pleading with him not to go. She could not tell what it was that made her feel this way; it was simply "an intense presentiment of evil." But Mary had had idle forebodings before. Shelley smiled and promised to return within a few days. As he pulled the *sandolino* aboard *Ariel* and waved to the shore, Mary turned away in tears. By two in the afternoon they had picked up Captain Dan Roberts in Lerici, and *Ariel*'s topsails were disappearing behind the looming ramparts of the old fortress.

Mary and Jane settled back to wait. The days dragged, and the weather did not improve. On Monday evening, July 8, a violent thunderstorm swept over the bay, sending big seas smashing against the house. July 9 was one of those sparkling days that follow storms. By now the women were watching for *Ariel*. The tenth and eleventh followed with no sign of her. A few fishing boats came riding into the bay; they had sailed up from Leghorn, and one captain reported that *Ariel* had left ahead of them. Was it mistaken identity? Mary and Jane had no way of knowing. The watching and waiting continued. The sea churning and hissing at their very door began to get on their nerves. Mary described it later: ". . . prognostics hovered around us. The beauty of the sea seemed unearthly in its excess: the distance we were at from all signs of civilization, the sea at our feet, its murmurs or its roaring for ever in our ears,— all these things led the mind to brood over strange thoughts, and, lifting it from everyday life, caused it to be familiar with the unreal. A sort of spell surrounded us, and each day, as the voyagers did not return, we grew restless and disquieted. . . ."

By Friday Jane Williams could stand the suspense no longer; she was ready to go to Leghorn herself. But Friday was so stormy that no boatman would venture out, so she was forced to wait. That day a letter arrived. It was addressed to Shelley. Mary opened it. As Jane watched, the letter fell from Mary's hands. Jane scooped it up and read the lines: "Pray write to tell us how you got home, for they say that you had bad weather after you sailed on Monday, and we are anxious." It was from Leigh Hunt.

Shelley and Williams had had an easy sail down to Leghorn from Lerici, with *Ariel* footing along at five and six knots, leaving a white curling wake in the blue Mediterranean. At dusk they had passed the purple *pineta* near Pisa, and by early evening the winking harbor lights had signaled to them that they were approaching Leghorn.

In the harbor, riding to her anchor, Byron's yacht *Bolivar* waited for them, her tall masts rocking slowly across the curtain of stars as she moved with the swells. Williams brought *Ariel* to, astern of *Bolivar*, and Vivian, the young hired hand, let the anchor splash over the side. On *Bolivar*'s quarterdeck, silhouetted by the cabin lights, was the lean figure of Trelawny. At his hail Shelley and Williams rowed over. They could not go ashore at this hour, Trelawny explained, because it was 9:30 P.M. The port health office had closed at nine, and they would have to stay aboard ship until they could get their clearance papers. After a short reunion, Shelley and Williams returned to *Ariel* with pillows borrowed from *Bolivar*. They settled down on deck to sleep, lulled by the swish of the waves against the breakwater, the croon of nesting gulls and the slap-slap of the *sandolino* tied astern.

Lord Byron was in an inhospitable mood. The Villa Dupuy, outside Leghorn, which he had rented to be near the cooling sea, had proved a disappointment. It sat on a hill south of the town, and in the cool dusk he and Teresa, who had moved in with him, could look out past the olive trees to the houses of the city and the sea beyond while they played cards (Byron cheated and Teresa pretended not to notice). But in midday the villa's pink walls were found to be thinner than those of the big palazzo farther inland at Pisa, and the hot June and July days were nearly unbearable, even when they hung damp green boughs against the windows and spent the airless afternoon sipping water ices. Trouble followed trouble, to nag at him along with the heat. Byron's cook turned out to be a spy for the stubborn old Count Guiccioli, and on a tip from the cook the count reported to the Vatican that Teresa was living openly at the Villa Dupuy. The Pope, "in order to dissuade the imprudent young woman," suspended her allowance from the count.

On top of everything else, the villa's water gave out. The nearest supply was a mile away. So Byron gave up. He was in the aggravating process of packing up his cumbersome equipage to leave Leghorn and move back to the Palazzo Lanfranchi, when a brawl broke out between Gamba's servants and his. Count Gamba was stabbed; one of the servants threatened Byron's life. And now the Hunts arrived, with six unmannerly children released like wild animals from the confines of their ship. Faced with the prospect of quartering them in Pisa, and realizing that he could not go back on his promise, Byron sulked.

The Hunts were still recovering from a horrendous voyage. Eight months earlier they had confidently set out from London, only to plunge into the worst winter storms of the century; their ship, reeling and lurching before the storm, her decks and even cabins awash, had been forced into shelter at Dartmouth, and they had not been able to sail again until late spring. After such an odyssey they were dismayed and hurt at their inhospitable reception. Somehow Shelley humored Byron, soothed Hunt and restored equanimity. But it took nearly a week for Byron and the Hunts to move up to Pisa and install themselves in the ground floor of the Palazzo Lanfranchi. Williams became impatient with the delay. Shelley too was disturbed by the state of affairs he found in Pisa. The local authorities decided that the unseemly brawl at the villa was the excuse they were looking for to banish the Gambas from Tuscany. Byron was outraged, but decided to follow them. So he fretted about his unwelcome new boarders. Marianne Hunt complained that the Palazzo Lanfranchi was damp and gloomy and the furniture unsuitable. She was pregnant and ill. When she started spitting blood, Pisa's Dr. Vacca came down, examined her and sadly announced that she was the victim of a debilitating, incurable disease and could not live for more than a year (she died in her seventies, thirty-one years after Dr. Vacca). The rioting, unrestrained Hunt children taunted Byron's animals and drove Byron nearly mad. He stationed his bulldog Moretto at the stairs to his floor, with the orders: "Don't let the little cockneys pass!" Moretto took it upon himself to attack the Hunts' pet goat, chewing off its ear. The children cried. Mrs. Hunt whined. Byron swore.

And through the hot, dry nights priests walked the streets praying for rain. An ominous air hung over everything. Shelley decided he had done all he could, and must sail next day.

> The hours are flying
> And joys are dying
> And hope is sighing.
> There is
> Far more to fear
> In the coming year
> Than desire can bear
> In this.[56]

Shelley and Hunt went for a walk. They toured Pisa's cathedral and Campo Santo, studied the frescoes of Benozzo

Gozzoli and the paintings of Andrea del Sarto. They strolled past the Leaning Tower. As they walked back along the Arno, the night was bright with fireflies. They talked of Plato. They laughed at a joke Hunt had brought from London. He had also brought a copy of Keats's last volume of poems. Shelley asked to borrow it, promising to send it back as soon as he had returned to Lerici. The two friends parted affectionately, after Hunt had asked Shelley to promise that he would not sail next day if the weather was stormy; he was worried about the thunderstorms that had been threatening the coast. Shelley promised. Hunt paused at the steps of the palazzo to watch his friend climb into the chaise and disappear down the curving street along the Arno. Then he went in and closed the big iron-bound door.

Five nights later, at midnight, the same big door boomed with frantic pounding. Hunt had gone to bed. Byron was up, and Teresa was with him. As Teresa came smiling forward to greet her visitor, she stopped dead at the sight of the disheveled figure stumbling up the wide staircase and the pallid face and wild eyes of Mary Shelley, who was gasping: "Where is he? Where is he? Where *is* he?"

Byron said later: "Light seemed to emanate from her features. . . . I never saw such a scene nor wish to see another." He could only send Mary on to Leghorn. The carriage clattered into Leghorn at two in the morning, stopping in front of the best inn. But neither Trelawny nor Captain Roberts was there. Exhausted by the trip, Mary Shelley and Jane Williams asked for a room, where they stretched out on the beds, still dressed, and tried to sleep. But sleep would not come, and with the first glimmerings of dawn they were on their way to the next inn, where they located Roberts.

Both Trelawny and Roberts had been in Leghorn harbor on

July 8, when *Ariel* had sailed. Now, in his blunt, straightforward fashion, Roberts told Mary and Jane what had happened so far as he knew.

Shelley had borrowed £50 from Byron and had done some last-minute shopping—some household items, a few bottles of beer, a hamper of wine for his friend the harbor master at Lerici—and it was noon by the time he walked out to the long stone pier. There had been thunderstorms in the morning. The weather seemed to have cleared, but Captain Roberts still did not like the look of it; the breathless heat followed by sporadic thunderstorms could be a weather breeder. Shelley paused. But Williams was insistent; the breeze was freshening from the west. At this rate, he argued, they could be home by seven. Shelley did not relish the prospect of sitting another day in Leghorn any more than Williams did. He decided to go.

Trelawny went aboard *Bolivar* to accompany *Ariel* out of the harbor. Shelley and Williams made ready to sail. There was a great thrumming of canvas as the sails went up, then the clank of the hoisted anchor chains and the sudden silence of the sails as they filled and the two ships heeled over and headed out of the harbor.

But at the end of the mole they were met by the guard boat and signaled to halt. With more rattling of spars and canvas, *Ariel* and *Bolivar* came up into the wind. The health officers demanded clearance papers. Shelley and Williams had theirs, but Trelawny had none. The officers made Trelawny turn back. As he put *Bolivar*'s helm over, he saw Shelley wave to him. *Ariel* sailed swiftly out past the mole.

Standing on *Bolivar*'s quarterdeck, Trelawny watched *Ariel* through his glass. As the wind freshened more, he estimated her speed at seven knots. At his side the Genovese mate of *Bolivar* muttered something about the blackness of the sky and the foolishness of going to sea in such weather with topsails set. Trelawny swung his glass across the horizon. Now he could see it coming.

The long, thin sea haze in front of a storm was sweeping toward the shore. *Ariel* was out there in its path, already setting her course up the coast for Lerici and still flying her topsails. With that guard in the way at the harbor entrance, there was nothing Trelawny could do but wait until the storm passed, and hope they could weather it. He angrily snapped his glass shut and went below.

Captain Roberts watched as the haze continued to roll in. The sky darkened, then turned a yellowish brown. The sea's inshore green and offshore blue gradually changed to dark blue, to purple, and to oily black. The fog became more like smoke as it took on the dark tints of the water and the sky. It danced in swirls and eddies and the black sea broke out with innumerable little crests of white, with the first faint stirrings of the approaching winds. In the harbor the still water looked like a sheet of lead. The first fat drops of rain plopped onto the surface and rebounded. One by one the fishermen came racing into shelter.

Roberts walked out the long pier to the lighthouse and climbed to the tower. Dimly through the upper layers of the low-lying haze he thought he could make out *Ariel*. They seemed to be taking in her topsails as she bucked through the rising waves. Then the last of the blackening haze swept in and enveloped her like the curtain of eternity.

The storm, Trelawny later recalled, lasted only twenty minutes. As he came on deck, the fishermen who had raced into the harbor were putting out double anchor lines. The sudden, screaming winds drowned out even the rattle of anchor chains and the shouts of sailors. Rain lashed the decks and waves washed over the mole. The storm's full violence was spent in

those few minutes; but through the evening there followed a
succession of gusty showers, and lightning stabbed the darkness
all along the coast.

> 'Tis the terror of tempest. The rags of the sail
> Are flickering in ribbons within the fierce gale:
> From the stark night of vapours the dim rain
>   is driven,
> And when lightning is loosed, like a deluge
>   from Heaven,
> She sees the black trunks of the waterspouts spin
> And bend, as if Heaven was ruining in,
> Which they seemed to sustain with their terrible mass
> As if ocean had sank from beneath them: they pass
> To their graves in the deep with an earthquake of sound,
> And the waves and the thunders, made silent around,
> Leave the wind to its echo. The vessel, now tossed
> Through the low-trailing rack of the tempest, is lost
> In the skirts of the thunder-cloud: now down the sweep
> Of the wind-cloven wave to the chasm of the deep
> It sinks, and the walls of the watery vale
> Whose depths of dread calm are unmoved by the gale,
> Dim mirrors of ruin hang gleaming about;
> While the surf, like a chaos of stars, like a rout
> Of death-flames, like whirlpools of fire-flowing iron
> With splendour and terror the black ship environ,
> Or like sulphur-flakes hurled from a mine of pale fire
> In fountains spout o'er it. In many a spire
> The pyramid-billows with white points of brine
> In the cope of the lightning inconstantly shine,
> As piercing the sky from the floor of the sea.
> The great ship seems splitting! it cracks as a tree,
> While an earthquake is splintering its root, ere the blast
> Of the whirlwind that stripped it of branches has passed.
> The intense thunder-balls which are raining from Heaven

Have shattered its mast, and it stands black and riven.
The chinks suck destruction. The heavy dead hulk
On the living sea rolls an inanimate bulk,
Like a corpse on the clay which is hungering to fold
Its corruption around it. . . .[57]

Next morning Trelawny searched the horizon for a sign of *Ariel*, and questioned returning fishermen, without success. Then he went to Pisa to tell Byron.

The handsome, self-confident face paled. Byron's lip quivered and his voice faltered. First Allegra; now Shelley. He questioned Trelawny. How far out had they sailed? Could they have run in somewhere? What had Trelawny done to search farther north? He agreed with Trelawny's plan: send *Bolivar* along the shore, and dispatch a courier to the seacoast towns as far north as Nice. Trelawny also posted a reward, and then rode north himself to see what he could find.

At the little fishing town of Viareggio, about halfway between Leghorn and Lerici, he found what he had feared: one of the Italians told him that a punt, a water keg and some bottles had washed onto the beach. Trelawny went to look at them. Immediately he recognized the *sandolino* and the water keg from *Ariel*.

When the lamp is shattered
The light in the dust lies dead—
When the cloud is scattered
The rainbow's glory is shed.
When the lute is broken,
Sweet tones are remembered not;
When the lips have spoken,
Loved accents are soon forgot.

As music and splendour
Survive not the lamp and the lute,
   The heart's echoes render
No song when the spirit is mute:
   No song but sad dirges,
Like the wind through a ruined cell,
   Or the mournful surges
That ring the dead seaman's knell. . . .[58]

Here Mary and Jane, returning from their fruitless race to Pisa and Leghorn, caught up with Trelawny. He accompanied them home. Trying to keep hope alive, he told them of similar cases in which vessels had been blown far to sea and had found refuge in some distant harbor. . . . Perhaps *Ariel* had been driven to Corsica, or farther up the coast, even to Nice. . . . He had sent a courier that far north because there was still the chance . . . *Ariel* had sailed safely through some heavy weather on her way to Lerici from Genoa; she could have weathered this storm with a little luck. . . . But he knew the weight of the evidence. As he rowed the women across the bay to the little house, even in the dusk he could read Mary's thoughts in her face when she looked out past the harbor to the open sea. Mary wrote later: "A voice from within me seemed to cry aloud: 'that is his grave.' "[59]

And all that hot, sticky night, through the open windows came the bouncing lights of bonfires and the wild songs of the Italians who were celebrating a *festa,* unmindful of the lonely, voiceless grief in the house above the beach.

Trelawny stayed six days, helping with what he could, consoling as much as he could, arguing that it was too soon to give up hope. By the time he left Lerici, Mary had begun to hope against hope, though Jane seemed beyond consolation.

Then, back in Leghorn, Trelawny learned the worst. Two bodies had washed up on the shore, one at Viareggio and one at Migliarino. He rode up to make sure. At Migliarino, near the mouth of the Serchio, where Shelley and Williams had sailed so recently, Trelawny found a body partly consumed by fish. It was identifiable by the black silk handkerchief with the initials EEW. One of Williams' boots was off and his shirt was pulled partly over his head, as if he had been stripping to swim for it. The other body, six miles up the beach, was mutilated too. But the familiar double-breasted jacket, the nankeen trousers, the boots and the white silk socks told who it was. And in one pocket, doubled back as if hastily thrust away, was the volume of Keats's poems which Leigh Hunt had lent Shelley on that warm, calm night when they had walked home through the fireflies along the Arno.

Trelawny had the bodies buried temporarily above the tide line and then raced for Lerici; he wanted the women to learn this final news as softly as he could break it to them, though he had no idea how he would tell them. At Lerici he left his horse in the village and walked quickly along the path to the lonely house. Before entering the house he stopped a moment to steel himself for the ordeal. Looking out on the quiet bay, he thought back to the evenings he had enjoyed when he had visited the house on the beach—of Jane's guitar and Shelley's high-pitched laugh and "the general *buona notte* of all the joyous party."

Then, from behind him, came a scream.

The nurse, Caterina, had chanced upon him; immediately she knew what he had come to say. Trelawny climbed to the main room. Looking at Mary and Jane, he could not bring himself to speak. Looking at him, they did not need to be told.

"Mrs. Shelley's large, grey eyes were fixed on my face," Trelawny wrote later. "I turned away."

Mary finally broke the silence. In a low voice, taut with the effort of self-control, she asked: "Is there no hope?"

Still Trelawny could not speak. Head bowed, he left the house and walked back down the twisting path to Lerici.

A third body, little more than a skeleton but presumed to be Charles Vivian, was found and buried on the beach nearby. But Mary wanted Shelley buried in Rome near their son, and Jane wanted Williams buried home in England. These arrangements could not be made, however, because of Italy's complicated quarantine laws. Trelawny got in touch with the British chargé d'affaires in Florence, Edward Dawkins, and talked him into obtaining special permission for the bodies to be cremated; then the ashes could be shipped out of the principality. So on August 15, 1822, Trelawny, Byron, Hunt and a quarantine officer and crew, equipped with spades, mattocks, long-handled tongs, nippers and hooks—"so fashioned as to do their work without coming into personal contact with things that might be infectious"—assembled on the beach at Migliarino, where Williams' body had been temporarily buried.

The spot was marked by a fence running down the beach into the sea, forming the boundary between Tuscany and Lucca. Trelawny had had a "furnace" built at Leghorn—a black iron frame "five feet long, two broad, with a rim around it, supported by legs two feet high . . . such things as were said to be used by Shelley's much-loved Hellenes on their funeral pyres." He erected it on the sand, while the soldiers gathered driftwood and dug up Williams' remains. Trelawny described what they found: "It was a humbling and loathesome sight, deprived of hands, one leg, and the remaining leg deprived of the foot—the scalp was torn from the head, and the flesh separated from the face, the eyes out, and all this mutilation not by time the destroyer—but fish-eaten—it was in the worst state of putrefaction—a livid mass of shapeless flesh."

Byron watched. At the sight of the moldering corpse falling to pieces as it was lifted, he was appalled. "Are we all to resemble that?" he asked. "Is that a human body? Why it might be the carcase of a sheep, for all I can see." He pointed to Williams' black handkerchief. "An old rag retains its form longer than a dead body. . . . This is a satire on our pride and folly." He mumbled on as if to himself: "Don't repeat this with me. Let my carcase rot where it falls."

The funeral pyre burned high. When it subsided, Trelawny approached the flames and tossed salt and frankincense into the fire and poured wine and oil on the body. "The Greek oration was omitted," he wrote later, "for we had lost our Hellenic bard." Byron began to feel ill. He stripped, waded into the water and swam far out. Trelawny followed him, noticed how sick he was and persuaded him to come back. As the fire burned low, Trelawny had the furnace lifted with long poles and dipped sizzling into the sea to cool. He then gathered the ashes and fragments of bone and put them into an oaken box with a brass plaque. The box was placed in the back of Byron's carriage, and Byron and Hunt rode back to Pisa.

Next day, August 16, they all assembled again, five miles farther up the coast. The spot was a few hundred yards from the main square of Viareggio. By the time Byron's carriage had arrived and Trelawny had gathered his helpers again, a small group of villagers had assembled to watch. They stood at a distance, respectful and silent, awed by this pagan ceremony that was forbidden by their faith.

The day was hot and breathless. The sun made heat waves dance above the sand. The sea hissed along the shore, a long, yellow ribbon rimming the Mediterranean's blue. Back of the people on the shore stood a row of stunted pines, twisted by the force of the storms, and behind the pines rose the towering Apennines, crowned by the white of Carrara marble.

> There is a pleasure in the pathless woods,
> There is a rapture on the lonely shore,
> There is society, where none intrudes,
> By the deep Sea, and Music in its roar:
> I love not Man the less, but Nature more,
> From these our interviews, in which I steal
> From all I may be, or have been before,
> To mingle with the Universe, and feel
> What I can ne'er express—yet can not all conceal.[60]

Shelley's grave was marked by three white stakes in the sand. But they were so far apart that the digging went on for nearly an hour. Then there was the thud of a mattock on a bone. The body was quickly uncovered. It was in better condition than Williams' had been, though the lime thrown into the grave had stained the flesh a dark indigo. Trelawny had his furnace ready, and once again the fire burned brightly.

Byron, watching, stood silent and contemplative. Hunt stayed in the carriage, as he explained, "now looking on, now drawing back, with feelings that were not to be witnessed." Trelawny had brought oil, salt and wine, and, he wrote, "more wine was poured over Shelley's dead body than he had consumed during his life." The quivering flames turned yellow, orange and blue. The corpse fell open. Trelawny reported: "The frontal bone of the skull, where it had been struck with the mattock, fell off; and as the back of the head rested on the red-hot bottom bars of the furnace, the brains literally seethed, bubbled and boiled as in a cauldron, for a very long time." And over the fire a solitary seagull whirled and circled, throughout the afternoon.

Again Byron could not stand it. Again he retreated to the sea. Swimming three miles out to where *Bolivar* was anchored, he stayed in the water until he felt better. On the beach the helpers moved into the shade and away from the white-hot furnace. Then Trelawny noticed an extraordinary thing about his friend's corpse.

Nearly all of Shelley's remains had by now been reduced to gray ash—all except the heart. Probably gorged with blood, the heart refused to burn. Looking around and noting that he was not being watched at the moment, Trelawny reached quickly into the fire and snatched out the heart, burning his hand in the process. He slipped Shelley's heart into his pocket and waited for the fire to burn down.[61]

Byron staggered out of the water, trembling from the ordeal. Saying scarcely a word, he dressed and climbed into his carriage, where Leigh Hunt waited. That evening on the way home Byron and Hunt drank too much, and Byron became hysterical. For days he was severely ill. Never after that day was he completely well.

Trelawny gathered up the ashes of Shelley, placed them in another box and sent them out to *Bolivar*, which would take them to Leghorn. From there the remains of Percy Shelley would be taken to Rome's Protestant Cemetery, to be buried alongside his son. Edward Williams' ashes would later go to England, accompanied by his widow, Jane. And in Pisa, where she had gone to put Lerici forever behind her, Mary Shelley wrote: "They are gone to the desolate sea coast to perform the last offices to their earthly remains. . . . His rest shall be at

Rome, beside my child, where one day I also shall join them.
. . . They are now about that fearful office, and I live!"

And Byron, still trying to recover from the experience, wrote
Tom Moore: "You will have heard by this time that Shelley
and another gentleman (Captain Williams) were drowned.
. . . There is thus another man gone about whom the world
was ill-naturedly, and ignorantly, and brutally mistaken. It
will perhaps do him justice *now*, when he can be no better
for it."

In Rome came an ironic denouement. Trelawny sent
Shelley's ashes to Joseph Severn, the Englishman who had
come to Italy as Keats's companion and had stayed on after
Keats's death. As a last favor to Shelley, Severn agreed to
oversee the burial in Rome's Protestant Cemetery. Some weeks
later Severn wrote Trelawny of a surprising discovery. There
was no room beside the grave of William Shelley, so Severn
obtained permission to have William's body moved to a new
site and reburied alongside the ashes of his father. But, Severn
wrote, "on opening the grave, we discovered a skeleton 5½
feet." The bones of little William Shelley were not there. "To
search further we dare not," continued Severn, "for it was in
the presence of many *respectful* but wondering Italians."
Sensing the restlessness of the watching crowd, Severn realized
that "it would have been a doubtful and horrible thing to
disturb any more stranger's graves in a foreign land. So we
proceeded very respectfully to deposit poor Shelley's ashes
alone."

Puzzled and troubled, Trelawny went to Rome. There in
the tree-shaded Protestant Cemetery was the headstone of
William. It still stood over the ground where only the skeleton
of a full-grown man had been found. Trelawny left it as it was,

but he disliked the spot chosen for his friend Shelley. So he had the ashes disinterred and buried on a slope next to the old Roman wall. At his direction a flat marble slab was placed over the grave. It read:

PERCY BYSSHE SHELLEY
Cor Cordium
Natus IV Aug. MDCCXCII
Obit VIII Jul. MDCCCXXII
"Nothing of him that doth fade,
But doth suffer a sea-change
Into something rich and strange"

Trelawny planted six young cypress trees and four laurels around the spot. He then had another slab placed beside Shelley's, a plain marble one that would wait for him.

[XI]

With Shelley gone, the soul went out of the Pisan Circle. Mary refused to return to the cottage on the bay, even to close the place up. In Pisa she sat and brooded about the past months, trying to recover but unable to. Finally she decided that even Pisa was too full of memories, and prepared to move on, to Genoa and perhaps finally back to England.

Byron fretted and fussed about the big palazzo, nearly as unhappy and listless as Mary. The Gambas had been notified that they must move on again, both because of the local officials' concern over Count Gamba's revolutionary reputation and because of their assumption that this was the best way to rid the area of Byron as well. For the time being, and for want of any other attraction, Byron stayed in Pisa. He and the Hunts annoyed each other more and more. The Hunt children still ran wild, nearly driving Byron out of his mind. They were, he said, "dirtier and more mischievous than Yahoos. What they can't destroy with their filth they will with their fingers—six little blackguards." In her journal, Mrs. Hunt wrote: "Can anything be more absurd than a peer of the realm—and a *poet* —making such a fuss about three or four children disfiguring the walls of a few rooms? The very children would blush for him."

Partly out of defensiveness, Mrs. Hunt maintained her prior pose of gentility, making no pretense of accepting the fallen woman who was Byron's mistress, sneering at Byron's nocturnal writing habits and complaining querulously about everything around her. Even on the few occasions when Byron attempted to make conversation, Marianne Hunt turned him away with her sarcastic tongue. Directing the talk to the Pisan Circle's favorite scapegoat—Trelawny—Byron said one day: "What do you think, Mrs. Hunt, Trelawny has been speaking against my morals. What do you think of that?" Even from Shelley he could have expected a laughing comment on who should cast the first stone. But Mrs. Hunt's reply was a sniff and: "It is the first time that I ever heard of them." Byron could only walk off in silence, to retire to his study, his gin and water and the next cantos of *Don Juan*.

And when he rose for breakfast next day, sometime after noon, his indolent, patronizing attitude angered Leigh Hunt even more. The great man would announce his rising by singing loud arias from Rossini in his bath, then descend to the garden just outside the window where Hunt was, or pretended to be, hard at work on an article for their joint magazine, *The Liberal*. "Leontius!" Byron would shout; this would never fail to remind Hunt that it had been Shelley's affectionate and playful name for him. Grudgingly Hunt would go out into the garden, only to wince as Teresa joined them, "with her sleek tresses," gleaming from her bath. This open dalliance always offended Hunt's moral sensibilities, and he suspected Byron of knowing how much it annoyed Hunt to parade his mistress before him. Hunt stood it as long as he could, and finally moved out, crowding the family into a few rooms at a local inn. Byron was so pleased to be rid of them that he sent them eighty crowns, by his secretary. Hunt turned to Mary Shelley, who agreed to take them in with her when she moved to Genoa.

Byron too had had enough of Pisa. The effects of the scene on the beach at Viareggio would not dissipate. He lost weight. He drank more than he had before. He gave up his daily horseback rides, unable to enjoy the exercise any longer. Nor was he interested in going down to Leghorn to sail aboard his yacht. Since Shelley's drowning, he said, he had "taken a disgust to sailing."

Teresa noticed the "shade of melancholy diffused over Lord Byron's face," and she worried about it. But she was pleased to see how Byron's expression changed on one particular day. It was September 15, and they were sitting in the garden of the Palazzo Lanfranchi when a servant announced the unexpected arrival of Hobhouse. Byron's melancholy "gave instant place to the liveliest joy," Teresa recalled; "but it was so great, that it almost deprived him of strength." As Byron greeted the companion he had not seen in four years, his cheeks turned pale and tears came to his eyes. "His emotion was so great," Teresa wrote, "that he was forced to sit down."

But the two old friends had been parted so long that a cool formality came between them for a while. They rode together, were caught in a thunderstorm and took refuge in a cottage; next day they rode out again. And that night after dinner they settled back over the brandy and talked as they always had before. Byron spoke of England, asking questions and showing how well he had kept up with events at what he still thought of as home; he even talked of returning next spring, if only for a visit. Hobhouse stayed for five days, and on the last night they sat up until 2 A.M., early for Byron but late for Hobhouse, who had to be on the road next day. Their talk ranged over the whole world, and settled on Greece.

> The dead have been awakened—shall I sleep?
> The World's at war with tyrants—shall I crouch?
> The harvest's ripe—and shall I pause to reap?
> I slumber not; the thorn is in my Couch;
> Each day a trumpet soundeth in mine ear,
> Its echo in my heart—[62]

More and more Byron had been thinking of Greece. Trelawny wrote of a conversation with Byron in which "his thoughts veered round to his early love, the Isles of Greece, and the revolution in that country—for before that time he never dreamt of donning the warrior's plume, though the peace-loving Shelley had suggested and I urged it."

> The Isles of Greece, the Isles of Greece!
> Where burning Sappho loved and sung,
> Where grew the arts of War and Peace,
> Where Delos rose, and Phoebus sprung!
> Eternal summer gilds them yet,
> But all, except their Sun, is set.
>
> The Scian and the Teian muse,
> The Hero's harp, the Lover's lute,
> Have found the fame your shores refuse:
> Their place of birth alone is mute
> To sounds which echo further west
> Than your Sires' "Islands of the Blest."

> The mountains look on Marathon—
> And Marathon looks on the sea;
> And musing there an hour alone,
>   I dreamed that Greece might still be free;
> For standing on the Persians' grave,
> I could not deem myself a slave. . . .
>
> Must *we* but weep o'er days more blest?
> Must *we* but blush? Our fathers bled.
> Earth! render back from out thy breast
> A remnant of our Spartan dead!
> Of the three hundred grant but three,
> To make a new Thermopylae! [63]

The preparations for any such expedition would take time. Meanwhile Byron felt that he had to get out of Pisa. Genoa seemed the place. Mary Shelley was in Genoa, and she had agreed to take in the Hunts; so Byron would not really be deserting his responsibility if he found a villa nearby and continued to help put out *The Liberal*. Genoa might be more comfortable than Pisa in the coming winter, protected as it was by the mountains rising steeply between the city and the wintry winds of northern Europe. Genoa was a *new* place; it had none of the associations of Ravenna with Allegra or Pisa with Shelley. And Genoa was a major port; it could serve as a likely starting place for a voyage to Greece.

Even the move to Genoa was a major logistical exercise. After a pandemonium of packing, Byron finally rolled away in his Napoleonic carriage, followed by two other carriages carrying some of his massive collection of furniture, his menagerie and other personal effects. The remainder was taken to Leghorn, to be shipped aboard *Bolivar* (to Trelawny's disgust that she should be reduced to a freighter). The Gambas followed Byron in their carriage. The Hunts followed in theirs. Everyone, including Trelawny aboard *Bolivar*, met in Lerici, a logical stopover before starting the tedious climb through the Apennines. There Trelawny took Hunt around to see Shelley's cottage.

It was as if Mary and Jane—and Shelley and Williams—had left only temporarily. There was dust on the furniture, and the pounding sea had broken a window or two. But the two men almost expected to find Shelley on the upper porch looking out across the bay. A sense of Shelley pervaded the house. As Hunt described it, they "paced over its empty rooms and neglected garden. The sea fawned upon the shore, as though it could do no harm."

At Lerici, Byron, still feeling oddly out of sorts, swam too far out to sea and became so sick that he spent four days in agony "in the worst inn's worst room" before he was able to continue the journey. When he finally got to sleep on the fourth night, he was so exhausted that he did not awake despite an earthquake that sent nearly everyone else screaming into the streets. Realizing that Byron still had not recovered from the traumatic cremation ceremony on the beach, Trelawny urged him to continue by sea instead of attempting the climb through the mountains. Off the flotilla went, one ship carrying Byron and the Gambas, one carrying the Hunts, and Trelawny continuing aboard *Bolivar*.

They put in at Sestri, the next village up the coast. Already the sea had made Byron feel a little better. But Mrs. Hunt enjoyed neither the voyage nor the rough landing, when "a dozen odiously dirty men with beards unshaven and long shaggy hair, up to the middle in water, began fighting for me and Mr. H. to carry us through the water." Her composure was at length restored. The carriages were put ashore. The furniture sailed on up the coast. Byron, the Gambas and the

Hunts rode the rest of the steep, winding trail over the mountains—"great doughy billows, like so much pudding or petrified mud," Hunt called them; but Mrs. Hunt shut her eyes "as the carriage went within a yard or not so much of some frightful precipice." At last they rolled into Genoa and up the steep hill to the area called Albaro, back of the city.

Teresa's brother Pietro had found them an impressive villa, the Casa Saluzzo, high on a hill overlooking Genoa and the sea. Byron settled down in one apartment and the Gambas in another. There was plenty of space; the villa contained forty rooms. One mile down the hill, the Hunts moved into Mary Shelley's Casa Negrotto. Byron tried to get back to concentrated work on *Don Juan*. He continued to support the Hunts, despite the fact that the first issue of *The Liberal* was a flop in London. He sent some stanzas of his poetry to Mary Shelley to transcribe, since she needed the money. And after the reunion Mary noted in her diary that the old magic had not gone completely: "I do not think that any person's voice has the same power of awakening melancholy in me. . . . I listen with an unspeakable melancholy that yet is not all pain." Byron's voice reminded her of Shelley, but there was that about Byron himself that still stirred her too.

Mary had no such effect on Byron. To his mind she was petty, talkative and a perpetual whiner. It seemed to him that she was forever complaining about something; it was almost as if God had gone out of His way to provide Mary Shelley with a truly magnificent grief in which she could luxuriate for the rest of her days. Byron was gentlemanly enough in Mary's presence, and she continued to see in him the romantic image of days gone past, until the day Leigh Hunt blurted out the truth.

Hunt had accused Byron of not helping Mary enough

financially, and had threatened to turn to Trelawny if Byron would not give her more money. Byron's angry reply was that he should go to Trelawny by all means, no doubt adding some of his less flattering opinions of the entire assemblage in the Casa Negrotto. Hunt, exasperated as he often was, tactlessly went to Mary to recount the episode, which ended, Hunt reported, with Byron's statement that he would give Mary more money but would be glad never to see her again.

Mary was shocked and hurt. Teresa heard of it and tried to recover the situation. She wrote a note to Mary that reflected her own growing concern: "Dio buono! I don't know what to say to you, my dear, for I can't do anything. I feel that I can be of little use, that L.B. will not take advice, that he is very much irritated. . . . I venture to offer, if I can do so in any way, to be of help to you. If only my usefulness and my circumstances were as strong as my good will!"

Mary's answer showed how much she had been hurt and how she had retired behind her prim defenses: "Dear Contessina . . . it is a great relief to me to find that the poison has not reached you, too. I thank you for your kind offer, but if I am to understand that you wish to be a peace-maker between me and Lord Byron, you will not succeed. I felt no repugnance at the idea of receiving obligations and kindnesses from a friend. . . . But now all that is over—a man who does not esteem me cannot be my benefactor. . . ."

In such bitterness, the relationship between Byron and Mary Shelley came to an end. He kept to his villa and she to hers. They never saw each other, alive, again.

In the high-ceilinged, drafty, stone-floored Casa Saluzzo the cold became almost unbearable as autumn storms off the Mediterranean smashed against the hillside. The winter was the worst in years, with icy gales sweeping over the Apennines and down onto Genoa. Byron shivered and still tried to concentrate on *Don Juan*. He suffered from chilblains and a nagging inflammation of the face. Things were even worse in the Casa Negrotto. The only fireplace was in the room the Hunts used for their parlor. Hunt tried not to mind when everyone crowded around the fireplace on the howling winter days, but Mary noted with self-pity that it was "the annihilation of study, and even of pleasure to a great degree. For after all Hunt does not like me; it is both our faults, and I do not blame him, but so it is. I rise at 9, breakfast, work, read, and if I can at all endure the cold, copy my Shelley's MSS in my room, and if possible walk before dinner. After that I work, read Greek etc. till 10, when Hunt and Marianne go to bed. Then I am alone. . . ."

The Hunts continued to infuriate Byron. He and Hunt went on exchanging notes, overtly on the business of *The Liberal* but covertly exchanging insults and fencing with double meanings. "I'll trouble you for another cool hundred," wrote Hunt with mock superciliousness when out of cash, knowing full well how parsimonious Byron had become recently. When Byron addressed him as "Dear Leigh," Hunt replied with feigned delight that the great man should be so informal and friendly. When Byron wrote a stiff note and Hunt replied with a "Dear Lord Byron," Byron countered with a sarcastic "Dear Lord Hunt." Mrs. Hunt complained: "What a pity it is that the good actions of *noblemen* are not done in a *noble manner!*" At the same time Byron complained in a letter to his publisher: "I cannot describe to you the despairing sensation of trying to do something for a man who seems incapable of doing anything for himself." Through the fall and winter the two men nagged at each other continually.

In Trelawny's phrase: ". . . without Shelley, we all degenerated apace." Byron lost interest in *The Liberal*, and after four issues it collapsed. He lost interest in riding, in swimming, in his early-morning writing sessions. He even, finally, lost interest in Teresa.

She had seen it coming, but she had refused to face it. Now, at the Casa Saluzzo, the Gambas and Byron kept to their separate apartments. Byron dined alone, and Teresa joined him only when he asked her. They met in the garden in the afternoons. She came to him at night less and less frequently. When her younger sister Carolina died of consumption in Ravenna, Byron only sent Teresa a note, though they were in the same house. She knew why: he could not stand her tears. But still she realized how distant he had become. It did not help to have her father itching to go back to Ravenna. He had petitioned for permission to return home, and to his delight it had been granted. Hardest of all for Teresa to take was the excitement of her brother Pietro, whom Byron had promised to take to Greece. Pietro could hardly wait to go.

On one spring afternoon Byron and Teresa sat in the garden looking out on the sails in the harbor. Byron suddenly said: "I have not even got a portrait of you which is like you. A miniaturist has been recommended to me; will you sit to him for me?" So he *was* going away, and he wanted a memento to take along. No doubt Byron was startled at Teresa's response, which was to break into tears and run from the garden.

It was now a matter of time. There were less painful afternoons in the garden, and still the good-bye was unspoken. But the realization was undeniable. Weeks went by before the final decision was made. Friends came and went. A Lady Blessington arrived from London, full of gossip about home.

Byron was entranced with her, more because of what she had to tell him about England than because of herself; but both she and, more important, Teresa, took it for infatuation. Lady Blessington talked her husband into buying *Bolivar*. She also made note of Byron and his way of life and later recorded it all in an intimate, revealing—and gossipy—book. When she left, Byron's eyes filled with tears as he said good-bye. He knew now that he was also saying good-bye to his plans to return to England.

Trelawny had laid up *Bolivar*, paid off the crew and gone off on horseback "to take a cruise inland." At his hotel in Rome, in June, he found a letter waiting for him: "Pray come, for I am at last determined to go to Greece. . . . I am serious, and did not write before, as I might have given you a journey for nothing; they all say I can be of use in Greece. I do not know how, nor do they; but at all events let us go. . . ."

But first Trelawny went back again to Lerici, for a last look. He checked into an inn and then walked down the narrow, twisting path along the rocky shore. Out on the bay the fishermen were drifting in from the sea, their sails catching the sunset. The waves lapped at the rocks below. Trelawny walked a few hundred yards, rounded the high promontory and stopped for a moment. The house still huddled at the water's edge, its base in the bay, dwarfed by the wooded hill rising steeply behind it.

Trelawny walked on. As he drew closer he could see that the house was still deserted, as it had been when he had brought Hunt here to see it. Now the door hung open. All the windows along the ground floor were smashed. Trelawny walked in and waited a moment for his eyes to adjust to the gloom. On the dirt floor lay the canvas-bottomed skiff that Shelley and

Williams had sailed on the Serchio. The oars and mast were broken, no doubt by marauding boys. The ladder-like stairs were still there. Trelawny climbed to the open center room above.

Its walls were splotchier, but otherwise everything seemed the same. He walked over to one of the doors opening onto the terrace, looked out across the darkening blue toward the line of islands and the sea, and let the quiet scene call up his memories of beauty and companionship, of creation and tragedy.

It was nearly dark as he turned away from the door and crept down the trembling steps. In the growing darkness he could just make out the shadowy shape of Shelley's skiff. Then, with this stage of his life at an end, he walked back along the path to Lerici, to leave in the morning and ride to Genoa to rejoin Byron.

In Genoa things were going with a rush. Byron had been communicating with various "committees" supporting the Greek patriots. Ever since the Greeks had risen against their Turkish masters, and had been savagely counterattacked by the Turks, Greek exiles and sympathetic Britons had rallied to their cause. Shelley had written in his preface to *Hellas:* "We are all Greeks. Our laws, our literature, our religion, our arts have their root in Greece." Byron had known this before Shelley had; Byron had agreed with Shelley; now he felt it as keenly as Shelley ever had, perhaps partly because of Shelley.

Almost surely Shelley would have played a major part in the plans now afoot. Captain Roberts set out to locate a vessel for the voyage. He found the brig *Hercules,* a commodious craft which Trelawny lost no time in characterizing scornfully as a tub. But she satisfied Byron. Supplies were gathered. A crew, even including a doctor, was enlisted, Byron at last prepared to bring his Italian epoch to an end.

Teresa still could not let herself admit it. She knew Byron well enough to realize that there would be no dramatic parting, no final happy hours, no offer to take her along. She knew that it would do her no good to protest, and in fact would only make matters worse. Yet, when the time came, she could not help herself. She cried. She pleaded. She asked to be taken along, protesting that no hardship was too great to keep her from her lover's side. All this served only to antagonize Byron more, as she had known it would. But she simply was unable to accept the inevitable.

The result was an anticlimactic, bitter end. Byron tried to get her brother to break the news of the decision. He avoided Teresa more and more as the time grew short. At last, on the day of his sailing—he had deliberately chosen July 13—they had their ultimate parting. At her urging he did promise to return—one day, when Greece was independent. No doubt Teresa had told herself that this once she would not cry or plead. But she watched through tears as Byron went limping away from her for the last time.

Mary Shelley knew how Teresa felt. She came to comfort her, and the two ladies stood alone on the terrace on the hill, watching the brig move slowly out of the harbor. Next morning Teresa was in a carriage with her father, going home to Ravenna. Climbing the twisting road through the mountains, she began to feel physically ill. Her father had to order the coachman to stop. Teresa climbed out and sat on a rock beside the road. As her faintness diminished, she took her diary out of her purse and wrote: "I have promised more than I can perform, and you have asked of me what is beyond my strength. . . . I feel as if I were dying, Byron, have pity on me. . . ."

The brig was beset by calms and contrary winds—the thirteenth proved unlucky after all—and had to return to port. Byron was about to return to the Casa Saluzzo, but when he learned that Teresa had gone, he instead went with Trelawny and Pietro Gamba to nearby Sestri, where they sat in the garden eating cheese and fruit and waiting for a wind. None came, and they returned on board *Hercules* for the night. Next day the wind came on so strong that as soon as they were out of the harbor the horses below panicked and kicked down their stalls. Back they sailed into the harbor so the stalls could be repaired. Trelawny stayed aboard to supervise the repairs, and this time Byron, with Pietro and Charles Barry, a friend who had promised to close up the Casa Saluzzo for him, went back up the hill to the empty house.

They walked through the echoing rooms, already stifling from being closed up. The furniture that was left was mostly under shroudlike covers. Byron, Pietro and Barry went out onto the terrace where two days earlier Teresa and Mary had watched their sails move out of sight.

They sat on the terrace, ate some lunch and drank their wine. Byron wandered back into the house, and was gone more than an hour. Pietro used the time to send a note to his sister Teresa: "Keep up your spirits, find comfort in your hopes, wait for our letters . . ." Then he went looking for Byron to ask him to add a postscript. He found him sitting alone at his writing desk in his study, writing nothing, looking off into space. But he would not add a note to Pietro's letter; what was there to say? Next day, as Barry was clearing things out of the palazzo, he found, in the drawer of the writing table where Byron had sat all afternoon, a lock of Teresa's hair.

The wind finally turned favorable. The brig *Hercules* made her clumsy way down the coast. As she worked through the

Strait of Messina, Trelawny looked back on Italy for the last time. Byron stood silently beside him.

"Nature," said Trelawny, "must have intended this for Paradise."

Byron replied: "But the Devil has converted it into Hell."

Epilogue

The sirocco which had been lashing Missolonghi for days was becoming a full hurricane. Rain drove against the narrow windowpanes, and wind screeched around the gables and towers of the big house on the beach. From the bedroom on the second floor the waters could be seen surging in across the marsh and around the house. Waves crashed against the dunes farther out, and sometimes their thunder could be heard above the whine of the wind. But inside the bedroom were only the hushed sounds of sickness. On his bed Lord Byron moved feverishly in his sleep. His servant Fletcher occasionally moved a blanket back in place or dabbed at Byron's perspiring brow, while he waited for the next visit from the doctors.

Byron had been unwell much of the time since he had arrived in Greece. The shock of the cremation on the beach at Viareggio seemed still to be with him, and he rarely showed the spirit he had during the earlier days in Italy. The pestilential Greek climate had lowered his spirits even more, and he had not been in the country long before having his first serious seizure. In Cephalonia, where he spent five months before moving on to Missolonghi, he was suddenly attacked by a series of stomach spasms which drove him temporarily insane. Barricading himself in his room, he screamed and threw furniture at everyone who tried to calm him. At Missolonghi he apparently had an epileptic fit, going into convulsions, foaming at the mouth and thrashing about, and then suddenly recovering. The local doctor, following medical custom of the day, prescribed the application of leeches to draw off some of Byron's blood. When the leeches were removed, the blood would not stop; Byron fainted before the doctor was able, after ten hours, to stanch the bleeding. He came out of it pale and weak. Some days later he complained to Gamba of unpleasant nervous sensations and attacks of vertigo and "frequent oppressions on his chest." He slept poorly. He seemed always on edge, always at the brink of a temper tantrum. When one of his doctors pleaded with him to take better care of himself, Byron answered: "Do you suppose that I wish for life? I have grown heartily sick of it, and shall welcome the hour I depart from it. . . . Few men can live faster than I did. I am literally speaking, a young old man."

In the spring rains of 1824, days went by during which Byron could not enjoy his daily horseback ride. When, on Friday, April 9, it was momentarily clear, he insisted on going out, although the skies still looked threatening. He and Pietro Gamba rode through the sparse, rolling countryside outside Missolonghi, and were on the way back, three miles away from the city, when a rainstorm hit them. They were soaked through, and when they reached the city walls Pietro proposed that they ride on through town to the house instead of following the usual custom of taking a boat through the lagoon and across the marsh. Riding would at least keep them moving, while sitting in a rain-swept boat in wet clothes would be risky. Byron was affronted. "I should make a pretty soldier indeed," he said, "if I were to care for such a trifle."

He did change his clothes as soon as he had returned, at the insistence of the worried Fletcher. But two hours later he was shuddering with fever and rheumatic pains. By morning he felt better and characteristically decided to ignore his pains. The weather was clear, though threatening again, so he went out a few hours earlier than usual. With Gamba he rode through the nearby olive groves, this time returning without getting caught in the rain. But he complained that the saddle was still wet from the day before, and that the dampness had aggravated the pains in his hips. He then tried to forget about it. But late that night he gave up and sent for the doctor.

Now, on Sunday, April 11, the doctor convinced Byron that he was a sick man. He had not slept more than a few brief periods the nights before. The pains and fever were worse. His bedclothes were soaked with perspiration. His friends became alarmed to the extent of making preparations to get him out of swampy Missolonghi, to drier Zante, where there were better medical facilities. Byron agreed to this plan, but he refused to listen to the doctor's request to bleed him again. Before he could be moved, he became even worse. And the sirocco started to blow.

The frustrations and the disillusionment had started almost from the beginning. The Greek people had welcomed Byron like a messiah. But the many Greek leaders were still feuding among themselves over how to fight the Turks, and Byron's promise of help only served to whet the competition among them. At first Byron's natural cynicism served him well; he expected the different factions to vie for his favor, and he had no illusions about all Greeks working together even against the common enemy. But on the other hand, Byron was swept up in his own enthusiasms for the Greek cause, and he gradually came to despise those who were too obviously putting their own personal goals first. Byron spared nothing himself in putting everything he had into the battle. He wrote his London friend Douglas Kinnaird from Missolonghi: "The Greek Cause up to this present writing hath cost me of mine own monies about thirty thousand Spanish dollars *advanced*, without counting my own contingent expenses of every kind." He asked Kinnaird to help him obtain "all possible credits to the extent of my resources, for I must do the thing handsomely." One of his aides in Greece estimated that Byron was spending two thousand dollars a week on rations alone. Byron was giving and loaning money to Greek leaders who showed some promise of gains against the Turks; he was training a fighting force of his own; he was subsidizing Greek propaganda. In fact, he was making a more effective use of his resources than the entire Greek government itself. No wonder then that he soon became irritated when he realized that, as one of his aides put it: "The Greeks seemed to think that he was a mine from which they could extract gold at their pleasure." And as Byron grew sicker, the doctors gave orders that no more haggling Greeks could visit their patient. Byron's only visitors were to be William Parry, a firemaster who had become Byron's chief lieutenant now that Trelawny had gone off on his own, the servants Tita and Fletcher, and Pietro Gamba.

Pietro Gamba was even more disillusioned than Byron. The grasping Greeks sickened him, and the contrast between what he had dreamed of and what he and Byron were now doing was more than he could bear. He wrote home his personal opinion of the Greeks: "They are and always will remain the scum I have described to you. . . . If they remain independent, it will be because nobody wants them." It was Pietro who kept the only ties to Italy and Teresa, and occasionally he induced Byron to add a brief postscript. Teresa was in Bologna, under the protection of family friends, while her husband continued his campaign to bring her back to the Palazzo Guiccioli. Sitting in the swamps of Missolonghi, besieged by the Greek leaders of this faction and that, Byron must have thought back fondly to Teresa and Italy. He admitted to a friend that: "I left my heart in Italy." But when he did write to Teresa his tone was more friendly than ardent. "Pray be as cheerful and tranquil as you can—and be assured that there is nothing here that can excite anything but a wish to be with you again. . . ." "The Spring has come—I have seen a Swallow today. . . ."

He was neglecting his poetry even more than his lost love. Not since he had left Italy, in fact not since he had stood on the beach and watched the fire burn away the remains of Shelley, had he written a serious poem. Now, on the eve of his thirty-sixth birthday, he took gloomy stock and, perhaps remembering *Macbeth*, wrote:

> . . . My days are in the yellow leaf;
>   The flowers and fruits of Love are gone;
>   The worm, the canker, and the grief
>   Are mine alone!
>
> The fire that on my bosom preys
>   Is lone as some Volcanic isle;

No torch is kindled at its blaze—
A funeral pile. . . .

Seek out—less often sought than found—
A soldier's grave, for thee the best;
Then look around, and choose thy ground,
And take thy Rest.[64]

Dr. Francesco Bruno, the Genoese physician who had served and treated Byron since the start of the expedition, had been joined by Dr. Julius Millingen, a young Briton who had also come to serve in the Greek cause. Together Bruno and Millingen argued for the panacea of the time, bleeding. Byron was against it on general principles, answering stubbornly that: ". . . the lancet has killed more people than the lance." He took the medicines they prescribed for him—castor oil, antimony powder, extract of henbane, arrowroot, Epsom salts, bark—but he continued to hold out against being bled.

Steadily he grew weaker. He lapsed into periods of delirium. He dozed but scarcely slept. Coughing started—"violent, spasmodic coughing which finally caused him to vomit." The doctors persisted in their arguments for bleeding him. Millingen accused him of toying with his life; obviously the doctors knew more than he did, and he was simply being perverse in the face of all science and sense. Then Millingen "touched the sensible chord": often Byron had repeated his one great fear—not of death but of madness or senility; how he dreaded the thought of "dying first at the top." Millingen turned the point against him. "He might not care for life, it was true," the doctor argued; "but who could assure him, unless he changed his resolution, the disease might not operate such disorganization in his cerebral and nervous system as entirely to deprive him of his reason."

Byron pondered this a moment and then angrily thrust his arm out. "Come; you are, I see, a damned set of butchers. Take away as much blood as you will; but have done with it." Quickly, before "the honorable patient" could change his mind, the doctors opened his vein and "drew out a full pound." But Millingen admitted: ". . . the relief we obtained did not correspond to the hopes we had anticipated." So they talked the weakened patient into another bloodletting two hours later. Byron fell into a near coma, then went into more delirium.

As the news of Byron's illness spread through Missolonghi, an air of uneasy dread hung over the town. On Easter Sunday, the eighth day of Byron's illness, the town fathers called off the annual festivities and the firing of cannon. Instead an artillery brigade marched out of town, to lead the crowds away from the center. And patrols went through the streets, asking everyone to be as quiet as possible so as not to disturb their benefactor.

Pietro Gamba had sprained his ankle. He could hardly walk, and he used this as an excuse for keeping out of the sickroom. Actually he could not face the sight of Byron sinking slowly into death. When he finally did force himself to hobble to the bedside and explained his absence, Byron said: "Take care of your foot; I know by experience how painful it must be." At one point, suddenly, Byron raised himself, swung his feet to the floor and called for his servants to help him walk. Leaning on them, he stumbled into the next room. Others remade his bed with dry, cool linen. Dr. Bruno went into the next room with his patient and pleaded again to be allowed to draw away more of his blood. Byron's refusal was weaker this time, and he asked wearily to be helped back to bed. To the old soldier Parry it seemed that Byron was weak not only from fever but also from loss of blood. When he mentioned this to the doctors, he was politely told to mind his own business. Byron's man-servant Fletcher noticed that his master's hands and feet had the coldness of death; but the doctors convinced him that the only hope for his lordship was more bleeding. By now Byron was delirious much of the time, and Dr. Bruno became so worried that he ordered Tita to remove Byron's pistols from his bedside table.

There was one last flash of Byronic character. At the death-bed stood Millingen, Fletcher and Tita. None could hide his tears. Fletcher and even Millingen turned and fled. Tita could not—because Byron held him by the hand. As Tita turned his head away and wiped at his eyes with his free sleeve, Byron pulled at his hand to make him turn back. Summoning his last smile, he said: *"Oh, questa è una bella scena."*

And gradually, almost unnoticed by those inside the house, the hurricane subsided.

Late in the afternoon of April 18, Byron looked at Fletcher, said, "I want to sleep now," and closed his eyes. He lay still, breathing with an occasional rattle—while the doctors applied fresh leeches to his temples, bleeding him freely now that he could no longer protest.

At six o'clock the next evening, Fletcher was still at his bedside when Byron opened his eyes again for the last time. When he closed them again, Fletcher cried out: "Oh, my God! I fear his lordship is gone!" The doctors came forward, felt the still wrist and said: "You are right. He is gone."

That day a letter had arrived from Hobhouse. "Your monied matters, Kinnaird will tell you, are going on swimmingly—you will have, indeed you have, a very handsome fortune," his old friend wrote. ". . . and if you have health—I do not see what earthly advantage you can wish for that you have not got. . . ."

Minute guns tolled through the wind-battered, half-flooded town. The rains finally stopped and the winds diminished. The servants and the aides-de-camp gathered in the room overlooking the lagoon to assemble Byron's personal effects. And among them they found his last poem.

> I watched thee when the foe was at our side,
>   Ready to strike at him—or thee and me.
> Were safety hopeless—rather than divide
>   Aught with one loved save love and liberty.
>
> I watched thee on the breakers, when the rock
>   Received our prow and all was storm and fear,
> And bade thee cling to me through every shock;
>   This arm would be thy bark, or breast thy bier.
>
> I watched thee when the fever glazed thine eyes,
>   Yielding my couch and stretched me on the ground,
> When overworn with watching, ne'er to rise
>   From thence if thou an early grave hadst found.
>
> The earthquake came, and rocked the quivering wall,
>   And men and nature reeled as if with wine.
> Whom did I seek around the tottering hall?
>   For thee. Whose safety first provide for? Thine.
>
> And when convulsive throes denied my breath
>   The faintest utterance to my fading thought,
> To thee—to thee—e'en in the gasp of death
>   My spirit turned, oh! oftener than it ought.
>
> Thus much and more; and yet thou lov'st me not,
>   And never wilt! Love dwells not in our will.
> Nor can I blame thee, though it be my lot
>   To strongly, wrongly, vainly love thee still.[65]

Edward Trelawny was fording the river Evenos on his way to Missolonghi when a messenger reached him with the news. He raced to the town, which he had never seen before. The sight of it appalled him, perhaps more so now. To him it seemed to be:

. . . on the verge of the most dismal swamp I had ever seen. . . . I waded through the streets, between wind and water, to the house he had lived in. . . . Now that death had closed the door, it was as silent as a cemetery. No one was within the house but Fletcher, of which I was glad. As if he knew my wishes, he led me up a narrow stair into a small room, with nothing in it but a coffin standing on trestles. No word was spoken by either of us; he withdrew the black pall and the white shroud, and there lay the embalmed body of the Pilgrim—more beautiful in death than in life.

Trelawny's famous and self-revealing account of what he did next—sending Fletcher for a glass of water so he could sneak a look at Byron's lame foot—has often been discounted; in any case, considering Trelawny's nosy curiosity, it is doubtful that he needed another look at the leg of a man with whom he had gone swimming so many times.

The autopsy was crude even by the standards of 1824. Studying the bones and viscera of the "respected cadaver," as Dr. Bruno recorded, the doctors found a cranium "of a person eighty years old." But their findings were so sparse that diagnosticians reading the full report today cannot determine accurately the cause of Byron's death; one British doctor guesses at either typhoid fever or pernicious malaria, while an American doctor thinks it might have been "uremic poisoning . . . with his death hastened at the end by the numerous bleedings and purgings by strong cathartics." The internal organs were placed in separate containers. The body itself was sewed up and lowered into a tin-lined chest. When at last the weather had cleared enough and the town had recovered some order, the funeral was held. Through lines formed by Greek soldiers and Byron's own guard, the roughhewn coffin was borne to the church. And in towns throughout the land Greeks gathered at similar memorial services. In death Byron did more to unite Greece than he had been able to in life.

The brig *Florida* arrived at Zante, bearing British contributions to the Greek cause. The wooden coffin and the containers —all save the jar holding his lungs, which were left to be buried in Missolonghi in answer to the townspeople's pleas— were ferried to Zante and taken aboard the brig. Holes were bored through the wood and tin of the coffin and it was submerged in a cask of spirits. Minute guns fired again, and a salute of thirty-seven cannon paid Greece's final tribute to Byron. His servants and his dogs went aboard *Florida* for the voyage to England. But Pietro Gamba stayed behind to take passage on another ship; he explained in a letter to his father: "I know it is feared that my accompanying it openly might produce gossip and bitterness in Byron's family, on account of his well-known relations with Teresa."

Teresa was still in Bologna. Evidently her father went to her immediately, to be sure she did not hear the news from someone else first. It was morning and she was still in bed. She said nothing, but turned on her side, her face to the wall, alone with her grief and her memories.

It was morning too when a loud knocking on the door awakened John Cam Hobhouse in London. A messenger brought the news from Greece, with the announcement that the coffin was on its way to England. Hobhouse went down the

Thames to meet the brig *Florida* on July 2. As she swung at her anchor, a horde of small boats swarmed around her. Along both shores of the Thames stood lines of Londoners—silent and respectful. Hobhouse was rowed out to the brig. He climbed the gangway steps to the deck and stood at the rail looking about him. There on the deck was the huge cask holding the heavy wooden coffin.

"I cannot describe what I felt," he wrote later. "I was the last person who shook hands with Byron when he left England in 1816. I recollected his waving his cap to me . . . and here I was now coming back to England with his corpse. . . ."

As the poet's executor, Hobhouse supervised the removal of the coffin to a house on Great George Street, where it lay in state. Hobhouse arranged the funeral procession through the streets of London. At eleven on the morning of July 12, 1824, Hobhouse was in his carriage as the bells of Westminster Abbey tolled and the procession set forth, led by the High Constable in mourning and the riderless State Horse. The hearse was covered with a black pall and surmounted by black plumes. Following in a long line were the carriages of England's nobility—empty except for their pages. Thus England's lords and ladies gave notice that they had not forgotten nor forgiven the scandal of their fellow peer.

But all along the route of the procession the streets were lined with people, so many that in the narrower passages the funeral's pace was slowed even more. All were quiet as his lordship passed by. The only sounds were the creak and rattle of the carriages crossing the cobblestones, and in the distance the dying boom of the great bells of Westminster Abbey.

The procession rolled through Oxford Street, up Tottenham Court Road and up Highgate Hill. At the edge of the city the cobblestones gave way to a dirt road. The carriages with the armorial crests turned back. But the people on foot continued to follow the hearse, finally falling back themselves, one by one, as the body of Lord Byron moved up Pancras Turnpike on the journey to its last resting place at Newstead Abbey.

When Byron, Trelawny and Gamba had set out from Genoa for Greece, Byron had asked: "Where shall we all be one year from now?" It was one year plus two days as Byron's funeral cortege rolled through London. And watching at a window, with Jane Williams, stood Mary Shelley, who then sat down and wrote: "What should I have said to a Cassandra who three years ago should have prophesied that Jane and I—Edward and Shelley gone, should watch the funeral procession of Lord Byron up Highgate Hill. . . ."

Mary, like Teresa, had her memories of those Italian years. Mary, more than Teresa, recognized the poetic heritage those Italian years had left for the world. But at this final scene her reaction was still a poignantly personal one: ". . . how young, heedless & happy & poor we were then," she wrote; "& now my sleeping boy is all that is left to me of that time—my boy— & a thousand recollections which never sleep."

On the Italian Trail

To read all that has been written about Byron and Shelley would take more than a lifetime. I certainly haven't touched more than the high spots in a quarter century of reading the poets and the books about them. This cannot be a complete bibliography, and I doubt that a really complete bibliography has ever been put together, or ever could be, if only because new entries appear every month. If you are tempted to plow through most of the books and essays on the poets, I recommend the bibliographies in Leslie Marchand's *Byron* and Newman Ivey White's *Portrait of Shelley*. If, on the other hand, you are content to hit the high spots first, here are my recommendations.

There are four books that might be classed as "required reading" for anyone who wants to learn more about Byron and Shelley and particularly their Italian period. The first is the aforementioned *Byron, a Biography*, by Leslie A. Marchand.

There have been many biographies of Byron through the years, but none is so complete, so accurate and so readable as Marchand's; this classic study is the definitive work on Byron. It fills three volumes, but I defy you to skip a page.

The second "required" work has also been mentioned above: *Portrait of Shelley*, by Newman Ivey White. It was first published in 1940 in two volumes, and a shorter one-volume edition was published in 1945. The one-volume work has virtually all of the essential information, but the two-volume work has those extra little details, plus some fascinating notes, plus the bibliography. If Marchand is Byron's best biographer, White does the same for Shelley.

The other two books of "required reading," particularly on the Italian years, are Peter Quennell's *Byron in Italy* and Iris Origo's *The Last Attachment*. The former is a masterly combination of scholarship and narrative. Quennell is, of course, famous for his other studies in the field of English literature, notably his works on Ruskin, Hogarth and his new book on Shakespeare; and he has done equally good books on other periods of Byron's life, including *Byron, the Years of Fame*; *Byron, a Self-Portrait*; and *To Lord Byron*, in which Quennell joins with George Paston in depicting some of the women who became fascinated by Byron, as they revealed themselves in their letters to him. And by far the best portrait of the last of these women is Iris Origo's *The Last Attachment*. Marchese Origo studied letters, journals and notes which no scholar of her stature or writer of her ability had ever seen, and composed from Teresa Guiccioli's writings a fascinating narrative of Byron's last and greatest love affair.

But don't stop with these books. Certainly you should read Isabel C. Clarke's *Shelley and Byron, a Tragic Friendship*. The author, who had previously written books on the Brontës and Elizabeth Barrett Browning, in this case put together an admirably coordinated narrative of the interrelationships between Shelley, Byron, Claire, Allegra, Trelawny and all the other characters on this colorful stage. Byron does not perhaps come off so well in this account as in others, but Isabel Clarke's account still makes good reading.

A lot less accurate, but just about the most fascinating author on the subject—because he was there—is Edward Trelawny. His most famous book is *Recollections of the Last Days of Shelley and Byron*. Some of the details were altered by the author himself in later works, such as his *Records of Shelley, Byron, and the Author*, and his *Letters*, published many years later. But contemporary accounts and later research tend to support the general story told by Trelawny; and no one at the time described the dramatic events of those Italian years with as keen an eye for the colorful incident as did Trelawny. Read his account with reservations, but read it just the same. And for a clear-eyed account of Trelawny himself, with a sober assessment of his accuracy, read Margaret Armstrong's *Trelawny*. Then, if you haven't had enough Trelawny (and that may well be the case), turn to Margaret Armstrong's bibliography for the full listing of everything by and about Trelawny that has been published.

There are hundreds, perhaps thousands, of other books on Byron, Shelley and the people who gathered around them. Here are only a few recommendations:

Leigh Hunt, the poet and critic whom Shelley urged to come to Italy, and whom Byron grudgingly helped out, wrote his own account of the Italian visit, in his *Autobiography*, in his *Correspondence* and in a memoir entitled *Lord Byron and Some of His Contemporaries*. And for the best book on Hunt, see Edmund Blunden's *Leigh Hunt* (Blunden, well known as an English poet himself, also wrote a warm and informative biography of Shelley).

Some of the best contemporary accounts besides Hunt's and Trelawny's: Hobhouse's *Recollections of a Long Life* (by then he was Lord Broughton); John William Polidori's *Diary;* Mary Shelley's *Letters* and *Journal;* Marguerite, Countess of Blessington's *The Idler in Italy,* which has a revealing, if gossipy, account of Byron's last few months with Teresa in Genoa; Tom Moore's *Memoirs, Journal and Correspondence,* plus his *The Life, Letters and Journals of Lord Byron;* Pietro Gamba's own book: *A Narrative of Lord Byron's Last Journey to Greece;* and the English version of Teresa's account: *My Recollections of Lord Byron.* Be careful with Teresa's recollections, in whatever form. She was sometimes more concerned with telling the story as she would have liked it to be than with telling what actually happened. In fact, virtually the only person who seemed determined to tell the story of Byron without any gloss was Byron himself, and so his own letters are often the best source materials of the time; even here, however, make some allowance for his tendency to exaggerate his misbehavior. Try Teresa and Byron, one after the other; the truth lies somewhere in between, and rather closer to Byron's account than Teresa's, especially if the incident concerns Teresa's morals.

There are many other biographies of the two poets—Edward Dowden's *The Life of Percy Bysshe Shelley;* André Maurois' *Byron,* and his *Ariel, the Life of Shelley,* both of which are highly readable if not always entirely accurate. There is no better account of Byron's last months in Greece than that of Sir Harold Nicolson: *Byron, the Last Journey.*

A few more recommendations: C. L. Cline's *Byron, Shelley and Their Pisan Circle;* R. Glynn Grylls's *Claire Clairmont,* and her *Trelawny;* Austin K. Gray's *Teresa, or Her Demon Lover.* And among the many books about the dramatic last few months before Shelley's death, try these: Ivan Roe's *Shelley, the Last Phase*; Guido Biagi's *The Last Days of Percy Bysshe Shelley*. If you can read Italian, try Alieto Benini's *Byron a Ravenna*. For the Pisan period nothing is better than the beautiful, heavily illustrated *Shelley and Byron in Pisa*, by Vera Cacciatore, curator of Rome's Keats-Shelley Memorial.

Desmond King-Hele has some stimulating insights and observations in his *Shelley, the Man and the Poet*. So does Mario Praz in his *The Romantic Agony*. The years before Italy, in particular the sensational breakup of Byron's marriage, have been commented on even by Harriet Beecher Stowe, in her *Lady Byron Vindicated*, which led to Sir John C. Fox's *The Byron Mystery*. But the most illuminating book on this subject, though by no means confined to this subject, is one of the most recent books on Byron, Doris Langley Moore's *The Late Lord Byron*; concentrating on the immediate aftermath of Byron's death, and sifting through the evidence, including some hitherto unpublished papers, Doris Langley Moore has produced a true literary detective story.

Besides the books devoted to Byron and Shelley, there are the many essays on them, their lives, their work and their Italian adventure—essays by Browning, Ruskin, Blunden, Macaulay, Eliot, Origo, Marchand, Nicolson. You can find them in any big library. And they may logically lead you to the next step: reading some of the poets' original manuscripts and letters. There are more of these in the U.S. than you might suppose—in the Berg Collection in the New York Public Library; in New York's Pierpont Morgan Library; in the Yale Library; in Harvard's Houghton Library; in the University of Texas Library; and in California's Huntington Library.

After you have gone this far, there will be no stopping you from the inevitable trip to England and the Continent. And for a rewarding vacation project I suggest the following:

London, for a study of the Byron and Shelley materials in the British Museum and the Byron Collection at the offices of Sir John Murray; a drive to Shelley's Eton and Oxford and to Byron's Harrow and Cambridge; on to Newstead Abbey and a look at the Roe-Byron Collection, as well as the Byron Oak and Byron's and Allegra's graves.

Then: down to Venice, where you can still see the Palazzo Mocenigo and the incredible sunset across the lagoon that still makes the city look like "fabrics of enchantment piled to Heaven"—not to mention "The Bridge of Sighs, a palace and a prison on each hand." La Mira bears little resemblance to the summer resort of Byron's day, and the Lido is nothing whatever like the sandspit where Byron took Shelley horseback riding. But Ravenna is little changed; the Palazzo Guiccioli is there, now an army administration building but looking much as it did when Byron lived in the rooms looking down on the courtyard and Count Guiccioli sulked in the rooms below; you can walk through the courtyard and see in your mind's eye Byron's livestock strutting about, the count's coach rattling off to the theater, even the hasty flight of Teresa when she received word that the Pope had granted her separation. Outside Ravenna, still shading the Po but no longer reaching to the retreating sea, are the umbrella pines where Byron and Teresa used to ride. And a few miles from Ravenna: Bagnacavallo, with its high brown walls, its arcaded streets and the bare, forbidding convent with the simple plaque above the entrance, noting that here Allegra, daughter of the English poet Byron, died.

Byron was not long in Rome, and there are few reminders of the Shelleys' tragic time there. But Rome is an important stopping point for anyone on the trail of Byron and Shelley, because here, in the little house where Keats died, is the Keats-

Shelley Memorial, packed with books, manuscripts, pictures and memorabilia of Byron as well as Shelley and Keats. The library is presided over by Dottoressa Vera Cacciatore, herself an often-published authority on the poets.

In Pisa the imposing Palazzo Lanfranchi still stands by the Arno; it now houses state archives. Shelley's house was bombed during World War II. But at the head of the Bay of Lerici the little house still stands on the shore. A road has been built in front of it, and a squat third story has been added to the building. Still you can stand in front of the house and look out across the bay, as Trelawny did on that awful night when he came to tell Mary the truth; and you can see what moved Shelley to call it "this divine bay"—in good weather; in a storm you can sympathize with Mary.

There is a jam of modern shipping in the harbor at Leghorn now. But the old stone pier is there; so is the lighthouse, with its view across the Mediterranean; imagine standing up there and watching a friend of yours out in his boat heeling over before one of the Mediterranean's howling *ponènti*. Then go up the coast only a few miles, to the beach near Viareggio. Today the shore is lined with honky-tonk beach-front hotels and restaurants. Yet if you go there when the summer visitors have departed, you can stand on the lonely beach, as I did, and look out across the sea, then back at the soaring Apennines, and imagine the flaring flames of the funeral pyre, with Byron limping away into the water and Trelawny reaching into the fire to pluck out the heart of Percy Shelley. And there, more than in this book or even the classic books on Byron and Shelley, you may for a moment sense the grandeur of that tragedy, and finally understand what—to Byron and Shelley—was indeed Italy's fatal gift of beauty.

Notes

I have resisted the temptation to include in the Notes all the fascinating little details that could be added to the story of Byron and Shelley in Italy. All of the facts essential to the story are, of course, in the narrative itself. But there are many tangential stories, for which I refer you to the books mentioned in the bibliographical chapter that precedes the Notes.

1. Byron: *Childe Harold*, IV.
2. Shelley: *Julian and Maddalo*.
3. Byron: *The First Kiss of Love*.
4. It was Hobhouse who, when Byron sent him some maudlin lines about the death of his dog, responded with the famous epitaph often credited to Byron:

> Near this spot
> Are deposited the Remains of one
> Who possessed Beauty without Vanity,

284

Strength without Insolence,
Courage without Ferocity,
And all the Virtues of Man without his Vices.
This Praise, which would be unmeaning Flattery
If inscribed over human ashes,
Is but a just tribute to the Memory of
BOATSWAIN, a Dog . . .

5. Byron: *Lines to Mr. Hodgson.* Francis Hodgson, resident tutor at King's College, Cambridge, was a slightly stuffy friend of both Byron and Hobhouse. Byron enjoyed offending him with his behavior and his outspoken language.

6. Byron: *Childe Harold*, I.

7. These were the famous marble statues and friezes which the Greeks have been trying to get back ever since, so far without success.

8. Byron: *Written after Swimming from Sestos to Abydos.*

9. Byron: *Maid of Athens, Ere We Part.*

10. Byron: *Stanzas for Music.*

11. Byron: *Fare Thee Well.*

12. Since this book is about the Italian years, it can only sketch in the high points of Byron's earlier experiences. The best books on the subject are Marchand's *Byron, a Biography;* and Peter Quennell's *Byron, the Years of Fame.* A fascinating study of the breakup of Byron's marriage is in Doris Langley Moore's *The Late Lord Byron.*

13. The story of Shelley too in the years before Italy must be covered lightly, to sketch the background to Italy. The best book on the early years of Shelley is the late Newman Ivey White's *Portrait of Shelley,* followed closely by Kenneth Neill Cameron's *The Young Shelley.*

14. Byron: *Childe Harold*, III.

15. From Mary Shelley's Introduction to *Frankenstein.*

16. Polidori drifted away from Byron's entourage, reappearing once or twice. He committed suicide in 1821.

17. The monks of San Lazzaro still show visitors Byron's library and the terrace where he sat reading by the lagoon.

18. Byron: *So We'll Go No More A-roving*.
19. Byron: *Childe Harold*, IV.
20. Byron: *Childe Harold*, IV.
21. Byron: *Manfred*, III, 1.
22. Byron: *Manfred*, II, 4.
23. Byron: *Childe Harold*, IV.
24. Byron: *Childe Harold*, IV.
25. Shelley: *Passage of the Apennines*.
26. Shelley: *To Mary Shelley*.
27. Shelley: *Prometheus Unbound*, I.
28. Shelley: *Julian and Maddalo*.
29. Shelley: *On a Faded Violet*.
30. Shelley: *Lines Written Among the Euganean Hills*.
31. Shelley: *Stanzas Written in Dejection, Near Naples*.
32. Shelley: *Stanzas Written in Dejection, Near Naples*.
33. Shelley: *Ode to Naples*.
34. Shelley: *Prometheus Unbound*, II, 5.
35. Shelley: *To William Shelley*.
36. Byron: *The Prophecy of Dante*, Dedication.
37. Byron: *Don Juan*, II.
38. Byron: *Stanzas*.
39. Shelley: *Ode to the West Wind*.
40. Shelley: *The Indian Serenade*.
41. Shelley: *To a Skylark*.
42. Shelley: *The Boat on the Serchio*.
43. Byron: *Don Juan*, III.
44. Byron: *Sardanapalus*, V, 1.
45. Shelley: *Adonais*.
46. Byron: *Stanzas Written on the Road Between Florence and Pisa*.
47. This coincidence has been questioned. But there is good evidence that Claire was indeed in the coach from Pisa to Florence that day, and it is known that Byron's caravan forced it to the side of the road. Claire's reaction need only be imagined.
48. Shelley: *Evening: Ponte al Mare, Pisa*.
49. Shelley: *To Night*.

50. Shelley: *With a Guitar, to Jane.*
51. Byron: *The Island,* I.
52. Byron: *Don Juan,* VI.
53. I realize that many of the experts on Byron and Shelley refer to Shelley's boat as *Don Juan,* and that there is no evidence that Shelley himself referred to her as *Ariel.* Still it seems to me that Shelley's efforts to remove the name *Don Juan,* and his remark that the "superscription of my poor boat's infamy is erased," indicate his preference for the name *Ariel.*
54. Shelley: *Lines Written in the Bay of Lerici.*
55. Shelley: *A Dirge.*
56. Shelley: *A Fragment.*
57. Shelley: *A Vision of the Sea*—written, of course, before this storm, but prophetic in illustrating Shelley's fascination with death by drowning, as his reaction had been that day in the forest pool with Trelawny.
58. Shelley: *Lines: "When the Lamp Is Shattered"*—another example of the prophecy of Shelley's poetry of the time.
59. Half a century after *Ariel* went down, a mysterious story began to go up and down the Italian coast. An English traveler picked it up near Lerici. Trelawny's daughter heard it in Rome. The tale told of an aged Italian seaman who confessed to his priest just before dying that he and his fellow crew members of a felucca had sunk *Ariel.* They had thought Byron might be aboard, he said, perhaps with a chest of money. But as they tried to get alongside, the felucca's bow smashed *Ariel*'s gunwale and she immediately filled and sank.

Trelawny believed the story and put it in one of his later books. It tended to confirm a suspicion he had had ever since *Ariel* had been raised, two months after Shelley's death. As a sailor Trelawny realized that certain characteristics of the sunken schooner indicated foul play. When *Ariel* had been located on the sea bottom, two miles off Viareggio, Trelawny's friend Captain Roberts helped raise her. He found that while floating objects like the *sandolino* and the water keg had washed ashore, the heavier objects—a chest with clothes and some money, another chest with Shelley's books, the hamper full of wine which Shelley had bought that morning for Lerici's harbor master—were still in the bottom of the boat, waterlogged and mixed with the blue clay of the Mediterranean bottom. That meant that the schooner had not capsized —had she been knocked over and sunk on her side or bottom up, objects like these would almost certainly have tumbled out. As Roberts reported to Trelawny: "Everything is in her and clearly proves that she was not capsized. I think she must have swamped in a heavy sea. . . ." But shortly Roberts dispatched another letter, with this ominous postscript: "On a close examination of Shelley's boat, we may find many of the timbers on the starboard quarter broken, which makes me think for certain that she must have been run down by some of the feluccas in the squall."

Other bits and pieces of evidence added to the suspicion. Young Thornton Hunt, Leigh Hunt's son, had been on the pier when *Ariel* sailed from Leghorn; he remembered thinking it odd that, with everyone warning Shelley not to sail, two feluccas followed *Ariel* out of the harbor and were still on the same course as she when the haze swept in from the sea. Trelawny recalled that one of the seamen aboard *Bolivar* said, when they questioned the crew of a fishing boat after the storm, that he noticed in the boat an English-made oar resembling those of *Ariel*. The Italian crew, however, protested that the oar was theirs. A final factor was that this coast was known to be plagued by *arrisicatori*, piratical sailors who made a business of wrecking and looting ships in stormy weather; like the wreckers of Cornwall and the New England coast, the *arrisicatori* were expert seamen who were able to maneuver their sturdy craft no matter how wild the storm.

All this evidence did tend to indicate that Shelley, Williams and their hired hand had been sent to the bottom by piratical fishermen who tried to board *Ariel* but succeeded only in smashing her starboard quarter with the heavy bow of their felucca. Under such circumstances the open-decked schooner would have filled and sunk immediately.

Yet for most of the evidence there was counterevidence or explanation. The mysterious old sailor was never identified despite a thorough search for him. An Italian naval officer reported to the British magazine *Atheneum,* for example, that no one along the coast "knows anything whatever about the old sailor, or the strange confession he is said to have made on his deathbed." The officer went on to remind English Protestants that no Catholic priest "would betray the secrets of the confessional." As for the objects that remained aboard the schooner, they would not have fallen overboard if *Ariel* had simply shipped a heavy sea, filled and sunk, instead of capsizing. And the damage to her starboard quarter, despite Captain Roberts' suspicions, could have been done by the grappling gear while *Ariel* was being raised. Her timbers would have been weakened considerably after two months on the bottom of the Mediterranean. As for the oar found aboard one of the feluccas, there is no proof, nor is it known that *Ariel*'s oars were imported from England when she was built in Genoa. And as for Thornton Hunt's suspicions, he was twelve years old at the time.

That leaves the *arrisicatori.* But there is another clue, a final piece of evidence that seems to suggest that Shelley's death was not murder, but suicide. Four years after the event, John Taffe, of the Pisan Circle, reported that two fishermen from Leghorn told him they had sailed near *Ariel* as the storm was breaking upon them. The fishermen were reefing sail and running for shelter, but *Ariel* was plowing ahead under full sail, even including her topsails. She came plunging up the coast, pounding into each mountainous wave, shuddering with the impact and throwing sheets of spray from her bow. As the fishing boat raced past, a huge wave broke over *Ariel,* and one of the fishermen bellowed above the howl of the storm: "For God's sake reef your sails or you are lost!" One of *Ariel*'s men could be seen jumping up to let go the topsail halyard. But then a slighter man, evidently Percy Bysshe Shelley, stood up, grabbed his companion and pulled him back onto his seat, as *Ariel* went plunging down the back side of a wave and out of sight.

60. Byron: *Childe Harold*, IV—Byron could be prophetic too.
61. Trelawny later recalled that he offered this blackened memento to Mary Shelley, but that she recoiled at the sight of it and that he then gave it to Hunt. But Mary later asked Hunt if she could have Shelley's heart, and Hunt refused. Mary enlisted Byron's help, thereby adding to the estrangement between the two men. Hunt wrote Mary a stiff note: ". . . With regard to Lord Byron, he has no right to bestow the heart. . . . If he told you that you should have it, it can only have been from his thinking that I could more easily part with it than I can. . . ." Only after the whole group disagreed with him, and after Jane Williams had chided him with "how grievous it was that Shelley's remains should become a source of dissension between his dearest friends," did Hunt relinquish Shelley's charred heart to his widow.

    Mary tucked it away in a silk pouch attached to her copy of *Adonais*, and after her death in 1851 it was found there, now disintegrated into a pinch of dust. When Sir Percy Florence Shelley died thirty-eight years later, at the age of seventy, his father's heart was at last buried with him.

62. Byron: *Journal in Cephalonia*.
63. Byron: *Don Juan*, III.
64. Byron: *On This Day I Complete My Thirty-Sixth Year*.
65. Byron: *Love and Death*.

Index

ABOUT THE AUTHOR

A. B. C. Whipple's interest in Byron and Shelley has been of long duration, and his research for *The Fatal Gift of Beauty* has taken him to Byron and Shelley sites in England and throughout Italy, where most of the landmarks known to the two poets are still preserved.

Mr. Whipple has been a correspondent and writer for *Life* magazine, and has contributed articles to *Harper's, Fortune,* and *Reader's Digest.* He is the author of four books, including *Yankee Whalers in the South Seas* and *Tall Ships and Great Captains.* Mr. Whipple, editor, Life International Editions, lives in Old Greenwich, Connecticut, with his wife and two children.

Format by Gayle Jaeger
Set in Caslon Old Face
Composed, printed and bound by American Book–Stratford Press, Inc.
HARPER & ROW, PUBLISHERS, INCORPORATED